The French Road to
European Monetary Union

David J. Howarth
Lecturer in European Politics
Queen Mary and Westfield College
University of London

First published 2001 by
PALGRAVE
Houndmills, Basingstoke, Hampshire RG21 6XS and
175 Fifth Avenue, New York, N. Y. 10010
Companies and representatives throughout the world

PALGRAVE is the new global academic imprint of
St. Martin's Press LLC Scholarly and Reference Division and
Palgrave Publishers Ltd (formerly Macmillan Press Ltd).

ISBN 0–333–92096–1

This book is printed on paper suitable for recycling and
made from fully managed and sustained forest sources.

A catalogue record for this book is available
from the British Library.

Library of Congress Cataloging-in-Publication Data
Howarth, David J., 1967–
    The French road to European Monetary Union / David J. Howarth.
        p. cm.
    Includes bibliographical references and index.
    ISBN 0–333–92096–1
    1. Monetary policy—France—History—20th century. 2. Economic and
Monetary Union—History. 3. European Union countries—Economic
integration—History—20th century. 4. France—Foreign economic
relations. I. Title.
HG979.5 .H69 2000
332.4'944—dc21
                                                00–033358

10 9 8 7 6 5 4 3 2 1
10 09 08 07 06 05 04 03 02 01

Printed and bound in Great Britain by
Antony Rowe Ltd, Chippenham, Wiltshire

The French Road to European Monetary Union

French Politics, Society and Culture Series

General Editor: **Robert Elgie**, Senior Lecturer in European Politics, The University of Nottingham

France always fascinated outside observers. Now, the country is undergoing a period of profound transformation. France is faced with a rapidly changing international and European environment and it is having to rethink some of its most basic social, political and economic orthodoxies. As elsewhere, there is pressure to conform. And yet, while France is responding in ways that are no doubt familiar to people in other European countries, it is also managing to maintain elements of its long-standing distinctiveness. Overall, it remains a place that is not exactly *comme les autres*.

This new series examines all aspects of French politics, society and culture. In so doing it focuses on the changing nature of the French system as well as the established patterns of political, social and cultural life. Contributors to the series are encouraged to present new and innovative arguments so that the informed reader can learn and understand more about one of the most beguiling and compelling of all European countries.

Titles include:

David J. Howarth
THE FRENCH ROAD TO EUROPEAN MONETARY UNION

French Politics, Society and Culture
Series Standing Order ISBN 0–333–80440–6
(*outside North America only*)

You can receive future titles in this series as they are published by placing a standing order. Please contact your bookseller or, in case of difficulty, write to us at the address below with your name and address, the title of the series and the ISBN quoted above.

Customer Services Department, Macmillan Distribution Ltd, Houndmills, Basingstoke, Hampshire RG21 6XS, England

To the memory of Vincent Wright, an excellent teacher and a most charming man

Contents

Acknowledgements

There are numerous people whom I would like to thank for commenting on the various drafts of the chapters of this book. These include my former supervisor Jack Hayward, my former employer Vincent Wright, Jonathon Story, Robert Elgie, Kenneth Dyson, David Goldey and Mike Sutton. Numerous colleagues at Nuffield College, ENA and Aston University have provided support, intellectual and otherwise, over the years. My friends and above all my parents and Gilly have helped a great deal along the way.

List of Abbreviations

BIS	Bank for International Settlements
CAP	Common Agricultural Policy
CDU	Christlich Demokratische Union (Christian Democratic Union (Germany))
CERES	Centre de recherche et d'études socialistes (Centre for Socialist Research and Studies)
CNPF	Conseil national du patronat français (National Council of French Employers)
CRU	Composite Reserve Unit
CSU	Christlich-Soziale Union (Christian Social Union)
EC	European Communities
ECB	European Central Bank
ECOFIN	Council of Ministers of Economics and Finance
ECU	European Currency Unit
EEC	European Economic Community
EIB	European Investment Bank
EMCF	European Monetary Co-operation Fund (FECOM)
EMI	European Monetary Institute
EMS	European Monetary System
EMU	Economic and Monetary Union
ERM	Exchange Rate Mechanism
ESCB	European System of Central Banks
EUA	European Unit of Account
FNSEA	Fédération nationale des syndicats d'exploitants agricoles (National Federation of Farming Unions)
G-7	Group of Seven (USA, Japan, Germany, France, UK, Italy, Canada)
GDP	Gross Domestic Product
GNP	Gross National Product
IGC	Intergovernmental Conference
IMS	International Monetary System
INSEE	Institut national de la statistique et des études économiques (National Institute of Statistics and Economic Studies)
MCA	Monetary Compensatory Amount
MEP	Member of the European Parliament

PCF	Parti communiste français (French Communist Party)
PS	Parti socialiste (Socialist Party)
PU	Political Union
RPR	Rassemblement pour la république (Rally for the Republic)
SGCI	Secrétariat général du comité interministériel des relations économiques européennes (General Secretariat of the Inter-ministerial Committee for European Economic Relations)
SEA	Single European Act
SEM	Single European Market
SPD	Sozialdemokratische Partei Deutschlands (Social Democratic Party of Germany)
TEU	Treaty on European Union (The Maastricht Treaty)
UDF	Union pour la démocratie française (Union for French Democracy)
UDR	Union pour la défence de la république (Union for the Defence of the Republic)
VSTF	Very Short Term Loan (Ortoli) Facility

1
The Analytical and Conceptual Framework

The principal motive behind French policy on monetary co-operation and integration in Europe between 1968 and the start of Stage Three of Economic and Monetary Union (EMU) on 1 January 1999 was the pursuit of monetary and economic power.* The French sought to maximise national control over monetary and macroeconomic policymaking by minimising the impact of American and German monetary policies upon the franc and the French economy, and by maximising French influence over the establishment of American and German monetary policy. Their objective was to preserve national control in an increasingly integrated world economy, in which developments in larger national economies had increasing influence over domestic economic developments. The failure to improve monetary co-operation at the international level increased French efforts to compensate for this within Europe.

A small élite of government ministers, Treasury and central bank officials determined the most appropriate mechanisms by which international and European power was to be enhanced. The motives which have shaped the precise content and timing of this élite's policy initiatives can be divided into three categories: monetary and economic power at the international and European levels, and domestic political considerations. The perception of these motives has been shaped by particular attitudes towards economic policy and the process of European political

---

* Monetary co-operation refers here to European agreements to maintain intra-parity stability and develop the use of the ECU without the loss of *de jure* monetary autonomy. Co-operation involves both informal and formal consultation and co-ordination of policy. Monetary integration refers to European agreements which involve the loss of *de jure* monetary autonomy.

integration. Minimising the impact of American monetary policy upon the French economy can be categorised as the major international monetary power motive. Minimising the impact of German monetary policy was part of the larger goal of containing the independent expression of German economic and political power within a European framework. This can be categorised as the most important element of France's European strategy. These international and European power motives were rooted in more specific economic motives: to increase French power in relation to the Americans and Germans in order to pursue certain economic goals. The French also saw monetary co-operation and integration as a means to achieve certain domestic economic goals not directly linked to the strategic objectives, notably to control inflation and reform the domestic economy. A set of core economic attitudes and an acceptance of limited further European integration by the French policymaking élite made support for European monetary co-operation and integration possible. Domestic political motives were less important in terms of shaping the direction of policy but, nonetheless, had limited impact on the details and timing of specific French policy initiatives.

The existing literature is limited to studies of particular periods but fails to explore analytically French motives and attitudes.[1] The most detailed studies of the political and economic motives of national foreign monetary policy focus upon the United States. It is, therefore, useful to turn to the literature on American foreign monetary policy for inspiration as to an appropriate analytical framework. The motives used here to structure this analysis of French policy on European monetary co-operation and integration are modifications of the factors formulated and applied by two authors writing on American policymaking. Odell (1982) examines three policy shifts in American international monetary policy during the 1960s and early 1970. He presents five perspectives to structure his analysis: international market conditions, international security and power structures, domestic politics, organisation and internal bargaining, and men and ideas. Bergsten (1975; 1996) presents three factors in his study of the costs and benefits of past and future alternative monetary arrangements to the United States: economics, political goals and political power.[2] The five factors formulated and applied by Odell were modified and re-applied by Story (1988) in his study of four factors which led the Germans and the French to launch the EMS in 1979. The frameworks applied by these three authors have considerable explanatory merit but none can provide a complete explanation of the development of French policy on monetary co-operation and integration without considerable modification.

Motives should be distinguished from explanatory factors. Policy-makers develop motives in order to deal with the pressures created by the different factors. For example, while Odell presents international market conditions as a potentially useful explanatory factor of French policymaking, the policy motives explored here include the desire to minimise the negative impact of these conditions upon the French economy and to maximise France's competitive position. Different policymaking actors faced with a set of conditions may advocate distinct policies for very different reasons depending upon the institutions that they represent and their different attitudes. An explanation of policy outcomes through an examination of motives and attitudes provides a more accurate description of why particular policies were developed than an examination of the relative importance of the factors identified.

In order to understand the temporal interplay of these different motives of French policymaking, five distinct periods can be distinguished and used as comparative case studies. These are: French attempts from 1968 to 1981 to establish a satisfactory form of European monetary co-operation which culminated in the creation of the EMS (Chapter 2); the Socialists' first two years in government to the March 1983 decision to keep the franc in the Exchange Rate Mechanism (ERM) of the European Monetary System (EMS) (Chapter 3); the period of the entrenchment of the strong franc policy and French demands to reform the EMS from 1983 to 1988 (Chapter 4); the discussions and negotiations leading to the agreement on EMU at the Maastricht Summit of December 1991 (Chapter 5); and the post-Maastricht period leading to the start of Stage Three of the EMU project on 1 January 1999, during which the French struggled to keep the EMU project on track yet continued to seek to increase their monetary and economic power in relation to the Germans (Chapter 6). Throughout all five periods, international and European monetary power motives were closely inter-linked. The French sought greater power in relation to the Germans in part to increase their power in relation to the Americans. Domestic political considerations influenced policymaking in a myriad of ways, although they were always of secondary importance.

This analysis begins in 1968 for several reasons. This was the year of the first major initiatives on EMU, notably the Werner plan for action, followed a month later by a Commission memorandum and different plans submitted by various German sources. These proposals were timed to coincide with the completion of the EC customs union and the start of common agricultural prices in July. Previous initiatives – for example, the 1964 proposals of Valéry Giscard d'Estaing, as Minister of Finance, and André de Lattre, the head of the French Treasury – were half-hearted and poorly formulated. 1968 was noteworthy for the impact of international monetary instability upon European currencies, which also encouraged initiatives on EMU. Attempts to reform the International Monetary System (IMS) during the mid-1960s failed to prevent this instability. The Bretton Woods system was approaching collapse with the *de facto* end of the dollar's convertibility into gold in March 1968 through the creation of a two-tiered gold market. International monetary instability – especially the November 1968 speculation crisis – demonstrated the unequal attractiveness and strength of the mark and the franc and, correspondingly, the relative strength of the French and German economies. The franc, already the clear underdog of the two currencies, was considerably weakened by the inflationary impact of the May 1968 Grenelle Accords. Dealing with the economic and political implications of this unequal strength was to be a central theme in French monetary policy for the following two-and-a-half decades. Moreover, starting in 1968, the mark began to replace the dollar as the franc's principal money of reference. The impact of German interest rate changes on French monetary policy increased substantially from this moment. Finally, the Grenelle accords marked a decisive relaxation of the French government's approach to inflation, the subsequent reaction to which involved turning to European monetary arrangements in order to constrain domestic economic policymaking. The analysis ends at the beginning of 1999 because the start of Stage Three of EMU represents the attainment of French monetary and economic power objectives. However, this is not to suggest that French governments and central bank officials will cease to attempt to maximise French influence in the formulation of European monetary policy.

International and European monetary power

The three authors who develop frameworks for the examination of foreign monetary policymaking each specify an international monetary power factor. Bergsten applies a 'national power' perspective through which he analyses the different sources and expressions of American international monetary power (Bergsten, 1975; 1999, pp. 28*ff.*). Odell modifies this into an 'international security and power structure' or 'realpolitik' perspective which analyses the power relations between states. Story alters this into a 'power politics' perspective. Here this perspective is modified further into what can be dubbed monetary power motives. These motives cannot be distinguished from economic power motives, but for the sake of brevity the more restricted label is applied. It is also necessary to distinguish between international and European monetary and economic power motives in considering the development of French policy on European monetary co-operation and integration. The political and economic constraints and the precise objectives pursued at the international and European levels were very different.

French international and European monetary power motives can be divided into three types: positive, negative and veto (Bergsten, 1975; 1996, pp. 28–9ff.). A country has positive power to the extent that it is able to influence or even determine the behaviour of others. However, all countries, including France, have less international monetary power than the United States and are thus more likely to exercise the two other forms of power. A country has veto power to the extent that it can block actions desired by others. The degree of veto power depends upon whether the country can do so on its own or whether it requires the support of a certain number of other countries. A country has negative power to the extent that it can avoid external constraints on its behaviour.

Odell and Bergsten outline several elements which determine a country's international monetary power (Odell, 1982, pp. 31–3; Bergsten, 1975; 1996, pp. 33ff.). These are: the state's position in the general international power structure, determined by its share of world military and productive capabilities; the state's share of international transactions; the self-sufficiency or openness of the economy; the ability to finance or eliminate payments deficits. It is not the objective of this book to analyse France's position in any hierarchy of international monetary power. However, this relative power is particularly relevant to the extent that it shaped the expression of the international and European power motives of French governments. Notably, France was better able to shape European monetary developments than international ones because France had greater monetary power in relation to her European partners, most crucially Germany, than in relation to the United States.

The impact of attitudes

Attitudes on monetary and economic policy and European integration shaped the manner in which monetary developments were perceived and suitable policy was made by French political and bureaucratic leaders.[3] None of these attitudes was universally shared. Rather they were held by certain groups within and outside government advocating particular policies in competition with other groups holding different attitudes and advocating different policies. Political leaders also had their own particular set of attitudes which they brought with them to office and which shaped policymaking. Attitudes cannot, therefore, be considered in isolation: their influence on policymaking was determined by the degree of influence of their proponents.

Attitudes on economic policy

Five closely linked monetary and economic policy attitudes, entrenched more or less firmly in the French economic tradition, encouraged support for European monetary co-operation: opposition to floating currencies; support for a strong currency; preference for low inflationary economic growth; emphasis placed upon a trade and balance of payments surplus and support for an interventionist role of the State in the economy. Attitudes were shaped as much by politics and the public perception of previous decisions as by analysis of economic reality. A crucial feature of these attitudes was that they were more often rooted in the myths surrounding the impact of earlier monetary and economic policy decisions than in economic theory. Arguably, this was in part because members of the French financial policymaking élite were under-educated in economic theory. Their economics training at the *Institut d'Etudes Politiques* and the *Ecole Nationale d'Administration* focused principally upon public economic and financial management, as considered appropriate by the existing financial administrative élite.

Opposition to floating

Opposition to floating currencies stemmed from several beliefs. First, the currency was not to be considered a good like any other, subject to market pressures. In this respect, French thinking resolutely opposed that of the Friedmanite monetarist school which had considerable influence over the formulation of American policy and throughout the world from the start of the 1970s. Second, floating currencies led to monetary instability which discouraged international investment and exchange. The Gold Standard prior to World War II and the dollar–gold standard of the Bretton Woods system since were upheld as invariably beneficial. Third, floating was associated with poor financial management, inflation and a weak currency. *'Fluctuat et mergitur*. The franc floats and sinks.'[4] This was inaccurate in that the brief periods of floating this century, and the economic and financial difficulties to which they corresponded, took place because of previous developments: the outbreak of World War I, the necessary devaluation of an overvalued currency in 1936, and the start of the collapse of the Bretton Woods system in 1968 which coincided with high French inflation. However, the public and political association of the two remained strong.

E. H. Carr wrote: 'Laissez-faire, in international relations...is the paradise of the economically strong' (1946, p. 60). Floating currencies were a more attractive option to the Americans because the size and relatively closed nature of the American economy meant that it was less affected by the fluctuation of other currencies. Floating was less attractive to the French because the value of the franc in relation to the currencies of the major trading partners was greatly affected by uneven capital movements. Even when the franc left an exchange rate system – as in 1974 – it was never allowed to float freely. French authorities always intervened (a managed float) in order to prevent its excessive fall.

The preference for fixed exchange rate systems was not unqualified. First, until 1976, the French consistently argued in favour of the return to a gold standard which would not give any dominant currency country an economic advantage. The French were active in their criticism of the operation of the Bretton Woods system which, they argued, permitted the Americans to run unfairly large balance of payments deficits with little impact on the strength of the dollar (Bordo *et al.*, 1993). Likewise, in the post-reunification period, the operation of the EMS imposed the ill effects of German monetary policy upon the French. Second, there was disagreement as to the extent to which fixed exchange rate systems should be adjustable – and thus to what extent they should provide an external constraint on domestic economic policymaking. Third, fixed exchange rate systems were considered expendible when governments emphasized other economic and political priorities as was the case with French participation in the Snake mechanism in early 1974.

Support for a strong currency

A strong franc was traditionally valued by the financial and political élite as well as the public more generally. The financial élite focused principally upon the inflationary consequences of a weak currency subject to devaluation and the impact that this had on lenders. The political élite and the public tended to prefer a strong currency for political and patriotic reasons as much as for economic ones. In the public mind, a strong franc demonstrated the strength of the economy and that of the nation, as well as the managerial competence of the government. Support for a strong franc was also closely associated with a preference for exchange rate stability: it was believed that a floating franc was invariably a weak franc. The degree to which this goal was pursued also reflected the frequency of franc devaluations (eleven between 1914 and 1958). On occasion, the political importance of maintaining a strong franc resulted in the maintenance of an exchange rate which failed to consider the relative price of goods in France as compared to other countries. The Laval government of the mid-1930s maintained a strong franc – despite excessively high interest rates, deflation, economic stagnation and the rise of unemployment – largely because of the political importance of doing so. Moreover, this reflected a widespread political, public and academic consensus in favour of a strong currency.[5]

A strong currency was associated with periods of political strength and non-inflationary economic growth: the franc was not devalued between 1958 and 1969. Periods of political and economic instability were likewise associated with a weak currency: notably, the 1936 devaluation under the new Popular Front government and the repeated devaluations during the Fourth Republic, despite solid economic growth.[6] The 1936 devaluation remained, unfairly, a symbol of incompetent left-wing economic and financial management, which was to influence strongly Socialist government monetary policy in the early 1980s.[7] The image of the strong franc was as important as its reality. The low inflationary economic growth of the first four years of the franc Poincaré stood as a symbol of the merits of a strong currency. However, this success depended upon an initial devaluation of the franc when the gold parity was re-established in June 1928. The following period of economic growth and financial stability owed less to a strong franc than to other factors including a large devaluation which re-established the franc's market value.[8] Likewise, the low-inflationary economic growth of the first decade of the Fifth Republic followed a 17.5 per cent devaluation in 1958. De Gaulle's decision to create the new franc by removing two zeros from the old franc had both political and economic significance. Politically, this reform symbolised a departure from the weak currency of the Fourth Republic. Economically, it was perceived a useful psychological device to discourage future inflation (Valance, 1996, pp. 330–3).

Since World War II, the sliding value of the franc in relation to the mark was a preoccupation for many governments, and the worrying manifestation of growing German economic and potential political power in Europe. This preoccupation informed the stabilisation of 1958, the monetary policies of the late 1970s and the policy of 'competitive disinflation' embraced in the 1980s.

Preference for low inflation

The control of inflation had long been a priority of French governments, although they repeatedly met with limited success. Between World War I and the 1980s, inflation was successfully contained during only two periods.[9] One coincided with the period following the adoption of the franc Poincaré. However, this led into the period of the Laval Deflation which was remembered as even more economically and politically disastrous than any previous or subsequent periods of high inflation. Only the ten year period following the Pinay–Rueff stabilisation plan of December 1958 corresponded to stable, low inflationary economic growth. This lack of success is surprising given the political importance attached to a strong currency and the rhetorical emphasis placed on non-inflationary economic growth. However, these values competed with other political considerations and the structure of State credit policy, a central feature of the French 'overdraft' economy. First, inflation was politically expedient: 'it provided the means to dampen social conflict that would otherwise undermine economic modernisation and political stability' (Goodman, 1992, p. 110). The importance of such considerations was most obvious in the case of the immediate postwar period and after May 1968.[10] Second, attempts to reform the postwar provision of State credit met strong opposition from the financial policymaking and banking élite, which sought to ensure their extensive control over major investment decisions.[11] Third, France had never suffered from hyperinflation which meant that the French were less preoccupied with monetary targets than were the Germans. Into the 1980s, the general attitudes in French society, including most trade unions and many leading industrialists, remained tolerance or indifference to the problem of inflation, especially if combined with high levels of economic growth.[12] For French governments, the importance of anti-inflationary objectives became great enough to override political considerations only in the late 1970s and 1980s.

Maintaining a surplus

Prior to World War II, the trade balance of a country was an almost universal preoccupation. Equally, it was an almost universal assumption that an economy was in poor health unless the trade balance was in surplus.[13] In the postwar period, the trade (and even the overall payments) balance ceased to be a core preoccupation in several countries, notably the United States and Britain. However, in France, governments continued to uphold this as a principal objective of economic policy.

State intervention in industry was organised accordingly, culminating in the national champions strategy of the Pompidou and Giscard presidencies. Exchange rate stability, notably between the dollar and the franc and European monetary co-operation, were seen as necessary to ensure this surplus. 'Competitive disinflation', the major French macroeconomic policy of the mid-1980s onwards, rested upon a firm attachment of the financial and monetary policymaking élite to the abovementioned economic objectives: fixed exchange rates, a strong franc, low inflation and a trade surplus (Fitoussi, 1993; 1995).

Support for an interventionist State

French attitudes to a strong currency, monetary stability and a trade surplus also reflected a postwar tradition of assertive State intervention in the economy, labelled *volontarisme*. This tradition was rooted in an older mercantilist statist tradition dating to the *ancien régime* 'in combination with the Saint-Simonist anticipation of a technocratic managerialism' (Hayward, 1986, pp. 9–11). A core underlying assumption of this tradition was the mistrust of the capacity of the market to ensure the most appropriate use of resources to enable both strong economic growth and social harmony. This applied as much to exchange rate policy as to investment decisions. Speculative attacks against the franc, it was argued, often had little to do with the strength of the French economy or the level of inflation. Active intervention was, therefore, necessary to avoid the destabilising effects of international capital flows. However, as in most areas of economic management, the monetary policy of a *volontariste* State was influenced invariably by factors other than the effective use of national resources. Moreover, there was never agreement as to the appropriate balance between economic growth and social harmony. President Charles de Gaulle's attitude to the strong franc epitomised both this assertiveness as well as its potentially non economic nature.[14]

Liberal and left-wing opposition

Economic attitudes also discouraged support for monetary co-operation and integration. Fixed exchange rates were opposed by many liberal and left-wing economists and politicians. The former argued that only floating currencies properly reflected the market value of a currency. The latter sought the removal of the external constraint created by exchange rate mechanisms and the pursuit of redistributive reflationary economic policies. Both questioned the economic logic of focusing upon the strength of the currency. A few liberal economists did not see exchange rate mechanisms as useful anti-inflationary tools. Wage and price controls were the crucial policies that made domestic anti-inflationary policies successful. Left-wing economists and politicians generally refused to place a priority on the goal of stemming inflation. Certain liberal economists, influenced by Anglo-American thinking, also questioned the need to focus on the trade balance, while left-wing economists and politicians often argued that trade barriers could be raised in order to prevent a deficit in the trade balance in the context of reflationary economic policies. Many economists and politicians also placed greater emphasis on other goals, notably lowering unemployment, stimulating economic growth, and investment and redistributing wealth – regardless of the impact on inflation.

Attitudes on European integration

Attitudes on European integration more generally also shaped French policy on monetary co-operation and integration. These included attitudes on widening areas officially subject to intergovernmental policymaking at the European level – which involves extending the Commission's power of policy initiation – and widening areas of supranational control – either when member states lose their veto, or when Community institutions are granted specific powers to influence or to make decisions. From the early 1950s, the French political and administrative élite saw improved European co-operation and limited European integration as a useful channel for the pursuit of French economic and diplomatic interests. While there was always a small number of idealists (Euro-federalists) in French policymaking circles, most of the élite's support for European integration was consistently cautious and limited, and almost always intergovernmental. The emphasis that de Gaulle placed upon '*Europe des patries*' infused all French policymaking. French policy was positive only when developments clearly served French economic and diplomatic interests. This raises the difficulty of distinguishing between general attitudes on European integration and European monetary power motives. Pursuing limited further European integration was normally supported only to the extent that it was seen as an effective way to increase France's positive European and international power. Nationalist opposition to the transfer of State powers discouraged all forms of integration that went beyond the economic. Even the more 'Euro-friendly' of French policymakers were reluctant to support further political integration.

Limited supranational developments were perceived and defended as necessary in the context of major gains for France. In other words, concessions to German demands for greater political integration were minimal, limited principally to package deals leading to the new policies and the treaty reform sought by the French. Thus the ECSC created a High Authority with stronger powers. The nationalist reaction to this led the French government to insist upon strengthening the Council of Ministers – a purely intergovernmental forum – as the major decision-making body of the EEC. Attempts to move towards weighted majority voting in the Council were subsequently blocked by de Gaulle (the 'Empty Chair Crisis'), but it is very likely that less overtly 'nationalist' French leaders would have done the same. The adoption of Qualified Majority Voting (QMV) in the Single European Act (1987) was seen as necessary to overcome the potential obstructionism to the creation of the Single Market by competitively weaker countries.[15] French policy-makers only reluctantly accepted the gradual extension of the powers of the European Parliament. More recently, the acceptance of the term 'European Union' to describe the three pillars created in the Maastricht Treaty (1993) demonstrated the traditional Gaullist interpretation of the term 'Union', devoid of 'federalist' connotation, rather than any commitment to a federal state. The French joined the British in insisting upon the maintenance of member state vetoes on all advances in the intergovernmental policy co-operation covered by the two new pillars, Common Foreign and Security Policy and Home and Justice Affairs.

The underlying economic motives

French policymakers sought monetary power not only for power's sake, but in large part to achieve economic goals. Moreover, the economic attitudes of the policymaking élite were affected by the economic impact of previous policy decisions. Interdependence theories of European/regional integration emphasize the explanatory importance of economic motives. While progressive economic integration – the removal of tariff and non-tariff barriers to trade and then the liberalisation of capital flows and the attempt to move to financial integration – did not make necessary monetary co-operation and integration, co-operation and integration was provided a certain economic logic. Moreover, increased financial integration and the emergence of large-scale international capital movements during the 1960s made it increasingly difficult for countries to pursue an independent course in monetary affairs.

Odell and Story present a neoclassical liberal economic perspective which stresses international market conditions as a potentially useful explanatory factor for changes in foreign monetary policy content.

According to the neoclassical vision, 'the world is a market-place where rational actors respond promptly to evolving market conditions as relayed through changes in relative prices' (Story, 1988, p. 398). The supply of and demand for currencies in the foreign exchange markets depend upon the state of payments balances, which in turn relies on trends or cycles in relative prices, incomes, and national money stocks. International market conditions encourage foreign monetary policies to conform. 'Delays in adjustment by state institutions are deemed as irrational on the grounds that they involve rising costs' (Story, *ibid.*).

Both Odell and Story conclude that this market perspective is of limited explanatory value with regard to the development of foreign monetary policy. Notably, it provides a test of the neoclassical position. Its use as a tool to explain policy developments is invariably ambiguous for the following reasons (Odell, 1982, pp. 19, 25*ff* and 351). First, it permits numerous kinds of policy responses to market imbalances involving either less government intervention or different forms of government intervention designed to perfect the market. Liberals have tended to disagree as to the form of minimal intervention allowed. Moreover, the market perspective does not clarify whether or not a government behaving in accordance with market rationality is to act unilaterally, or through bargaining and organisation with other states. This perspective permits, therefore, floating, pegged or fixed exchange rates, co-operation on floating, or non co-operation, and the possible establishment or dismantling of multilateral institutions. The precise policy response will depend on other factors, above all attitudes. Only a Friedmanite position would insist upon floating and government non-intervention. Second, the explanatory power of the neoclassical position relies, to a large extent, upon the openness of the country in question to international market forces. Third, the market perspective alone fails to take into consideration previous international agreements which may constrain policymaking. Story also rejects the explanatory merit of international market conditions in his study of the establishment of the EMS: 'it provides a general explanation for divergent performances between the [French and German] economies; but even there, the market analysis provides no insight as to why policies in the past were adopted that generated divergent performances' (Story, 1988, p. 400).

The focus here is upon economic motives rather than the underlying international market conditions which influenced monetary policy-making. However, the economic motives were in large part shaped by these underlying conditions, notably the growing international and European economic interdependence and the consequently increased impact of economic developments in other countries upon the French economy. These conditions shaped motives both as a constraint upon policymaking and as a resource. The perspective applied by Odell and Story emphasizes the constraint aspect. Changes in international market conditions force governments to adapt policy and international market mechanisms constrain policy choices. Odell and Story neglect to examine the manner in which power motives encouraged French policymakers to use this constraint as a resource. Policymakers sought greater international and European monetary co-operation and integration in order to mitigate the negative impact of this international influence, to manipulate France's position in the international and European economy in order to place France in an economically advantageous position and to force through domestic economic reforms.

French policymakers have referred variably to seven closely related economic motives for supporting particular forms of European monetary co-operation and integration. It is necessary to consider both the manner in which international and domestic economic developments affected French economic attitudes but also the impact of economic attitudes upon the perception of these developments. The importance of these different motives varied considerably during the period under study. First, the core motive of all economic policy is to ensure economic growth, to which most of the other motives relate either directly or indirectly. Opposition to the EMU project grew following the Maastricht summit because the economic constraints of the project (the economic convergence criteria) combined with the asymmetric operation of the ERM required more austerity, menaced deflation and inhibited short term economic growth.

Combating inflation

In France, as in most advanced industrialised states, this larger encompassing objective was, by the late 1970s, transformed into ensuring non-inflationary economic growth. The spiral of inflation, devaluation, and then even greater inflation, threatened to develop beyond the control of policymakers. In the context of an increasingly open economy, devaluation became increasingly ineffective and even harmful.

[Its] effect on the price of imported products and the resulting [impact] on domestic prices greatly exceeds the positive impact on exports, which has become more haphazard in a world where technical standards, quality and reliability are for many products more important criteria than sale price: and in these areas and for a number of consumer goods, French industry does not perform well.

(Patat and Lutfalla, 1990, p. 234)

Monetary laxity thus risked weakening the competitiveness of French industry. In order to deal with this problem, Giscard and his prime minister, Raymond Barre, imposed two disciplines on the French economy: exchange-rate stability, and a lower rate of short term economic growth than that of France's principal trading partners.

Reforming the 'overdraft' economy

Once the need to combat inflation had been embraced by key French policymakers, they sought to reform the inherently inflationary and debt-ridden domestic 'overdraft' economy (Loriaux, 1991). The French economy was characterised by a high degree of dependence on institutionally allocated credit (the 'treasury circuits') – in 1976, 85 per cent of all finance provided to firms and households were accorded by banks or some other financial institutions.[16] The generous provision of credits resulted in excessively casual cash-flow management in both firms and banks which led to a high level of indebtedness of firms to banks, and banks to the Bank of France. Alternative sources of finance were severely underdeveloped – thus, for example, the virtual nonexistence of a financial market. The 'overdraft' economy was the product of the government's unwillingness to tackle the political legacy of the immediate postwar growth-oriented industrial policies. It created structures and patterns of financial behaviour that increased the difficulty of achieving monetary stabilisation in France and were politically difficult to change. It relied upon the *'encadrement du crédit'* or 'tightening of credit' – a clumsy weapon – to combat domestic inflation. Moreover, monetary policymakers of the 1950s and 1960s attributed endemic inflationary pressure in the economy to deficit spending, and therefore sought to use fiscal policy to fight it. While the 'overdraft' economy could be tolerated during periods of low-inflationary economic growth, the inflationary impact of the Grenelle accords and the rise in oil prices during the 1970s underlined its structural weakness.

French monetary policymakers came to see a European exchange rate mechanism – the Snake and then the EMS – as a useful disciplinary device that would help to enforce necessary anti-inflationary reforms which met the resistance of influential interests. In this way, they sought to increase their control over the domestic economy by surrendering some margin of manoeuvre over monetary policy. While the extent of reform was limited during the Barre government, the motive was nonetheless important in determining French European monetary policy. More serious reform had to wait until the Socialist government began its serious restructuring of domestic financial markets in 1984.[17]

Intra-European exchange rate stability

The French and most European governments also officially accepted the argument that European economic integration and increased international economic exchange required exchange rate stability to diminish uncertainty, to permit more successful trade and thus permit greater economic growth. This view was not, however, universally shared and relied upon a series of arguments about the merits of fixed or pegged (fixed-but-adjustable) exchange rates as opposed to floating currencies. In France, it relied on a firmly entrenched opposition to floating. If trade arguments motivated French policymakers to diminish exchange rate instability, it is important to note that companies involved in large-scale imports and exports never campaigned actively for improved European monetary co-operation.

Intra-European exchange rate stability was initially considered necessary to ensure the survival of the Common Agricultural Policy (CAP). For the French, the CAP was of considerable political and economic importance, due to the influence of the farm lobby and to the operation of the policy's provisions which ensured France a large net gain from the Community budget. In December 1964, Community member states agreed on common agricultural prices quoted in European Units of Account (EUA), but linked directly to the value of national currencies. A devaluation of 10 per cent would correspondingly increase agricultural prices and the reverse for revaluations, which provided additional incentive to avoid parity realignments (Gros and Thygesen, 1992, p. 11).[18]

However, the survival of the CAP – despite frequent claims to the contrary – did not depend upon intra-European exchange rate stability, due to the introduction of Monetary Compensatory Amounts (MCAs) in 1969–70. MCAs were far from perfect instruments, introduced to neutralise the impact of currency realignments on the competitivity of agricultural products from the different member states. A large devaluation or a free float still made the setting of agricultural prices exceedingly difficult.[19] Nonetheless, MCAs enabled French governments to forego participation in European exchange rate mechanisms – as when the franc left the Snake – without destroying the CAP. Indeed, protecting the CAP remained a consideration of limited importance in determining French policy on European monetary co-operation and integration.

French opposition to floating also stemmed from the impact that capital flows had upon the exchange rate of the franc in relation to the mark, with a nearly constant downward pressure placed on the franc. This created an additional motive for monetary co-operation: to diminish the cost of defending the value of the franc, notably the franc–mark parity. This motive is distinguished here from the larger objective of reforming the International Monetary System in order to ensure greater stability, which is considered in the international monetary section. The uneven impact of dollar fluctuations upon European currencies and the resulting speculation crises encouraged French governments to support European monetary co-operation. The more purely economic motives were to shield the franc from speculation and to spread the burden of defending the franc as a weak currency to strong currency country members of the EMS. This motive also encouraged the development of strong franc policies as a means of building the credibility of the franc in order to discourage speculation.

Lowering interest rates

In order to stimulate domestic economic growth, French governments consistently attempted to minimise real interest rates and, after having embraced anti-inflationary objectives, sought to do so without substantially increasing the money supply. Lowering interest rates involved lowering inflation and convincing international money traders of the credibility of the strong franc policy. For most of the 1970s and 1980s, international market conditions imposed relatively high rates on the French economy given high inflation, the expectation of devaluation, and then the lingering reputation for an addiction to high inflation and devaluation. In addition to the EMS constraint, the French were prevented from pursuing a low interest rate policy by a fear of inflation and by the need to attract international capital. Opposition to the EMS increased during the period following German reunification, when the system's asymmetric operation, combined with high German rates and low French inflation, led to excessively high real rates.

Aiming for a surplus

Finally, French support for European monetary co-operation was a response to the imbalance in the country's international payments position. French monetary and economic policy centred around the objective of reversing a chronic trade and overall balance of payments deficit. According to the economic perspective applied by Bergsten, the international monetary arrangements preferred by a particular country depends upon the priorities that it accords to four different responses to an imbalance in its international payments position.

> First, [a country] can finance the imbalance. ... Second, [it] can alter the course of its domestic economy in an effort to adjust the imbalance indirectly. ... Third, [it] can seek to suppress its external imbalance directly by adopting selective measures aimed at particular classes of international transactions. ... Fourth, a country can seek to adjust the imbalance directly by changing its exchange rate.
>
> (Bergsten, 1975; 1996, pp. 12–19)

French governments opted for all four responses at various times, depending upon the prevailing economic attitudes of the moment and the domestic political situation. However, their support for European monetary co-operation, the move from the fixed-but-adjustable EMS to the fixed exchange rate regime and then the EMU project, depended upon the increased emphasis placed upon the second response. To the extent that monetary co-operation involved the collective defence of weak currencies, the first response also encouraged progress in this direction. The French attempted the third response principally by resorting to capital controls. However, with increased dependence upon foreign capital to finance domestic industrial debt, and German and British insistence upon the liberalisation of capital movements within the Community – especially in the context of the Single European Market (SEM) programme – this response became increasingly difficult to defend. By the mid-1970s, the fourth response was considered ineffective due to the inflationary impact of devaluations.

The second response related to two closely linked motives. First, and most importantly, French governments sought to improve their trade balance by pursuing the policy of 'competitive disinflation'. Lower French inflation would make French products more competitive, both domestically and as exports, than the products of countries with higher inflation. Previously, the goal of redressing the trade balance encouraged the adoption of tariff or non-tariff barriers and considerable State assistance for particular national firms deemed able to compete in the world economy (the 'national champions'). Three developments during the 1970s and 1980s forced French governments to adopt a new strategy to improve the competitiveness of French companies: increasingly constraining European legislation on state subsidies and mergers; the inflationary impact and diplomatic difficulties created by large devaluations; and the Single Market programme which was to remove nontariff barriers to the flow of European products. This strategy was linked to the motive of reforming the internal structures and processes of the 'overdraft' economy. Second, French governments sought to protect France's competitive position by discouraging the devaluation of high inflation country currencies. These motives encouraged French governments to use European monetary co-operation as a constraint upon both themselves and other European countries.

Domestic political motives

Five domestic political motives influenced the expression of French policy on European monetary co-operation and integration, although they were secondary to international and monetary power motives. First, government members involved directly in monetary policymaking had to demonstrate some responsiveness to the demands and opinions of other leading politicians of the party or parties in government, the National Assembly party members and grassroots support. Party competition and party political strategy (linked closely to electoral considerations) also shaped policymaking. As a minimal reflection of this strategy, a government's policy choices were affected by its strength or weakness; that is, its margin of manoeuvre within the constraints of party competition. A third domestic political motive in pursuing European monetary co-operation and integration is that it provided a useful political, as well as psychological, constraint on economic policymaking, thus helping political leaders introduce anti-inflationary policies that otherwise might not be adopted for political reasons. Fourth, government policymaking was influenced by public opinion.

Finally, governments responded to the views of powerful groups which sought to influence policymaking in order to protect their interests. In theory, those groups which had the most to gain from exchange rate stability, notably large exporters and importers, should have pushed most actively for monetary co-operation. Interest group positions on monetary co-operation and integration should have roughly corresponded to their prioritisation of economic objectives, stressing anti-inflation or employment. On the one hand, groups which stressed anti-inflationary measures (notably the financial sector) should have supported constraining European mechanisms that discouraged currency devaluation. On the other, groups which emphasized employment and immediate economic growth as priorities (even at the expense of higher inflation) should have opposed mechanisms that prevented the adoption of macroeconomic policies that served these priorities.

One final point should be made before moving on to the detailed analysis of French policymaking. With regard to the source of policy positions, the terms 'the French', 'France', 'French government(s)' and 'French policymakers' are used interchangeably in the following chapters. They refer to official or unofficial French policy as approved by the president and/or the prime minister and/or the minister of finance. However, the purpose is never to treat 'the French' as a spuriously uniform whole. At different times, from 1968 to 1999, French politicians and administrative officials presented diverging positions on the same issue.

2
The First Steps to European Monetary Co-operation, 1968 to 1981

French policy on monetary co-operation and integration in Europe prior to 1968

Different French governments supported European monetary co-operation, and even integration, from the nineteenth century. The French sought the creation of the Latin Monetary Union in 1865 for a combination of economic and political reasons which included the rise of Prussian economic and military power (Dyson, 1994, pp. 26–8). While seriously disrupted in 1878, the Union continued formally until March 1929. After World War II, the European Payments Union was a successful form of monetary co-operation, essential for French and European reconstruction and economic growth and an important step towards improved economic co-operation (Lynch, 1997, pp. 122–5). During the 1950s, the French did not see the co-ordination of member state economic and monetary policies as a crucial factor in the establishment of the Common Market. The French and the other Community member states believed that the successful functioning of the IMS throughout the 1950s made efforts at the European level unnecessary. Moreover, the French supported the general consensus that existed on monetary policy in favour of international co-ordination and against European level co-ordination which would have excluded the dollar and pound (Tsoukalis, 1977, p. 51).

Nonetheless, certain provisions of the Treaty of Rome recognize the importance of some form of economic and monetary policy co-ordination to ensure the smooth functioning of the Common Market (Articles 103–109). However, despite these provisions and the creation of the Community Monetary Committee as a consultative body to help co-ordinate monetary policies, little co-ordination took place. During the first decade of the Common Market, most proposals for increased monetary co-operation came from the Commission, the new Monetary Committee and the European Parliament – for example, the European Reserve Union of January 1959. The Commission presented a bold, albeit vague, proposal for the creation of a parallel European currency in January 1965, but this was largely ignored. Between May 1964 and January 1968 there was an almost complete lack of progress in the monetary field at the Community level. Bloomfield (1973), among others, claims that European countries were content with the prolonged monetary stability of the period due to the continuing payments surpluses and the mounting reserves of EEC member states.[20] However, de Gaulle's determined opposition to the development of any new European policies was an important factor discouraging Commission activity.

Prior to 1968, French interest in European monetary co-operation and integration – to the extent that it was present – was due principally to negative international monetary power motives: to limit the impact of dollar fluctuations upon the stability of intra-European parities. Within the Bretton Woods system, each participating currency was allowed to fluctuate up to 1 per cent on each side of its dollar parity. This meant a possible 2 per cent fluctuation between two European currencies, which the French and other participating European countries found unacceptably large. They therefore signed the European Monetary Agreement in 1955, which, upon entering into effect in 1958, established ± 0.75 per cent fluctuation margins for participating European currencies. Until 1968, however, intervention by European central banks in order to respect these margins was minimal given the general stability in parities.

The Agreement also symbolised improved *de facto* French economic and monetary co-ordination with the European partners. Relatively high French inflation during the mid-1950s and an overvalued franc led to French reluctance to accept the Agreement's provisions which would render all participating European currencies freely convertible (for non-residents) with the dollar. The 1958 Pinay–Rueff stabilisation plan ensured French participation. However, the French, under de Gaulle, opposed the more far-reaching proposals for monetary co-operation of the Commission, the Monetary Committee and the European Parliament. They argued for momentary co-ordination only when irked by unilateral German action – the expression of minor European power motives – such as the mark/guilder revaluation of 1961.

De Gaulle's overall strategy to maximise the degree of French economic and monetary power in relation to the Americans did not extend to the development of policies in favour of greater European monetary co-operation – beyond the formulation of common European positions against the Americans – let alone monetary integration. During the 1960s, particularly after 1964, the United States increasingly became a source of international monetary instability by refusing to address its own payments disequilibrium. The dollar 'overhang' led to a number of speculative crises during the 1960s, while a more expansionist American monetary policy began to fuel global inflation. The decline in confidence in the dollar resulted in a massive capital flow to European currencies and securities. Moreover, the French disliked Bretton Woods because they felt that the United States exploited its situation to acquire real assets abroad in exchange for non-convertible dollars (Berger, 1972, pp. 348–58; Bordo *et al.*, 1993). The result was increased tension between the French and the Americans: the former blamed US policy for being the principal source of inflation in France, which was not actually the case. At his 4 February 1965 press conference, de Gaulle launched a direct attack on the dollar, sought to remove it as pivot of the Bretton Woods system, praised the virtues of the gold standard and started a gold war with the Americans: the French Treasury began converting its dollar balances into gold in order to decrease the value of the dollar.[21] According to the de Gaulle–Rueff strategy, the eventual return to the gold standard made enhanced European monetary co-operation unnecessary.

Although official French policy focused upon IMS reform, some leading French policy makers argued in favour of radical steps towards European monetary integration in order to ensure continued monetary stability and even, in the long term, challenge the hegemonic role of the dollar. As early as 1963, a French National Assembly commission supported the creation of a common Community currency, as one of several possibilities to counter growing IMS instability.[22] In 1964, Giscard, then minister of finance, and André de Lattre, the head of the French Treasury, proposed the creation of a parallel European currency, the CRU (Composite Reserve unit), the value of which would be determined by member state gold reserves. Their stated objective was to ensure the survival of the new CAP in the context of international monetary instability, as well as challenge the position of the dollar (and sterling) as the dominant international reserve currency. In January 1965, Giscard also indicated his support for Commission proposals for the rapid introduction of a parallel currency (to circulate in addition to other

European currencies) (*Le Monde*, 15 January 1965). However, neither the Commission nor the interested French officials made any detailed concrete proposals.

While both de Gaulle and Giscard were motivated principally by the desire to challenge unacceptable American monetary hegemony, their different policy responses were rooted in opposing attitudes to the loss of national policymaking autonomy and European integration. Giscard was generally favourable to limited further European integration. De Gaulle, his former prime minister, Michel Debré and other leading Gaullists were opposed to any further loss of national policymaking powers, particularly on a matter of such symbolic importance to the French nation. De Gaulle also tended to oppose the co-ordination of Community member state economic policies which involved quantitative targets which would thus limit national policymaking autonomy. The 1965 'Empty Chair' crisis put an end to all Commission monetary initiatives, while nationalist opposition silenced Giscard on the matter – one of several factors leading to his resignation in January 1966.[23] Out of government, he continued to call publicly for the creation of an EEC currency (*Le Monde*, 7 June 1966 and 1 November 1966).

This battle within the French government and administration over a European currency also reflected differing economic strategies, even though both Rueff and Giscard sought to entrench anti-inflationary measures. Giscard's opposition to the Rueffian project of the return to the gold standard was in part rooted in his belief that this would allow the government to avoid the austerity measures and structural reforms that were necessary to strengthen the French economy.

The monetary stabilisation of 1958 – which involved the devaluation of the franc – proved fragile. The global economic expansion of the early 1960s generated inflationary pressures from which the French 'overdraft' economy was poorly insulated. Giscard tightened the provision of capital (*encadrement du crédit*) in order to gain better control over inflation. To avoid the ill-effects of this policy, he also imposed fiscal restraint and transferred the financial responsibility for government programmes to parapublic or private agents (*débudgetisation*).

The financial reforms of 1966–67 were the culmination of the search for new, non-inflationary sources of capital that could be used to facilitate industrial investment (Loriaux, 1991, p. 174). The reforms were not, however, particularly far-reaching. A great deal of State financial support continued to be funnelled to both industrial modernisation as well as the more backward sectors of the economy. Despite all the good intentions and because of the government's failure sufficiently to reform the 'treasury circuits', the control of inflation proved difficult. Government austerity measures continued. Parsimonious wage increases in the public sector resulted in the strikes of 1963–64. Frustration over wages, combined with that over the more general effects of austerity, were two of the principal catalysts of the May 1968 uprising.

Establishing French policy on European monetary co-operation

During the period from 1968 to 1981 there was a gradual construction of the set of core motives and attitudes which shaped French policy on European monetary co-operation. The period begins in 1968 for the reasons discussed in the introductory chapter. The period ends at the May 1981 presidential elections, by which time the commitment of the Barre government to the new European Monetary System (EMS) and the anti-inflationary policies necessary to maintain the franc in it, had proven firm. The goal here is to explain both the transformation of French motives and attitudes, and the changes in the manner in which these motives and attitudes shaped policy. These changes depended largely upon developments imposed upon French policymakers: notably, the refusal of the Americans to reform the International Monetary System (IMS) to promote greater stability, the impact of instability, the decision by the Germans to float the mark with other European currencies in March 1973, and the impact of the rise in oil prices in autumn 1973 upon domestic economic growth and inflation. However, there was much margin for manoeuvre: these changes did not dictate the development of a particular French policy.

This chapter does not enter into the detail provided in subsequent chapters on specific policy decisions. In part this is because the failed negotiations on EMU, the functioning of the Snake arrangements and the successful negotiations leading to the establishment of the EMS have been thoroughly examined in several studies, including, notably, Dyson (1994), Kruse (1980), Ludlow (1982) and Tsoukalis (1977). These studies explore the positions of all the member states yet focus on French and German interests given their importance in influencing the direction of negotiations. They do not, however, examine French motives and attitudes systematically. The purpose of this chapter is to provide a structured analysis of the development of the core motives and attitudes which were to shape French policymaking during the 1980s and 1990s.

European monetary initiatives and developments

At the beginning of this period, increased international monetary instability sparked renewed interest in EMU at the European level. The Prime Minister of Luxembourg, Pierre Werner, published a plan in January 1968 calling for the creation of EMU. In February, the European Commission published a more cautious Memorandum which recommended the establishment of a Community mutual aid system but opposed the irrevocable fixing of exchange rates and did not mention the creation of any European Monetary Fund. In November 1968, in spite of unprecedented levels of speculation against the franc, the French government decided to maintain its parity with the mark. The Commission Memorandum of February 1969 (the first Barre Plan) recommended greater medium term economic policy convergence and compatibility, the improved co-ordination of short term economic policies and the establishment of short term monetary support and medium term financial aid. Following a French initiative, in July 1969, the Council of Ministers agreed to the extension of a May 1964 obligation to consult on exchange rate changes to cover all economic policy measures having impact upon other member states.

At the December 1969 European Summit in The Hague, President George Pompidou called for the creation of EMU, while Chancellor Brandt presented concrete proposals on a two stage development towards this goal. Pompidou called specifically for a pooling of foreign reserves which could be used for short term monetary support, the common administration of Special Drawing Rights, the need for a common policy and a single European spokesman on international monetary issues. In January 1970, the Ecofin Council agreed upon the creation of a short term monetary support mechanism which provided unlimited credit for up to 45 days. In March 1970, the Werner Group was created to 'prepare a report containing an analysis of the different suggestions and making it possible to identify the basic issues for a realisation by stages of economic and monetary union in the Community'.[24] An interim report was submitted in May 1970 and the final report was submitted in the following November. The major division in the Committee was between the 'monetarists' and the 'economists', the former consisting of the French, Belgians and Luxembourgeois, while the latter consisted of the Germans, Dutch and Italians. The former argued in favour of the immediate establishment of tighter fluctuation margins and the creation or enlargement of short term monetary support and medium term financial aid. The 'economists' insisted upon greater economic convergence and the improved co-ordination of economic policies prior to the tightening of fluctuation margins. The final report of the Werner Group achieved a delicate balance between these two positions, advancing the principle of 'parallelism' in the progress of both the economic and the monetary fields. The final goal of EMU was also defined and some specific proposals on necessary institutional reforms made: the creation of a 'centre of decision for economic policy' and the 'Community system for the central banks'. In February 1971, the Ecofin Council adopted a resolution, on the realisation of EMU by stages, and three decisions, on the improved co-ordination of short term economic policies, the strengthened collaboration between central banks and on the activation of the medium term financial aid mechanism (accepted in principle from the first Barre Plan). This mechanism allowed for a longer delay for the repayment of certain loans incurred during speculative attacks. Following the formal agreement of these measures in March 1971, the Community central bank governors agreed to reduce the intra-EEC fluctuation margins from ±0.75 – permitted by the European Monetary Agreement of 1955 – to ±0.60 per cent, to come into effect the following June.

The tighter fluctuation margins were not put into effect due to the monetary crisis of May 1971. The French blocked negotiations on EMU until the resolution of the international monetary crisis. In August 1971, President Nixon announced a series of measures – including the end of the dollar's convertibility into gold and of the American government's commitment to maintaining the 1 per cent fluctuation band with other currencies – which formally destroyed the Bretton Woods system. To deal with the increased instability, in September 1971, President Pompidou called for the creation of an executive organ attached to the Committee of the Governors of Central banks to manage 'in a concerted fashion' the monetary reserves of the EC. In December, Pompidou met with Nixon in the Azores and agreed upon the re-establishment of fluctuation margins of ±2.25 per cent between the dollar and other participating currencies. This was formally established in the Smithsonian Agreement later that month.

The new international arrangements permitted a maximum fluctuation of 4.5 per cent between individual European currencies which was considered excessively large to ensure the survival of the CAP. In a February 1972 meeting, Pompidou and Brandt agreed upon the tightening of European fluctuation margins to ±2.25 per cent between individual participating currencies, which the other Community member states and candidates agreed to at Basle later that month. This created a

European monetary arrangement within the fluctuation margins established with the dollar – thus the label 'Snake in the tunnel' – which entered into force on 24 April 1972. At Basle, the Council also adopted a Directive legalising the adoption of capital controls, which reversed the two Directives on the liberalisation of capital movements adopted in 1960 and 1962. In September 1972, the Ecofin Council agreed to establish by April 1973 a European Monetary Co-operation Fund (EMCF or FECOM) to be managed by the Bank for International Settlements. This was given no powers, serving principally to assist with the co-ordination of monetary policies. Instability during the first three months of 1973 and the refusal of the Americans to keep the dollar in the fluctuation margins of the Smithsonian Agreement led the Germans to decide to float the mark in a joint float of European currencies – removing the Snake from its tunnel on March 1973.

The French decided to float the franc outside the Snake in January 1974. In the following September, the French finance minister, Jean-Pierre Fourcade, presented a plan on a reform of European monetary arrangements (*Agence Europe/Documents*, 817, 17 September 1974). This was the most far-reaching French initiative on European monetary reform to date. However, few of the themes were new. It called for a 'concerted float' of all the Community currencies which would have involved close co-ordination between the five countries with currencies participating in the Snake mechanism and the other four member states, including France, the currencies of which floated independently. It proposed joint EEC interventions in the exchange markets in order to ensure greater stability in the parities of European currencies and the dollar; greater flexibility in intra-EEC exchange rate adjustments; an extension of Community credit facilities and the issue of Community loans; the definition of a new unit of account and co-ordinated European action in the Eurodollar market. For the first time, the French also proposed the establishment of a margin of fluctuation around a weighted average of Community currencies rather than between the strongest and weakest. In May 1975, Fourcade further argued 'that responsibility for intervention should not fall only on the central bank, the currency of which found itself at the lowest limit of intra-EEC margins' (Tsoukalis, 1977, pp. 156–7). These plans were opposed by the other member states. The French brought the franc back into the unreformed Snake in July 1975 but withdrew it again in March 1976. Subsequent proposals on the reform of European monetary arrangements – included in the June 1975 Commission report on 'European Union', the November 1975 *All Saints' Day Manifesto* and the 1976

Tindemans report on 'European Union' – were rejected by some or all of
the member states.

In 1978, upon the initiative of Chancellor Schmidt, discussions
between French and German representatives began on the creation of
a new monetary system. The Franco-German compromise was presented
to the other Community heads of State and Government at the July
Bremen Summit and negotiations on the new system were largely complete by the December 1978 Brussels Summit. The new system differed
from the Snake mechanism in the following ways. The margins of
fluctuation of ±2.25 per cent were established around the European
Currency Unit (ECU), a weighted basket of Community currencies.
The ECU would also be used in intra-Community exchange rate interventions. Moreover, the repayment period of credit supplied under the
short term monetary support mechanism was extended and medium
term financial assistance for this repayment enlarged. The member
states were unable to respect the 1 January 1979 deadline for putting
the new system into operation when the French tabled a proposal that
monetary compensation amounts (MCAs) be gradually phased out. On
14 March 1979, the EMS entered into operation. From this date to the
May 1981 presidential elections the franc's parity with the mark was
maintained.

Coping with the collapse of Bretton Woods

International monetary power motives – more important in shaping
French policy during this decade than during the following periods –
provided the logic for the first steps to European monetary co-operation.
International motives initially encouraged the French to pursue IMS
reform, which would have rendered developments at the European
level unnecessary. European monetary co-operation and integration
was considered secondary. The French supported fixed European parities
– which effectively existed during most of the 1960s – within a stable
IMS. Initial French interest in European co-operation was, therefore,
limited to the establishment of a common European position on IMS
reform. French interest in European co-operation to achieve international monetary power objectives grew as the possibility of desirable IMS
reform faded and the stability provided for at the international level,
and thus in Europe, decreased.

The manner in which international monetary power motives encouraged the French to support European monetary co-operation developed considerably during this period. Four specific motives can be

distinguished which varied in terms of their influence over the direction of French policy. First, as during the period prior to 1968, the French sought European support for their positions on IMS reform (positive power). This objective dominated France's European ambitions until the departure of the Snake mechanism from its tunnel in March 1973. It was subsequently of less importance given the improbability of IMS reform. One of the major French ambitions during the period was to create a 'European monetary personality' or 'identity' which would present with one voice common positions – ideally French positions – in relation to the rest of the world and in particular the Americans. The French argued that the proposed EMCF should have as its principal function the co-ordination of European positions for international negotiations.[25] Insistence upon common European policies structured French policy on European monetary co-operation most clearly during the period between May and December 1971. At this time the French refused to participate further in discussions on EMU without a satisfactory joint European agreement on international monetary reform.

There were three principal reasons for the lack of French success. First, they were unable to establish an 'identity' largely because of the consistently different reactions of the EEC member states to international monetary instability. Second, French views tended to differ from the European norm and were consistently more strident in relation to the United States. The French repeatedly took unilateral positions which contradicted those of their European partners.[26] Following the collapse of international arrangements, French demands became more modest – focusing upon increasing American responsibility for stabilising the dollar through the introduction of capital controls.[27] However, even on this point the Germans did not support the French. Third, the best way to ensure the eventual creation of an 'identity' was to establish EMU, the political and institutional implications of which the French refused to accept. The final report of the Werner Group only recognized the 'need for a progressive movement towards the adoption of common positions in relations with third countries and international organisations' (1970).

The French did succeed in establishing European unity on some major issues. First, after a month of considerable disagreement as to the appropriate European reaction to the Nixon measures, on 13 September the six EEC finance ministers agreed on a common position in the upcoming international negotiations, which largely satisfied the French.[28] The Smithsonian accord of December 1971 was the most significant joint European action at the international level. Following the Nixon measures and the French government's decision to block American–EEC trade discussions in retaliation, President Pompidou reached an agreement with Chancellor Brandt on the realignment of EEC currencies.[29] This enabled Pompidou to negotiate with Nixon in the Azores on behalf of the EEC in establishing a new international monetary arrangement which formed the basis of the Smithsonian accord.[30] Another example of successful joint European action was the Rambouillet agreement of November 1975. Here the French and Americans agreed on a series of measures for limited international monetary reform and the establishment of a co-ordination and intervention mechanism between the Snake currencies and the dollar. As with the Smithsonian accord, the French had reached prior agreement on a framework with the Germans and the compromise was later endorsed by the EEC Council of Ministers.

The second international monetary power motive consisted in diminishing the impact of dollar fluctuations by seeking agreement between EEC member states in order to increase intra-EEC parity stability (negative power). The French sought stability for several reasons: to challenge the international role of the dollar; to avoid attacks on the franc; and to protect the operation of the CAP. To accomplish this, the French sought first to improve intra-European consultation on monetary and economic policies and the co-ordination of monetary policies;[31] second, to tighten fluctuation margins; and third, to adopt a common European policy on increased capital controls.

French support for the gradual narrowing of intra-EEC margins was motivated by the impact of increased international and European monetary instability and the IMF discussions starting in 1969 on the possibility of introducing greater exchange rate flexibility at the international level. This objective was central to France's 'monetarist' strategy during the EMU negotiations. The maintenance of tighter margins and stable intra-EEC parities relied upon two developments: the establishment of guaranteed support mechanisms and the convergence of European economic policies (above all, on inflation and balance of payments). The French sought the former largely for European monetary power and economic reasons. They opposed the latter because convergence infringed upon autonomous economic policymaking.

The French were the principal catalysts behind the March 1971 agreement to tighten fluctuation margins. The collapse of Bretton Woods and the establishment of larger fluctuation margins in the Smithsonian agreement encouraged French demands to reinforce European arrangements to provide stability: which led to the creation of the Snake mechanism. The British decision to float the pound at the end of June 1972 placed both the Snake and the tunnel (the whole system of pegged exchange rates) at risk. The French were worried that other countries would follow the British precedent – the Germans were tempted to do so – and threatened to abandon the Paris Summit planned for October 1972 if the Six did not commit themselves to keeping their exchange rates fixed (*Le Monde*, 25 June 1972).

French support for tighter EEC fluctuation margins did not extend to support for a joint European float. However, the French had little choice but to participate in it. On the one hand, the Americans actively encouraged the collapse of international arrangements by refusing to respect the Smithsonian and other agreements to support the dollar. On the other, the Germans – on 4 March 1973 – informed the French that they would organise a joint European float with or without the participation of the franc. The French opposed the joint float because they believed that this would not help remove what they saw as the principal source of instability – dollar fluctuations. A joint float amounted to accepting the failure of French efforts to reform the IMS. However, French reluctance was only based partially on international monetary power considerations. European monetary motives, notably French fears of a mark-centred European float, were likely more important. This explains the preference the French expressed for the separate floating of European currencies: to avoid the pressure on the franc of a constantly revaluing mark. Subsequently, the French provided several reasons for supporting the joint float which were linked to strengthening their international monetary power. First, the joint float could provide greater stability between European currencies. Second, it could reinforce a European monetary 'identity' and be presented as an act of defiance towards the Americans. However, it is important here to distinguish between *a posteriori* justification and motives. Pompidou accepted the joint float because he had little choice but to do so.

The French also advocated the adoption of a more stringent system of capital controls in all the EEC countries. They began introducing controls in November 1968 and introduced a two-tiered market system (different rates for capital and current account transactions) in August 1971. The monetary crises of the late 1960s and early 1970s demonstrated the inefficacy of selective measures adopted in an uncoordinated fashion and only by certain member states. The French argued that the imposition of German controls was crucial to intra-EEC, and specifically franc, stability: by helping to stem the pressure to revalue the mark. Ironically, the French achieved a minor victory by gradually convincing the Germans, other Europeans and the Commission to introduce increased controls while the effectiveness of these controls decreased in the face of growing movements of speculative capital. Following the removal of the Snake from its tunnel, most of the EEC countries began slowly to dismantle controls. While the French lagged behind most of their European partners, Prime Minister Raymond Barre sped up efforts, and succeeded in removing all French controls by 1979.

The third international monetary power motive which encouraged the French to support improved European co-operation also involved increasing France's negative power *vis-à-vis* the Americans: to improve support mechanisms in order to discourage speculation against the franc and to ensure its defence. The French, initially opposed the development of an EEC mutual aid system – proposed by the Commission in February 1968 – because they did not see the need for it as the franc had hitherto been only moderately affected by speculative flows. Following the November 1968 and spring 1969 monetary crises, French interest increased markedly. A large amount of IMF credit was already available to the French. However, its provision was potentially slow and its required repayment rapid. Moreover, there was no absolute guarantee of the supply of credit, even though in practice this was not a problem. Establishing guaranteed credit was valued as a psychological weapon against the markets and would in itself discourage speculation. Furthermore, the bulk of support capital was American, which – especially for the French – created an undesirable dependence. Finally, to increase the pool of European reserves available for the defence of European currencies would help to build a European monetary identity and challenge American dominance. Because the development of European support mechanisms was also a means of increasing France's European monetary power, this is examined further in the following section.

The fourth international monetary power motive involved increasing France's positive power in relation to the Americans: to challenge directly the role of the dollar through European monetary co-operation. The French – perhaps incorrectly – saw tightening intra-EEC fluctuation margins as a principal way to diminish the use of the dollar as an intervention and reserve currency and as a means of international private transactions. In the context of the Bretton Woods system and the monetary arrangements of the Smithsonian accord, one reason for the preference given to the dollar was the lower exchange risk involved in holding dollar balances rather than other national currencies given the larger fluctuations possible between the latter (de Lattre, 1970). The French believed that if the intra-EEC margins of fluctuation were reduced, then the privilege enjoyed by the dollar for interventions in the exchange markets would be partially or totally eliminated. It was hoped that this would encourage the increased use of Community currencies in intra-EEC trade and holdings by Community central banks. On the Werner Group and later, the French argued that one of the main functions of the new EMCF should be to facilitate the use of Community currencies in the exchange markets and discourage the use of dollars.[32]

The French were unwilling to take dramatic steps resulting in the loss of monetary policymaking autonomy in order to challenge the international role of the dollar. During the discussions on EMU, they did not advocate the creation of a European single currency, even though the Commission presented this move as an effective way to challenge the dollar. Pompidou saw the creation of a single currency as a very long term objective and insisted on focusing full attention on the tightening of EEC fluctuation margins (Cousté, 1974, p. 110). Certain French policymakers – significantly Giscard – clearly did think in these terms. However, once elected president, Giscard ceased to speak publicly of the need to establish a single currency. The September 1974 French proposal and the following March 1975 Council decision to define the European Unit of Account (EUA) in terms of a basket of EEC currencies – the precursor to the ECU established in 1979 – was not conceived in this way, but rather in purely economic and statistical terms. Subsequent proposals to create a European currency – the 'Europa' presented in the Commission's report on *'European Union'* of June 1975 and the parallel currency of the *All Saints' Day Manifesto* of November 1975 – met with French indifference. They did publicly cite international monetary power motives in their decision to create the ECU in 1979. However, the desire to decrease the asymmetry of the Snake – European monetary power motives – was the immediate French goal.

French efforts to prevent the creation of a mark zone

European monetary power motives encouraged the French to pursue further European monetary co-operation only once this was seen as indispensable to control the expression of German monetary and economic power. Within the protective framework of the Bretton Woods system, the monetary impact of this power was negligible. Moreover, low French inflation and strong economic growth during most of the 1960s largely mirrored German economic developments. Growing instability in the IMS and the rapid increase of French inflation following the Grenelle accords, demonstrated for the first time the asymmetry in economic strength between France and Germany. The speculation crises of 1968 and 1969 provided the first monetary evidence of this asymmetry and demonstrated the impact of German monetary policy upon the franc. French economic growth during the early 1970s had been slightly greater than that of Germany, but French inflation had been considerably higher and this threatened a new wave of speculative attacks against the franc.[33] The French were facing a trade imbalance only three years after the large 1969 devaluation, while the Germans absorbed external shocks, pursued rigorous monetary policies and ran trade surpluses.

Improving European consultation and co-ordination

European monetary power motives led the French to seek four specific forms of monetary co-operation. First, they sought improved monetary and economic policy consultation and co-ordination with the Germans (and other European partners), principally to increase their control over German monetary decisions, notably realignments (positive power). Pressure on the franc to devalue increased substantially during the November 1968 monetary crisis and following the German government's decision to let the mark temporarily float without any prior warning to French officials. The French were left with little choice but to devalue the franc, although this was avoided only by Gaullist refusal to bow to a *fait accompli* partially imposed by the Germans.[34] The May 1969 crisis was precipitated by remarks made by the German finance minister regarding a likely mark revaluation which did not come to pass.

This negative experience led the French to demand the establishment of a system of obligatory consultations on parity realignments and the improvement of consultation and co-ordination more generally. During most of the period, the French saw consultation and co-ordination as a one way endeavour and sought to avoid as much as possible limits on French policymaking. Consultation ensured being informed of and having some say over German and other policy decisions. Co-ordination was seen as a means of extending this influence so as to make German policy decisions conform more to French interests. From 1968, the French sought improved co-ordination – on domestic monetary growth, credit and exchange rates – to encourage the Germans to adopt policies most conducive to exchange rate stability.

French support for economic co-ordination was limited to matters concerning budgets and balance of payments deficits. Principally, the French wanted the Germans (who purchased over 20 per cent of French exports) to reflate their economy in order to reduce both French balance of payments deficits and German surpluses. The French, like the others who defended the 'monetarist' position, argued that economic co-ordination should not precede monetary co-ordination. French opposition to extensive economic policy co-ordination was grounded principally on a refusal to restrict the national margin of manoeuvre on economic policymaking. However, in order to increase German flexibility on improved consultation and monetary co-ordination, the French also accepted some German demands for improved economic policy co-ordination. In January 1972, during the negotiations on the Snake mechanism, in return for German flexibility on French demands on capital controls, the French agreed upon the creation of a steering committee within the EEC responsible for the co-ordination of economic policies. There was no commitment that this co-ordination would actually take place, however. The French accepted co-ordination but only within an intergovernmental framework and with the maintenance of member state vetoes.

The French saw monetary consultation and co-ordination as a crucial element of European monetary co-operation.[35] In the context of the joint European float, Franco-German consultation and co-ordination was the only way to control German monetary policy. Following the departure of the franc from the Snake in January 1974 and again in March 1976, the French sought to be consulted and attempted to maintain co-ordinated EEC action in the exchange markets (buying and selling currencies) to maintain parity stability. They were particularly concerned by the increased influence of the Germans within the Snake, the uni-directional nature of consultations between the Federal Republic and the other smaller participating states and the limited consultation with non-participants. Given the minimal monetary support provided in the context of the arrangement and its asymmetry, the desire to participate in consultation and co-ordination was a principal reason for the French decision to return to the Snake in July 1975.

Increasing European support for the franc

European power motives also encouraged the French to demand improved support mechanisms. These were crucial to the participation of the franc in European exchange rate arrangements because the French opposed any significant restrictions on their economic policy-making autonomy that would otherwise be necessary to ensure stability between intra-EEC parities (negative power motives).[36] Several different mechanisms were established to facilitate the provision of potentially unlimited amounts of short term credit and the delayed repayment of

debts in the medium term. Throughout the period, the French continued to support the extension of credit granting mechanisms – for
example, the Fourcade Plan of September 1974 – and the organisation
of more generous debt repayment schemes (lengthening the settlements
period and relaxing the requirement that payments be made in the same
mixture of assets as the debtor's reserves). The EMS agreement involved
a substantial extension of the repayment period of credit and the enlargement of the amount of this credit provided for under the short term
monetary support mechanism. However, the extension of credit repayment schemes did not keep up with the rapid growth in speculative
capital flows and the amounts needed to defend the parity of the franc.
Moreover, French efforts to avoid convergence were foiled by German
insistence that the mechanisms designed to fend off unjustified speculation should not enable countries to avoid economic redressment or
realignment in the medium term. The French argued that no amount of
economic convergence could deter speculation. Thus, in order for
exchange rate arrangements to be credible it was necessary to demonstrate a financial capacity to withstand speculation.

The French were reluctant to extend this monetary support via the
pooling of reserves and opposed giving the EMCF control over these
reserves. As a debtor country, France, in theory, should have preferred
the multilateralisation of credit and debts with the EMCF because repayment conditions were normally more flexible. However, the French
opposed schemes to pool reserves largely because they did not wish to
immobilise a large percentage of national reserves at the European level,
especially with the advent of the energy crisis. Also, as one of the largest
Community reserve holders, France would contribute more than any
other Community country, except Germany. With large national gold
reserves, the French opposed schemes which proposed pooling a relatively large percentage of gold in comparison to dollars and European
currencies, as long as the price of gold was not clearly fixed (*Le Monde*, 5/
6 December 1973). In the EMS negotiations, the French accepted an
agreement on the pooling of 20 per cent of national gold reserves. This
was largely due to French support for the creation of the ECU, the
modification of the French position on a gold standard and a large
drop in the price of gold, which encouraged the French to get rid of
their reserves.

The French opposed Belgian and Italian proposals to strengthen the
EMCF by giving it control over pooled reserves and monetary support
mechanisms, because they did not want to give any powers to a supranational institution. This explains the apparent contradiction between

French insistence on the creation of the Fund – an agreement on it was considered as one of the pre-conditions for holding the Paris Summit of October 1972 – yet the refusal to grant it substantial powers. Established in April 1973, the Fund was only given minor technical functions – even fewer than those wanted by the French – due to German opposition. The French opposed subsequent attempts in 1973 and 1974 to expand its role. The agreement on reserve pooling in the EMS negotiations potentially gave the EMCF greater power. However, these reserves were effectively controlled within the intergovernmental framework of the Bank for International Settlements, as the EMCF was not given an independent status. Continued French opposition to the establishment of an independent Community monetary authority blocked any institutional progress, although as part of the EMS compromise package the French agreed to a statement committing the member states to establish a more powerful EMCF within the next two years.

French opposition to a joint European float

The third manifestation of European power motives was French resistance to German demands – from May 1971 – to organise a joint European float (negative power motives).[37] In addition to the international monetary motives for avoiding such a float, the French recognized that it would effectively create a mark zone in Europe and reinforce German power (Valance, 1996, p. 343). They saw a stable IMS as the best way to avoid the assertion of German power: German policy was effectively constrained in the context of international monetary arrangements because of the need to maintain the mark within the agreed upon fluctuation margins with the dollar. In a joint European float, the mark would be free to appreciate (in most cases) or depreciate in relation to the dollar to a degree considerably different than other European currencies, given different rates of inflation and the different attractiveness of the currencies to international capital. The franc would be forced either to follow mark movements or to realign. Without the convergence of economic policies to those in Germany, a joint float would thus result in greater potential instability between European currencies. Furthermore, in a joint European float, the compensating interest rate differential would have to be increased. German promises of increased support for weak currency countries were insufficient to compensate for the inherent asymmetry of a joint float.

Several French initiatives were designed in part to avoid a joint European float. These included efforts to promote stability – the introduction of capital controls and the maintenance of tighter parities – including the Nixon–Pompidou agreement and the following Smithsonian accord and perhaps even French insistence upon discussing EMU at the October 1972 Paris Summit. Faced with the German ultimatum of a joint float in March 1973, the French responded by proposing the separate float of individual currencies, even though the resulting instability would create difficulties for the operation of the CAP. French policy demonstrated that in spite of a strong opposition to floating and the objective of ensuring the stability of intra-EEC parities, European power motives had primacy. Moreover, the French decision to particip-ate in the Snake was also based on European power motives: faced with the German refusal to accept the separate float of European currencies, the French decided that participation was necessary in order to maintain influence over German policy and avoid the creation of a mark zone.

The first float of the franc outside the Snake in January 1974 was justified in power terms, although this was not directed specifically against the Germans or the asymmetry of the Snake: Pompidou argued that floating increased the French government's margin of manoeuvre in pursuing appropriate economic policies. In the context of the immediate post-oil crisis, the French wanted as much room to man-oeuvre as possible. Giscard, nonetheless, criticised the functioning of the Snake as 'a mechanism of European monetary prehistory' and advocated the creation of a more flexible system which would permit the participation of all the Community currencies (*Le Monde*, 3 May 1974). On the one hand, the French wanted to participate in consulta-tions at the European level, while on the other, they sought to avoid the constraint on domestic economic policymaking created by Snake mem-bership. The proposals of the Fourcade Plan of September 1974 reflected these two motives: the French sought to avoid re-entry into the Snake yet shape German monetary policy in the context of a 'concerted float' of the Snake and the four other EEC currencies floating independently (*Agence Europe/Documents*, 817, 17 September 1974).

When efforts to reform the Snake failed, the French decided to bring the franc back into the arrangement in July 1975 as the best way to prevent the establishment of a mark zone. Likewise, the French were adamant in their opposition to the 1976 Tindemans report on 'Europ-ean Union'. This reinforced the creation of a mark zone by supporting the idea of a two-tiered monetary Europe, originally proposed by Chan-cellor Brandt in November 1974. In March 1976, the French sought to camouflage the unavoidable devaluation of the franc by an enlargement of the Snake's fluctuation margins and a revaluation of the mark. The German refusal gave the French little choice but to remove the franc from the arrangement a second time. Given Giscard's preoccupation with German economic strength, this second departure sparked considerable fear in the Elysée that Germany was eclipsing France as the leader in European construction. The humiliation of the forced exit of the franc largely explains Giscard's changed economic policy, his decision to call in Raymond Barre as prime minister, the subsequent conversion to the strong franc and the creation of the EMS. The new system was seen as a dilution of the mark zone by adding the franc, lira and punt. Although sterling did not join the Exchange Rate Mechanism (ERM) of the EMS, it contributed to the basket of currencies which determined the value of the ECU.

Demanding a more symmetrical Snake

The fourth way in which European power motives shaped French policy on European monetary co-operation was, from September 1974, French insistence upon the creation of a more symmetrical Snake arrangement (positive power motives). Given the full awareness of the potential asymmetry of a joint European float, it is surprising that the French did not make this demand during the period leading to the decision to create the Snake and at the time of the decision to remove it from its tunnel. However, it was necessary to experience the impact of asymmetry first hand, with the difficulty of keeping the franc in the Snake in the face of massive speculation.

The French sought three reforms to diminish this asymmetry. They argued in favour of establishing target exchange rates between Community currencies and the dollar. This was intended to promote symmetry by forcing the Germans to block the upward pressure on the mark. The French also argued in favour of establishing fluctuation margins around a weighted average of Community currencies. This would decrease the necessity of weak currency countries adjusting in order to follow the strong currencies by permitting greater total fluctuation between strong and weak currencies. Moreover, the French insisted that strong currency central banks should also assume responsibility for maintaining weak currencies within Snake fluctuation margins.

The Germans blocked progress on the first French demand. The EMS incorporated the second by establishing 2.25 per cent fluctuation margins around the ECU, the value of which was to be set by a weighted average of European currencies. On the third, a condition behind French support for the EMS was that the Germans accept the obligation of strong currency central bank intervention (Ludlow, 1982). The French demanded compulsory unlimited intra-marginal intervention by strong currency central banks the moment a weak currency was attacked or at least once it crossed its 'divergence threshold' prior to reaching the floor of its fluctuation margins (van Ypersele and Koeune, 1985, pp. 53–7; Ludlow, 1982).[38] The Germans only accepted 'the presumption to act' when a weak currency had crossed its 'divergence threshold' and compulsory intervention once it had reached its floor. Although the unlimited nature of the intervention was stated in the Bremen accords, it was generally assumed that the Bundesbank did not permit any binding guarantee that would prevent the maintenance of price stability in Germany.[39]

In conclusion, French policy on European monetary co-operation appears somewhat contradictory from the perspective of European monetary power motives. The French could have improved the stability of intra-EEC parities and decreased the strength of the mark by supporting immediate moves towards economic convergence: the central demand of the 'economists' during discussions on EMU. It was unlikely that convergence would have led to a dramatic alteration of French economic policies, given that French inflation levels were near the EEC average, and well below it after the accession of the three new member states. The method of decisionmaking on co-ordination that the Germans proposed (majority voting in the Council of Ministers) would have precluded the possibility of convergence towards rigorous German policies. Indeed, German policy would have to have become more reflationary. Thus by not accepting the mandatory convergence of economic policies, French policymakers effectively eliminated any possibility of avoiding a mark-centred zone which required convergence to German economic policies to avoid pressure to devalue. French opposition to mandatory convergence is even more surprising given the clear preference of Treasury and Bank of France officials for economic convergence (on inflation and balance of payments) in order to promote stability in intra-EEC parities, and to ensure the survival of the Common Market and the CAP. The apparent contradiction can only be explained by the refusal to accept the loss of economic policymaking powers.

The difficult participation of the franc in the Snake arrangement and the decision to withdraw it in January 1974 altered the French position on economic convergence. Giscard – who had moved from being Pompidou's finance minister to his successor as president in May of that year – began to argue in favour of the increased co-ordination of economic policies because of the realisation that convergence towards an acceptable European average was preferable to forced convergence towards German economic policies (*Le Monde*, 3 May 1974). The Germans, however, were reluctant to consider this option outside the framework of discussions on EMU and, given the inflationary problems in several of the EEC member states, saw convergence to a European average as a far less acceptable plan for action than in 1970.

The French were more flexible on the issue of economic convergence during the discussions and negotiations on the EMS. It is odd, however, that they did not request economic policy convergence around a European average at this time. Possible explanations include the continuation of neo-Gaullist opposition to such constraints which limited Giscard's room to manoeuvre on the issue. More likely, the issue of convergence to an average was less important to Giscard and Barre, given their objective of emulating German economic policies. The EMS reflected a compromise between the 'monetarist' (French) and 'economist' (German) perspectives, which reflected the development of French thinking on the issue of economic convergence. However, progress from both the 'monetarist' and 'economist' perspectives was limited. On the one hand, support mechanisms were improved, strong currency central bank intervention ensured, albeit late in the day, and the fluctuation margins centred around the ECU. On the other, the French accepted the creation of the 'divergence indicator' that would warn countries of the excessive divergence of economic policies and lead to summoning economic co-ordination meetings at which recalcitrant countries would be encouraged to modify their policies in order to avoid realignments. Crucially, no obligation was placed on the modification of weak currency country economic policies.

From reflation to 'stop and go' to deflation

During much of this period there was a dialectic between the core economic goals of price stability and a trade surplus, on the one hand, and the desire to maintain high growth rates, create employment and permit wage increases, on the other. The goals of price stability and a trade surplus would enable the French to maintain a strong franc. Given the priority that the Germans placed on price stability, these goals were also crucial to the successful participation of the franc in European monetary arrangements – in particular after the decision to remove the Snake from its dollar tunnel. There was a major contradiction in French policy: on the one hand, French governments all proclaimed their desire to maintain a strong currency and to keep the franc in the Snake, even following its two departures; on the other, they sought to pursue growth and employment-oriented policies which weakened the franc and made floating a more acceptable option. The constraints imposed by the franc's participation in the Snake were only tolerable when these conformed to the economic priorities of the French government at the moment: which explains the decision to float the franc outside the Snake on two occasions.

After several years of negative experience, the French accepted that lax attitudes towards inflation made achieving a trade surplus very difficult. Devaluation was only a temporary solution to the balance of payments problem as it led to even higher levels of inflation which further contributed to the trade deficit. However, given domestic political constraints, which encouraged growth-oriented policies, the French only fully embraced the goal of price stability in August 1976 with the appointment of Raymond Barre as prime minister. From this date onward, European monetary co-operation was seen as desirable not only from the perspective of maintaining intra-EEC parity stability. It was also seen as a useful external constraint to reinforce national efforts to control inflation.

The dialectic between these two sets of economic goals – and the impact of the result of this dialectic upon French participation in European monetary arrangements – can be divided into three periods: the inflationary growth-oriented policies of the Pompidou presidency; the 'stop and go' policies during the first two years of Giscard's presidency to August 1976; and the pursuit of austerity by the Barre government from August 1976 onward.

Inflation was already increasing rapidly and the trade deficit grew considerably during the final months of de Gaulle's presidency. He refused, however, to accept a devaluation of the franc. Pompidou reinforced the shift from the policies of pre-May 1968, by arranging an excessively large devaluation in August 1969.[40] The commitment of the Pompidou presidency to strong economic growth in spite of rising inflation was in part rooted in political motives linked to the wage rises agreed upon in the Grenelle accords (Goodman, 1992, p. 110). It was the President's firm belief that immediate growth, investment and employment came before all other economic priorities (Valance, 1996, p. 347). Pompidou was apparently not preoccupied with inflation as an economic problem (Roussel, 1984, p. 474). His policies were far from controversial. At the time, most of French academic and business opinion – in addition to the trade unions – was inflationist.[41] Moreover, the franc remained strong until 1973, reinforced by the strongest economic growth since World War II and a trade surplus until 1972. Rising inflation and the evaporation of the surplus increased the difficulty of maintaining the franc's parity in the Snake. By February 1974, the mark had reached 1.833 francs, a 49 per cent increase since spring 1969.

The increase in oil prices in the autumn of 1973 and the subsequent rise in inflation, combined with a decline in economic growth. The French government failed to adopt measures to control inflation and decided that the best way to deal with the new recession was to continue with economic growth policies. As the Germans successfully contained inflation, this placed downward pressure on the franc in the Snake. Rather than modify economic policy, the French decided to remove the franc from the mechanism in January 1974. During the first four months of that year, inflation reached its highest level since the start of the Fifth Republic.

The second period of economic policymaking began shortly after Giscard became president. Three factors explain the policies adopted during this period. First, the deteriorating economic situation required firm action by the government: inflation was escalating far too quickly and the trade deficit threatened to reach record levels. Second, as president, Giscard was in a position to impose policies that Pompidou had previously refused. Third, Giscard had to compromise with a neo-Gaullist led government which tended to place greater emphasis on economic growth than controlling inflation. The combination of these three factors resulted in the adoption of 'stop and go' policies: the imposition of austerity measures in June 1974, which met with considerable domestic opposition, and the return to growth-oriented policies once the economic situation had stabilised.[42] The austerity measures of June 1974 were very successful. They permitted a return of the franc to the Snake a year later, a considerable drop in inflation and a trade surplus for 1975. In September 1975, Giscard could no longer resist the pressure from the Chirac government which insisted upon adopting measures to stimulate economic growth and combat rapidly growing unemployment. However, the government's reflationary package was excessive: inflation rose and the trade deficit exploded. Under such conditions the franc was again placed under downward pressure and on 12 March 1976, after a brief monetary crisis during which the Germans refused to revalue the mark, the French floated the franc. The Chirac government maintained these policies until the summer of 1976.

The worsening economic situation led Giscard to insist that the government adopt austerity measures. The Prime Minister Jacques Chirac resigned and the third period began with the appointment of Barre as prime minister. For the first time since May 1968, the French government was ideologically committed to antiinflationary measures. Barre succeeded in lowering inflation and the trade deficit, and the franc strengthened against the mark. With the brief exception of 1981 to 1983, this remained official government policy into the 1990s.

The reformulation of French economic priorities – or rather the increased determination to bear the economic and political consequences of stabilising the French economy – was due to a combination of economic, power and political motives. The economic motives included the desire to deal with the new problem of stagflation (inflation combined with low economic growth or negative growth), the worsening inflation/devaluation cycle in the aftermath of the oil crisis, a deteriorating balance of payments situation and the cost of defending a depreciating franc. The power motives principally concerned worries about growing German power. The political motives were largely linked to the humiliation of having to constantly devalue the franc.

Finally, French academic and business opinion was gradually turning against inflationary economic policies, influenced by the shift throughout the industrialised world due to the widespread problem of stagflation. In the Anglo-American literature, the concept of a trade-off between higher inflation and lower employment (the Phillips-curve), due to the stagflation of the 1970s, had slowly been modified by the consideration of factors affecting levels of employment other than monetary policy. However, as outlined by Dyson, the approach of French academics, bankers and administrators to inflation owed more to the influence of German policymaking – which 'had a long history of resistance to the postwar dominance of Keynesian economic ideas' – than trends in Anglo-American economic thought (Dyson, 1994, p. 252).

The preoccupation with the power balance with Germany, always encouraged the French to make comparisons with their more economically stable neighbour. From 1974, the structural weaknesses of the French economy in comparison to the German economy became increasingly apparent. In Germany, both inflation and unemployment were considerably lower than in France and economic growth higher. In terms of attitudes, the policy changes of 1976, which were so crucial to French participation in European monetary co-operation, involved embracing the 'German model' of low inflationary economic growth. This model became the lietmotif of the Giscard presidency. Yet the German reference did not necessitate this change. It had also been a priority of the Pompidou presidency to balance German power, although money was not seen as the lever with which to do so.

The crucial factor explaining the change in economic and monetary policies was the election of Giscard as president and his determination to impose change on a hostile neo-Gaullist coalition partner. Giscard, a member of the élite Finance Inspectorate and a former minister of finance, had a relatively good understanding of economics and extensive experience in economic management. However, his presence as minister of finance from 1969 to 1974 did not substantially modify the growth-oriented policies imposed by Pompidou and the neo-Gaullist dominated majority. As President, political constraints initially limited his ability to impose a decisive change in policy. The economic difficulties of summer 1976 can be seen as the threshold point at which Giscard became more willing to face the political consequences of policy change. His decision to appoint Barre as both prime minister and minister of finance was also important to the success of the change. In addition to Barre's well-known anti-inflationary views, his experience as a European Commissioner responsible for economic and financial affairs ensured his close familiarity with developments at the European level. Barre, an academic economist, was also a political outsider, comparatively free of the pressures of party politics. In his courses at *Institut d'Etudes Politiques*, he had taught a generation of top financial and banking bureaucrats. His ideas, therefore, both informed and largely conformed to those of the financial administrative élite of the country. Upon becoming prime minister, he stated categorically that the economic priority of the new government was to maintain price stability and the value of the franc.

The constraint of neo-Gaullist nationalism

Attitudes on European integration explain three developments in French policy on monetary co-operation and integration during this period. First, it is likely that the departure of de Gaulle facilitated monetary co-operation at the European level. Second, neo-Gaullist opposition to further European integration prevented French support for economic convergence and the political and institutional implications of EMU. Third, the arrival of Giscard to the presidency and subsequently Barre to Matignon, increased the probability of positive French initiatives on a substantial reinforcement of monetary co-operation. Nationalism and opposition to European integration clearly shaped French policy on monetary integration (the EMU project). It also made the adoption of austerity measures – if connected with French participation in European monetary co-operation – politically unmanageable.

If it is difficult to imagine positive French initiatives on EMU under de Gaulle's presidency, it is more problematic to claim that the General's departure in 1969 was essential for the development of positive French policy on monetary co-operation. As with the establishment of the CAP, de Gaulle could demonstrate considerable openness on European co-operation if this served French interests and if France maintained its veto on all decisions. Moreover, continued Gaullist opposition is hypothetical given the radical changes to the international and European monetary environment in the early 1970s. Given the French preference for monetary stability, it is highly improbable that de Gaulle would have blocked all efforts at improving co-operation at the European level. If all advance in monetary co-operation depended on the EMU project this would likely have been the case. However, the French would probably have sought the same co-operation without the EMU project: indeed, co-operation advanced despite the failure to agree on a second stage to EMU and French opposition to the political and institutional implications of the project. In any event, the departure of de Gaulle permitted progress on EMU discussions which in turn stimulated further European monetary co-operation.[43]

The election of Pompidou to the presidency permitted a more relaxed attitude to European integration and made possible Pompidou's surprising initiative on EMU and French participation in the Werner Group. Pompidou went further than de Gaulle on accepting some progress on European integration. Moreover, Pompidou reversed de Gaulle's opposition to British membership as a means to counter growing German influence in the EC. Nonetheless, he continued to defend the principle of *Europe des Patries* and oppose supranationalism (Cousté *et al.*, 1974, p. 113), as demonstrated unambiguously in the intergovernmentalist approach of French representatives on the Davignon Committee, established at The Hague Summit to examine steps towards political union.

The focus on the 'monetarist'/'economist' divide as the major division during the EMU discussions and negotiations detracts from an appreciation of the deeper divide which separated France from the other member states: notably opposition to the loss of national control over monetary and economic policy making. This explains French opposition to the co-ordination and convergence of economic policies, the establishment of a strong link between the first stage of the EMU project and the final goal, treaty revision, and the political and institutional implications of EMU. Given this opposition, it is necessary to raise the question of why Pompidou initiated discussions on EMU if he was not willing to accept the implications of the project. Indeed, given Gaullist opposition to supranationalism, the support of Pompidou and the UDR government for positions in favour of monetary union during the 1970–71 negotiations is surprising. The answer is most likely provided by an appreciation of the President's efforts to widen his support base to the pro-European Centre (discussed in the domestic politics section below).

His focus was on the short term implications of the project: notably, the establishment of support mechanisms and tighter fluctuation margins. It is possible that Pompidou's announcement for the need to establish EMU as a response to the collapse of the IMS reflected less a careful consideration of French interests, than a hasty reaction to the international monetary crisis of 1969 which placed unprecedented pressure on the franc. If Pompidou was strongly committed to the goal of EMU, he would have stood up to nationalist opposition.[44]

In any event, to contain the neo-Gaullist reaction, his tone on EMU changed shortly after the Summit meeting. In a 2 July 1970 press conference, Pompidou accepted the possibility of the harmonisation of monetary and economic policies but stressed the very long term nature of the EMU goal (Cousté *et al.*, 1974, p. 110). He cited the German example of the 40-year period between the *Zollverein* and the appearance of the mark as a single currency and then another 60 years until the central bank had a monopoly over the issue of the mark. At the start of 1971, Pompidou's tone had become even more negative, arguing that there was no point making theoretical speeches about what would happen in the next decade (Cousté *et al.*, 1974, p. 116).

French opposition to the supranational implications of EMU forced a vague compromise in the Werner Group which called for the creation of both a 'centre of decision for economic policy' and a 'Community system for the central banks'. The French insisted upon the former which was to consist of national government representatives with power over the macroeconomic framework in which monetary policy was to be made. The Germans demanded the latter which was to consist of independent European and national central banks controlling all areas of monetary policy except for exchange rate agreements with third countries.[45] The negative reaction of orthodox Gaullist opinion to these proposals forced the French government to take a stronger stand on supranationalism. During the EMU negotiations, which started in the autumn of 1970, the French sought to avoid the topic altogether or simply refused to discuss institutional questions, apart from the creation of the EMCF (which was to have minimal powers). France's stance created difficulties for attaining the monetary measures that it sought for the first stage because the Germans and Dutch disliked these measures and accepted them only with difficulty and because of their support for the overall goal of EMU.

Surprisingly, the French continued to adopt the rhetoric of advancing with EMU. Moreover, the January 1971 compromise between Pompidou and Brandt (formally agreed upon by the 22 March Council of Ministers) involved French commitment to the goal of reaching EMU by stages within a decade – although they again refused to discuss the institutional implications of the goal and any Treaty revision. Above all, the French sought to increase German flexibility on monetary support mechanisms and tighter fluctuation margins. Because of the French refusal to link the measures adopted in the first stage with the subsequent stages and the goal of EMU, the Germans insisted upon a safeguard clause. This clause limited the application of monetary measures to five years if no progress on economic policy co-ordination was achieved.

Opposition to further European integration did not extend to increased monetary co-operation – even though reaching the French goal of tighter fluctuation margins would invariably have reduced the scope for autonomous monetary and economic policymaking. Moreover, while the French saw tighter fluctuation margins as an end in itself, there was little opposition to the idea of tighter margins as a means to the end of 'fixed parities' (although this was not defined).

In addition to strategy, a major reason for the apparent contradiction in French policy was the serious disagreement within the government on both economic policy co-ordination and convergence, as well as the political and institutional implications of EMU, which occasionally manifested itself during discussions at the European level. The disagreement ran roughly parallel to the 1965 debate on the creation of the CRU. Michel Debré represented the opinion of the orthodox Gaullist majority and was highly reluctant on the loss of economic policymaking powers and refused all proposals containing any notion of supranationality. Giscard, the leader of the non-Gaullist coalition partners, supported by leading Bank of France officials, argued in favour of the adoption of a 'still not very ambitious plan' leading to EMU (*Agence Europe*, 15 December 1970). The confusion regarding the French position and the initial willingness to bend on institutional questions was due largely to the role played by Giscard and bank officials in the discussions; while the political weight of the Gaullist majority allowed the more restrictive vision to prevail.

Giscard's generally positive attitude towards limited further European integration, flexibility on the issue of policymaking autonomy, previous support for the creation of a 'common' currency – in addition to his economic attitudes – encouraged positive French initiatives on monetary co-operation. In early 1968, following the publication of the Commission Memorandum, Giscard and his Independent Republican party called for the creation of a common EEC currency (*Le Monde*, 7 December 1968). After the French presidential elections of 1969, Giscard returned to the ministry of economics and finance and shortly thereafter began to call for improved economic policy co-ordination. Indeed, Giscard's initial position on EMU more closely aligned with the 'economists' than the 'monetarist' French position. In a November 1969 speech to the National Assembly, he announced that the French government supported the creation of a European currency but that it was first necessary to co-ordinate economic policies (*Le Figaro*, 30 November 1969).

Given Giscard's political and economic attitudes, it is somewhat surprising that, upon becoming president, he did not publicly embrace the objective of EMU and push for the establishment of the much tighter co-ordination of economic policies. However, given the oil shock, he had other priorities in 1974. Giscard's European initiatives in other areas also suggested a greater willingness to accept the political and institutional implications of EMU. Interestingly, the French compromised little in institutional terms with the establishment of the EMS, while the Germans accepted improved support mechanisms and the creation of the ECU as the system's new standard. There are two explanations for Giscard's position. First, he might not have wished to push too far too quickly, especially given the setbacks in the past and the difficulties which plagued the franc in the Snake mechanism. EMU might have been his project for a second *septennat*. Second, as president, Giscard also might have adopted a more moderate position, recognizing the fragility of support for a single currency in France.[46] The EMS was seen as a gradual approach to EMU. The French would slowly conform to the German model, and upon convergence have fewer reasons to oppose a single currency.

Domestic political motives

Three domestic political motives were of particular importance in terms of encouraging French support for European monetary co-operation. First, the stability of the franc was preferred because devaluations were seen as involving large political costs. This was definitely the case with the de Gaulle presidency which had staked its prestige on maintaining the existing exchange rate of 1.20 francs to the mark. Pompidou was less concerned by this but, nonetheless, had to try to live up to the Gaullist precedent – even if economic policies made this problematic. In addition to the added stability, exchange rate co-operation was politically beneficial because it created the possibility of disguising franc devaluations within the co-ordinated realignment of several currencies or by the revaluation of strong currencies. However, the decision to devalue the franc twice outside the Snake mechanism demonstrated that this political motive was of secondary importance for many leading Gaullist politicians.

The support of most heads of industry – notably, large importers and exporters – and farmers was the second domestic political factor which encouraged a proactive French policy on the establishment of European monetary arrangements. These groups sought to ensure the stability of intra-Community parities. However, they did not consider the issue to be one of central importance and thus failed to organise any kind of concerted campaign to shift French policy. Farming representatives (notably, the FNSEA, the *Fédération Nationale des Syndicats des Exploitants Agricoles*) initially placed considerable pressure on the government to maintain stability in order to ensure the survival of the CAP. However, the successful operation of the MCAs rendered innocuous the threat of instability to food prices. Manufacturing interests saw EMU as the only way to provide a guarantee of fixed exchange rates. However, the passive support of the most important organisation representing these interests, the CNPF (*Conseil National du Patronat Français*), did not lead the government to adopt a more positive position on the issue. The CNPF did not organise any form of concerted campaign in favour of EMU and did not express any form of disapproval of the position of the French government.

The third domestic political motive was that, on particular occasions, party political strategy perhaps encouraged favourable initiatives on monetary co-operation and integration. The EMS initiative can perhaps be explained by Giscard's ambition to attract pro-Community Socialists to his presidency to build the centre in French politics 'while isolating the neo-Gaullists and Communists' (Story, 1988, p. 401). Pompidou's more positive approach on European affairs reflects in part his desire to compensate for the defection of left-leaning Gaullists by appealing to pro-European centrist voters. Such political motives partly explain Pompidou's strong rhetoric in favour of EMU at the end of 1969. However, given the inevitable Gaullist backlash on EMU, the political logic behind

Pompidou's rhetoric remains unclear. Giscard had imposed a French position in favour of British entry as one of his preconditions for supporting Pompidou's bid for the presidency (Abadie and Corcelette, 1994, p. 336). However, he did not insist upon a French policy in favour of EMU.

The backlash of orthodox Gaullists against the supranational elements contained in the Werner Group's Final Report effectively modified French policy on EMU and shaped the development of the following negotiations (*Agence Europe*, 21 October 1970). Their opposition centred upon the statement outlining the final objective which declared EMU 'a lever for the development of political union, which in the long run it cannot do without' (*Werner Report*, 1970, p. 12). The French government had already refused to accept the political and institutional implications of EMU. However, French representatives in the Group – led by top Bank of France officials – were more flexible on these questions than was dominant opinion in the UDR government. The Gaullist reaction broke the delicate compromise between the short term and long term, 'monetarists' and 'economists', and the French insisted upon renegotiation.[47]

While it is clear that the anticipation of domestic political difficulties shaped French negotiating positions, the importance of the backlash should not be exaggerated. It was not a case of domestic politics affecting the overall direction of French policy – which was consistently opposed to the political and institutional implications of EMU – but rather the nature of the compromise agreement (embodied in the Werner Report) upon which the European partners could agree. Moreover, the Gaullist reaction did not prevent the French government from making rhetorical commitments to the vaguely defined goal of EMU – as at the October 1972 Paris Summit – for strategic negotiating reasons.

Finally, the relative strength of the UDF and the RPR during Giscard's *septennat* likely had an impact on the President's willingness and ability to impose anti-inflationary economic policies and make positive initiatives on European monetary co-operation. The preference of the Chirac government to adopt reflationary measures – and Giscard's decision not to block them – led to the franc's second departure from the Snake. The President's subsequent insistence upon austerity led to Chirac's resignation, Barre's appointment, and a tenuous political situation in which the larger coalition partner was underrepresented in the government. While this probably did not undermine Barre's zeal in cutting inflation, it likely discouraged initiatives that would allow the re-entry of the franc into the Snake. The 1978 legislative elections – which increased the relative weight of the UDF in the government – considerably strengthened the position of Giscard and Barre in relation to the RPR. This better enabled the President to pursue a monetary deal with the Germans (Story, 1988, p. 401).[48]

Conclusion

Throughout the 1968–81 period, there was a consistency of French demands on monetary co-operation structured principally by international and European power motives. These motives called for the establishment of common European positions on developments in the IMS, improved monetary and economic policy consultation and monetary policy co-ordination, tighter fluctuation margins between European currencies and improved monetary support mechanisms. From September 1974, the French also argued for increased symmetry in European monetary arrangements: notably, establishing a margin of fluctuation around a weighted average of Community currencies rather than between the strongest and weakest, and increasing responsibility of strong currency countries to defend weak currencies. International monetary power motives were most important for stimulating initial interest in European monetary co-operation. European monetary power motives encouraged limited monetary co-operation but discouraged French support for a joint float of European currencies, which the Germans imposed upon the French. These motives became increasingly important with the creation of the joint float, the evaporation of hopes to reform the IMS, the full realisation of German economic, monetary and potential diplomatic power which the operation of the Snake mechanism made evident, and the negative impact of economic policies which diverged from those pursued in the Federal Republic. European monetary power motives encouraged the French to maintain the franc in the Snake and shaped French proposals on Snake reform. Throughout the period, opposition to limiting national control over economic policymaking discouraged French support for economic co-ordination and convergence demanded by German governments as a condition of their acceptance of French demands.

In spite of this consistent set of core French demands, there was considerable change in the intensity of French interest in further European monetary co-operation and the willingness of policymakers to adopt the necessary economic policies to ensure the participation of the franc in European monetary arrangements. These changes were due largely to the different attitudes of French policymakers on desirable economic policy and European integration. In part, they were also due to changes in the international economy. Under President Pompidou (1969 to 1974) the emphasis placed on growth-oriented economic policies made difficult the continued participation of the franc in European monetary arrangements, while neo-Gaullist opposition to further European integration precluded support for monetary integration and made further monetary co-operation more difficult. The franc was floated outside European monetary arrangements (the Snake) in January 1974. Giscard wanted to pursue anti-inflationary policies, was in favour of limited further European integration and firmly supported the participation of the franc in European monetary arrangements. However, from 1974 to 1976, he was unable to impose a determined anti-inflationary policy upon an unwilling government dominated by neo-Gaullists. Giscard's appointment of Barre as prime minister in August 1976 marked the beginning of a firm commitment to anti-inflationary economic policies, which made possible the franc's re-entry into the Snake, and more positive European initiatives generally.

The difference between accepting the desirability of monetary co-operation, on the one hand, and participating in European arrangements, on the other, is crucial to explain French policy during this period. The French initially opposed a joint European float but they chose to participate in it. Later, the French maintained a consistently positive attitude to the Snake even while pursuing economic policies which made the participation of the franc in this arrangement exceedingly difficult, and accepted two prolonged independent floats. Given the asymmetric operation of the Snake – and the resulting necessity to converge towards the German economic standard – the willingness and ability of French governments to participate in exchange rate agreements depended principally upon the economic attitudes of key policymakers. It is thus necessary to emphasize the role of Giscard and Barre in pushing through the low inflationary economic policies sought by the financial administrative élite in the Treasury and the Bank of France. They did so in the face of considerable opposition from within the government, their political opponents and the French population.

3
The Decision to Keep the Franc in the ERM, May 1981 to March 1983

Introduction

The gradual adoption of increased austerity during 1982 and 1983 and the March 1983 decision to keep the franc in the Exchange Rate Mechanism (ERM) of the EMS marked a major transition for the Socialist Party which had been radicalised during its long period in opposition. During the first two years of Socialist government, from May 1981 to March 1983, there was considerable political pressure from within the government to remove the franc from the ERM. Nonetheless, on at least four separate occasions President François Mitterrand made the decision not to float the franc – the immediate post-election period, and the three devaluations within the ERM of October 1981, June 1982 and March 1983. Keeping the franc within the mechanism was crucial for the development of Socialist government policy on European monetary co-operation and integration, European integration more generally, as well as overall economic policy. Due to the debate within the Socialist government regarding desirable economic policies, the official French position on the EMS was ambiguous prior to March 1983. However, following the third devaluation, the Socialist government fully embraced EMS membership, sought to increase the use of the European Currency Unit (ECU), and adopted the economic and monetary policies necessary to reduce the inflation differential with Germany and thus avoid the continued devaluation of the franc within the ERM. The March 1983 decision was therefore essential for widening the political support for European monetary co-operation and integration from a narrow pro-European and anti-inflationary centrist-UDF base to one encompassing the centre-left.

The precise combination of motives and attitudes which shaped Mitterrand's decisions to keep the franc in the ERM and pursue more determined deflationary economic policies is impossible to determine. Nonetheless, there have been numerous, mostly journalistic, accounts of the policymaking during this period which together help to provide a clear description of the motives and attitudes which shaped policymaking.[49] Most of these authors focus upon the debate on the economy within the Socialist government and stress the importance of international economic constraints which encouraged certain key policy actors to accept greater deflation and keep the franc in the ERM.

Monetary policy initiatives and developments

The interim Socialist government surprised most observers and shocked financial markets by deciding not to devalue the franc immediately following Mitterrand's election victory. During the pre- and immediate post-election period there was an attack of unprecedented scope against the franc.[50] International financial operators believed that the new Socialist government would devalue the franc as the start of a promised expansionist economic programme and the Socialists had themselves fuelled expectations that they would do so. A devaluation in relation to the mark was also necessary on economic grounds: to compensate for the cumulative inflation differential between France and Germany. International confidence in the Barre government's determination to avoid a devaluation and commitment to controlling inflation had discouraged speculation between 1978 and the start of 1981. The Socialists, however, lacked this credibility. Speculation subsided following the 21 May decision to maintain the parity of the franc.[51] The decision involved a temporary increase of short term interest rates to 22 per cent and the imposition of tight exchange controls. The huge Socialist success in the National Assembly elections further reinforced the strength of the franc.

With intense speculative pressure against the franc, the re-establishment of capital controls appeared the most economically sensible response. During his final months in office Barre considered that such measures would be contrary to his personal views on the necessity of the free flow of capital and would greatly anger large capital holders (an important UDF constituency) (Bauchard, 1986, p. 16). The Socialists, however, had no ideological or political reasons not to re-establish controls. Although Mitterrand chose not to do so immediately following his election – despite the recommendation of numerous financial experts, Socialist politicians and close advisers – controls were subsequently re-introduced (Bauchard, *ibid.*, pp. 29–30).

Speculation against the franc began again in mid-August 1981. The cumulative inflation differential did not set off the attack, even though this differential was the most important economic justification for a realignment. The principal catalysts were the contradiction between a strong franc and Socialist reflationary policies, the growing inflation differential between France and Germany, the trade deficit, and more specifically the official statements that there would be a record-breaking budget deficit in 1982. Attacks against the franc were also due to rising American interest rates and the resulting rise in the dollar, which in turn increased French inflation and the French trade deficit, principally because French energy imports were denominated in dollars.[52] This encouraged the unsuccessful Socialist efforts, culminating in the June 1982 Versailles G7 Summit, to reform the IMS.

The first devaluation within the ERM took place on 4 October 1981. A total realignment of 8.5 per cent was agreed upon in negotiations with the Germans and the other EMS partners. The mark and Dutch guilder were revalued 5.5 per cent, while the franc was devalued 3 per cent. A German condition for the relatively large revaluation of the mark was that France reduce expenditures by 10 billion francs and freeze another 15 billion of the 1982 budget.[53] The Socialist government accepted a minimum programme of corrective action that included a series of scattered price freezes and the establishment of a target of an average of 10 per cent increase in all prices.

Given the Socialist government's economic policies, the poor economic climate and Bundesbank reticence, the period was not propitious for progress in European monetary co-operation. Indeed, in December 1981 central bank governors quietly shelved the plans established in 1978 to reinforce European monetary co-operation through the creation of a European Monetary Institute (EMI) by 1983 (Begg and Wyplosz, 1992). Nonetheless, in March 1982, the European Commission presented its proposals on reinforcing the EMS (the Ortoli Plan), which the French supported and Germans opposed (*Agence Europe*, 3381, 1/2 June 1982). The Commission sought to reinforce the internal mechanisms of the EMS, improve the co-ordination of economic policies, develop the use of the ECU and improve monetary co-operation with third countries, especially the United States and Japan. Specifically, it proposed that the central banks of strong currency countries in the EMS spend more of their reserves to support weak currencies. Regarding the ECU, the Commission called for the removal of legal obstacles to its private use; the removal of controls on its circulation in EMS countries; an increase in the national reserve holdings of the ECU from 27 to 40 billion; an increase from 50 to 100 as the percentage of ECUs permitted in the repayment of credit to other national central banks lent through the Very Short Term Loan Facility (the VSTF or Ortoli facility); the establishment of an ECU interest rate at a significantly lower level than market rates; and the assurance of convertibility.

The announcement of large Socialist losses in the 21 March 1982 departmental elections encouraged renewed speculation against the franc. Continued reflation had worsened the trade imbalance and increased government debt and the inflation differential with France's largest trade partners.[54] The government responded by allowing the franc to slide to its ERM floor on 22 March, thus qualifying for the intervention of EMS central banks. On 24 March, the Socialists were forced to tighten exchange controls. Speculation subsided but increased in late May (on the eve of the Versailles G7 Summit) due in part to Mitterrand's mention of a possible float to American journalists, and other vague comments suggesting an inadequately firm commitment to the EMS (*International Herald Tribune*, 29 May 1982; *Washington Post*, 30 May 1982). For principally political reasons, the devaluation was delayed until after the Versailles summit.

The second devaluation of the franc took place in the context of the 14 June 1982 realignment which involved a 4.25 per cent revaluation of the mark and guilder and a 5.75 per cent devaluation of the franc. In nine months the franc had lost a fifth of its value *vis-à-vis* the mark. The Germans and the Dutch accepted the revaluation of their currencies on the condition that the Socialist Government adopt a severe austerity plan. The French drew up an 18-month to two-year plan, the objective of which was to limit the inflationary impact of the devaluation and, more generally, lower inflation (Hall, 1986, p. 200).

Nonetheless, in the international financial community it was widely considered that the realignment – which merely neutralised the Franco-German inflation/cost/productivity differential – and the significant but half-hearted plan were insufficient to defend the parity of the franc. Speculation against the franc thus began again less than two months later on 6 August, and continued in spite of a series of measures and announcements designed to discourage it.[55] This made clear to the Socialist government that in order to avoid periodic devaluations within the ERM a much more drastic austerity package was necessary.[56] Rumours of a planned float, the publication of a leaked Treasury document in *Le Canard Enchaîné* (2 March 1983) envisaging two franc devaluations in 18 months and conflicting figures for the French external debt contrived to put further pressure on the franc (*Financial Times*, 12 November 1982). In September, the government negotiated the largest line of credit in French history.[57]

By the end of 1982, the foreign currency reserves of the Bank of France dropped 50 per cent during 1982 and total reserves dropped 20 per cent.[58] On 17 December, the Bank of France announced to the government that it would soon lack sufficient foreign currency reserves to defend the franc. Just prior to the third devaluation, French foreign currency reserves reached a low of 30 billion francs – with the dollar at a very high 7.50 francs – and were rapidly diminishing (Bauchard, 1990, pp. 144–5). Over the period, interest rates were raised repeatedly to stem speculation, to 250 per cent on certain days.

In spite of the pressure to devalue the franc, the timing of the third devaluation was determined by political motives. Due to the upcoming German Bundestag elections of 6 March, the German Social Democratic government was not in a position to negotiate any realignment of currencies in order to keep the franc in the ERM. Following the CDU victory, the Bank of France decided to stop supporting the franc, partly because an excessively large proportion of its reserves had already been spent. Moreover, by allowing the mark to rise to its permitted ceiling against the franc, the Bank automatically acquired the right to draw on Community resources (the 45 day VSTF) and obtain assistance from other central banks. Mitterrand further delayed the decision on devaluation until after the 13 March second ballot of the French municipal elections.

The third devaluation of 23 March 1983 was the smallest, yet most economically significant, of the three. The Germans revalued the mark by 5.5 per cent in exchange for a mere 2.5 per cent devaluation of the franc, which compensated for most of the remaining Franco-German inflation differential that had accumulated since 1979.[59] In exchange for the large mark and guilder revaluation, the French were forced to devise a new, more far-reaching austerity plan. Therefore, more so than in 1981 or 1982, the decision to devalue the franc within the ERM required a dramatic alteration to Socialist economic strategy. Taxes were to be raised by 40 billion francs in 1983, public spending cut by 24 billion, and wages and price increases limited to 8 per cent (Hall, 1986, p. 200). In addition to a large mark revaluation, the Germans also conceded that France should be able to draw a 4 billion ECU loan from the VSTF.[60] However, they refused to accept the minister of finance, Jacques Delors' demands for wider fluctuation margins.

Mitterrand's March 1983 decision to keep the franc in the ERM

The clarification of the details of the March 1983 decision is necessary to understand the relative importance of the different motives and attitudes. There are several different, occasionally contradictory, accounts regarding Mitterrand's wavering on the ERM, the exact timing of his final decision, and the precise reasons for this decision. Four possible explanations for these differences can be provided. First, and most important, the President did not make up his mind on the ERM until just prior to the announcement of his decision. He had seriously considered both options, had decided to remove the franc and then changed his position. Second, the President's decisionmaking style created confusion as to his actual views. Mitterrand never brought his advisers together to discuss policy issues. To each visitor he gave the impression either that he had decided nothing or that he had decided against the position presented (see, for example Attali, 1993). Third, Mitterrand consulted with a wide range of economic experts and advisers, which could be seen as an indication of either a desire to find an alternative to the EMS option or a desire to confirm that this was the right option. Fourth, there was a certain attempt at revisionism on the part of leading Socialists following the March 1983 decision, in response to extensive opposition within the Socialist Party to the continued participation of the franc in the ERM. In order to stress the strong economic and diplomatic logic of the decision reached, revisionism involved deliberately under-emphasizing the significance of the President's wavering on reinforcing the policy initially adopted in June 1982.[61] The summary presented here is based upon an analysis of the different written accounts and interviews with many of the leading actors of the period.

The poor showing of the Socialists in the 6 March 1983 first ballot of the municipal elections led Mitterrand to endorse the removal of the franc from the ERM. He informed his special adviser Jacques Attali of his tentative decision on the day of the second ballot. However, during the following nine days, the President continued to meet with dozens of partisans of both options, determined to reach a final decision on the issue. One strategy for making this decision was to test the conviction of the two strongest opponents of floating: Prime Minister Pierre Mauroy and Minister of Finance Jacques Delors. On the morning of 14 March, the President announced to Mauroy that he had decided to leave the ERM and that he wanted him nonetheless to stay on as prime minister. Mauroy refused, as did Delors when the same proposition was made to him shortly afterwards. Moreover, both men threatened to resign from the government in the event of a float. Later that day, Mitterrand met with some of the leading partisans of leaving the ERM – ministers Pierre Bérégovoy and Laurent Fabius and the industrialist Jean Riboud – and asked them to draw up a detailed plan of action. He also met with other leading Socialists Jospin, Mermaz and Joxe to discuss the replacement of Mauroy. In the evening, the Prime Minister returned to the Elysée with his letter of resignation which Mitterrand again refused to accept, indicating that he was still open to the possibility of staying in the ERM. The two agreed on the '*Nouvel élan*' strategy, outlined by Jacques Attali and other Elysée staff, which required a large unilateral revaluation of the mark. That evening, Jean-Louis Bianco, the President's general secretary, left for Bonn. The German refusal to accept French terms on 15 March – although the negotiations on the size of the revaluation continued – discouraged the President from continuing with this strategy and he again received Bérégovoy, Fabius and Riboud to discuss the alternative policy.

Frightened that the President was very close to removing the franc from the ERM, Attali, Delors and Mauroy agreed that it was necessary to convince an important member of the other side to rally to the pro-EMS camp. They chose Fabius because of his moderate views on the subject and his close relationship with Mitterrand. Attali asked the Budget Minister to verify 'for the president' the state of French reserves with Treasury Director Michel Camdessus. At their 16 March meeting, Camdessus convinced Fabius with surprising rapidity of the need to remain in the ERM, because the negligible remaining foreign currency reserves made a float economically hazardous. Fabius contacted Mitterrand and stated that he would refuse to serve as Prime Minister if the franc was removed from the ERM. The President confirmed the reserve figures in a meeting with Gaston Defferre, the minister of the interior – another partisan of floating – who also concluded that it was necessary to remain in the ERM. Later the same day, Mitterrand told Delors to explore the conditions of a ERM realignment, and reaffirmed to Mauroy his decision that if Bonn agreed to a large revaluation of the mark to match a minor devaluation of the franc, a realignment within the system could be accepted. On 17 March, Mitterrand turned to Attali to find a means to conciliate increased austerity and industrial growth.

Fabius' change of position appears to have been the determining factor that led to Mitterrand's final decision. The President was impressed by the Budget Minister's willingness to sacrifice political ambition to economic prudence. He was also convinced by the arguments regarding low currency reserves, although they were not the decisive factor because Mitterrand was kept constantly informed of the state of French foreign exchange reserves and the heavy reliance on funds borrowed principally from the European Monetary and Co-operation Fund (EMCF) to support the franc. The President might have decided in favour of the ERM because of the determined opposition of Mauroy and Delors to a float at the risk of their political careers (Colombani, 1985, p. 65). However, their determination alone probably did not convince Mitterrand to support continued French membership, because it would not have come as a surprise to him – particularly given Delors' previous threats to resign over economic policy.

One important conclusion can be drawn: that Mitterrand's decision could probably have gone either way on the issue. His rather confused attitudes on desirable economic policy both encouraged and discouraged a float. His European attitudes – support for the *acquis communautaire* and belief in France's leadership role in Europe – encouraged continued ERM membership, although their importance is difficult to determine. He was convinced less by economic arguments than by the fact that Fabius was convinced by such arguments. Nonetheless, in spite of Mitterrand's hesitation on the issue, the March 1983 decision was definitive. With the subsequent improvement of the Bank of France's foreign currency reserve situation, the President did not take the opportunity to remove the franc from the ERM.

The political logic behind pre-1981 Socialist Party policy

Policy statements by Mitterrand and the Socialist Party on European monetary co-operation prior to 1981 demonstrated the preeminence of domestic political motives: criticising the RPR–UDF government and Mitterrand's attempts to win over left-wing socialist support for his leadership and communist voters to the Socialist Party and then to widen his appeal to centrist voters prior to the elections of 1981. In 1976, Mitterrand argued for French participation in the Snake and the creation of a more substantial system, principally as a means to ease the strain on the CAP created by the non-participation of certain Community currencies in the Snake arrangement (Huntzinger, 1981, p. 33). This support for the Snake was likely motivated more by the fact that French non-participation was an embarrassment for the Barre government, than any thought-out approval of the arrangement. However, Mitterrand was highly critical of French participation in the ERM (Mitterrand, 1979). Given his support for the Snake, which provided less financial assistance to weak currency countries, this can only be explained by political considerations: opposing the government and appealing to left-wing Socialists and communists. In order to maintain his control of the party leadership, Mitterrand needed to attract the support of left-wing Socialists dominated by the CERES group (*Centre d'Etudes, de Recherche et d'Education Socialistes*). Mitterrand and the Socialists sought to undermine the Communist Party by appealing to its electoral constituency. In the *Projet Socialiste* of 1979 – prepared by the anti-integrationist CERES leader Jean-Pierre Chevènement – the EMS was attacked because it was associated directly with the Barre government's liberal economic agenda to lower inflation and achieve financial equilibrium, which in turn tied France to the German standard (pp. 352–3). However, the Socialists did not oppose the creation of a European monetary system which involved 'concertation instead of harmonisation' (p. 181).

Electoral politics in 1981 required a different strategy again. The more moderate *101 Propositions* of the Mitterrand presidential campaign and the *Créteil Manifesto* of the National Assembly election campaign did not mention the EMS. Proposition 20 merely stipulated that the franc would be defended against currency speculation. To have written a commitment to the EMS into the *Propositions* would have been to contradict the *Projet*, which Mitterrand's manifesto was careful to avoid. However, it is clear that he was leaning towards support for the EMS. During his televised debate with Giscard, Mitterrand claimed that he was personally in favour of the EMS and that as long as the budget deficit did not become excessive and make membership impossible, the franc would remain in the ERM, and that he would do his utmost to make the system work well.[62] This modification of Party rhetoric reflected the change in Socialist Party strategy from the 1978 election to the 1981 elections: it was no longer necessary to appeal to communist support and more attention was paid to attracting centrist voters. Mitterrand presented himself as a cautious moderate – 'the calm force'. Moreover, he did not want to be challenged for making irresponsible statements that would encourage speculation against the franc. It is difficult to claim with certitude that Mitterrand's rhetoric on the EMS was motivated solely by electoral considerations. It is likely that he also wanted to keep his options open on EMS membership.

The failure of Socialist efforts to rebuild the IMS

As in the 1970s, American monetary policies continued to create disorder in international money markets. During this period, the contradictory economic and monetary policies pursued by the Reagan administration and the French Socialist government produced even greater friction between the two countries. The restrictive monetary policy pursued by the Federal Reserve Board forced a significant rise in interest rates throughout Europe, thus making the pursuit of reflationary economic policies difficult. The Socialist government insisted that speculative pressure against the franc was due entirely to American monetary policy.

As under the Pompidou presidency, the Socialist government made repeated, albeit unsuccessful, attempts to establish a common European front against the impact of American monetary policies. Specifically, they sought common policies on the reconstruction of the IMS, lower American interest rates and co-ordinated reflationary measures.[63] Indeed, during the Socialist government's first year, little good was said publicly about the EMS, except regarding its use as a counterweight to the influence of American monetary policy. More generally, Mitterrand recognized that France's influence as a middle power in the international economic system depended in large part upon maintaining close co-operation with the Germans – which a departure of the franc from the ERM would only damage – and strengthening the European Community's international presence.

The Socialist government's proposals on the reconstruction of the IMS were closely linked to its ideas on EMS reform. First, Delors proposed the establishment of a new IMS based around a triad of currencies consisting of the dollar, yen and ECU. Second, he argued in favour of the adoption of a two-tiered interest rate system in European countries as well as the United States, which would more effectively control capital movements than the unilateral European efforts of the early 1970s. Third, he sought the establishment of international obligations for the intervention of strong currency countries – now the dollar and the mark – to maintain weak currencies within the established fluctuation margins. The Socialists also sought to diminish the impact of American monetary policies with proposals to stimulate economic growth by a joint European effort to lower interest rates, increase consumption and adopt measures to create a 'Social Europe'. The Americans continued to refuse both the modification of their interest rate policies and the reconstruction of the IMS. The Germans agreed that American interest rates were excessively high. However, they refused to join the French in any concerted struggle against the Americans, to support French IMS demands or to modify their own deflationary economic policies.

Economic attitudes determined the manner in which international power motives shaped French policy on European monetary co-
operation. Those Socialist politicians and their advisers who advocated
greater restraint in domestic economic policies accepted that the international constraint of high American interest rates was a burden, but
argued that the removal of this burden by floating, and the free pursuit
of reflationary policies, would lead to financial ruin. Those Socialists
who sought to continue reflationary measures argued in favour of the
removal of the franc from the ERM as the best way to increase France's
negative international monetary power. They argued that it was the
ERM constraint which imposed the full brunt of high American rates
upon the French economy (because the Germans also maintained high
rates) and that a float would permit much lower rates. For these policy
actors, international monetary power motives concerned less the stability in intra-European parities than the ability to follow desirable economic policies.

The rapid growth of international capital movements also increased
French reliance upon EMS facilities to defend the parity of the franc. The
extent to which France had used these facilities prior to each of the three
devaluations demonstrated that withdrawal from the ERM was problematic on financial grounds, as it would mean that France would
instantly become liable for reimbursement of European funds, which it
would have difficulty to repay. Moreover, the Socialist government
would have trouble finding further lenders. Outside the ERM, France
would lose the triple A credit rating it still held on the international
loans market and the unacceptable spectre of IMF intervention loomed
large (*Financial Times*, 7 April 1983).

The Socialist government did not actively seek to strengthen EMS
support mechanisms, although it supported Commission proposals to
do so. These included the establishment of an ECU interest rate at a
significantly lower level than market rates, and the increase from 50 to
100 of the percentage of ECUs permitted in the repayment of credit to
other national central banks lent through the VSTF. This would have
effectively eased the financial burden of weak currency countries. Moreover, there were good economic reasons behind Delors' decision to
accept the special loan from the new VSTF of ECU 4 billion in May
1983: it saved France from the difficult task of raising another large
international loan and ensured a decreased debt servicing burden.[64]

A final international monetary power motive encouraged continued
French participation in the EMS. Delors argued in favour of increasing
the use of the ECU so that it might eventually become an international

reserve currency capable of rivalling the dollar in international financial markets (Riboud, 1983, p. 55). This theme is developed further in the following chapter because it was only after the March 1983 decision that the French began a determined campaign to expand the use of the new currency unit. It should be noted that this objective was of little significance in shaping the opinions of EMS opponents, was a secondary concern for EMS supporters and did not directly influence Mitterrand's decision to keep the franc in the ERM.[65] Still, the attraction of this objective explains the speed at which the Socialist government embraced the idea of strengthening the ECU following the March 1983 decision.

The debate on enhancing French European power

As prior to the creation of the EMS, negative European monetary power motives led to French demands to create a more symmetric system. Economic attitudes determined the manner in which these motives shaped French policy on European monetary co-operation. Those Socialists and their advisers who supported less reflationary policies tended to emphasize the importance of the EMS in shaping German monetary policy (positive European power) as evidenced by mutual realignments in the ERM. They also emphasized the impact that a departure from the system would have upon French leadership in the Community and how it would lead to increased German influence in Europe. Although such claims were probably exaggerated for effect, the departure from the ERM would have been potentially more damaging to French influence than had been the departure from the Snake in 1974 and 1976. Such claims were also of some importance in encouraging the President to keep the franc in the ERM. Those Socialists who supported continued reflation were motivated more by negative European power motives. They argued that because the Germans were unwilling to create a more symmetric EMS, it was necessary to leave the system in order to avoid the convergence of economic policies towards the German standard.

In the first few months following the Socialist election victories, Delors made several proposals for improving symmetry in the EMS, by requiring strong currency countries to intervene to support weak currencies prior to their reaching their fluctuation margin floor and to provide unlimited guaranteed support.[66] After the failure of initial efforts, he ceased to raise the issue publicly. He continued to do so privately in meetings with the Germans, notably during the negotiations leading to the three realignments in order to increase German flexibility on the revaluations of the mark. Delors claimed that the objective of the EMS was not to force member states to conform to the standards of the stronger currency countries – even though this was a principal reason why Giscard and Barre agreed to establish the system. He recognized, however, that the Germans – both the government and the Bundesbank – could not be expected to provide a guarantee of unlimited support for the franc given Socialist government economic policies.[67] Further attempts to reform the EMS would have to wait until after the March 1983 decision and the substantial change in French economic policies.

Those who sought to keep the franc in the ERM argued that continued participation was the best way to influence German monetary policy-making and bring about future reforms. However, more was potentially at stake than monetary power. Given the political dynamic of the period, and the close association of floating with the continued pursuit of reflationary economic policies, competitive devaluations and even the possible establishment of trade barriers, a departure from the ERM menaced a certain diplomatic isolation of France within the Community. Even without this tension, there was an inherent contradiction between the roles of European political leader and economic maverick. French leadership in the Community provided France with disproportionate influence at both the European and international levels. The pursuit of an alternative policy and the potential strains that this would have created with France's neighbours would have increased German influence over the direction of future Community developments and might even have encouraged a more independent German foreign policy – a growing concern of French governments.[68] Most Socialists did not share Giscard's goal of emulating the German economic standard as a means of maintaining French leadership in the Community. Still it was clear that following a completely different economic path would have weakened French influence in the EC. Pro-EMS politicians and advisers argued, particularly in March 1983, that to maintain the franc in the ERM was to 'choose Europe'. Officially, this was presented as one of the most important motives for keeping the franc in the ERM.[69]

Even without the accompanying reflationary policies, there are three principal reasons why a decision of the Socialist government to float the franc would have been perceived as more damaging to French leadership in the Community than the previous decisions of Pompidou and Giscard. First, the Snake was not seen as a crucial pillar of integration, whereas the EMS was created during a period of European idealism and was an important symbol of Franco-German leadership in the Community. The creation of the EMS in 1979 was one of the most important initiatives promoting European integration since the signing of the Treaty of Rome in 1957. The symbolic significance of the System was also derived from its creation following a prolonged period of stagnation in European integration, or 'Eurosclerosis'. Moreover, the ERM included a larger number of Community currencies than the Snake, making the new system a more important part of the Community.

Second, the potential diplomatic damage of removing the franc from the ERM was greater than the impact of leaving the Snake because the EMS was a more substantial monetary system than its predecessor. It involved a greater degree of commitment from all the participating countries, particularly through the obligatory financial assistance of strong currency country central banks, strengthened loan facilities and co-operative realignments. From the French perspective the EMS was also of greater significance than the Snake largely because, by March 1983, the franc had managed to remain in the ERM during a period of four years, a far more successful record than it's participation in the Snake. Diplomatically, it would have been easier for Mitterrand to have devalued the franc outside the ERM immediately following his investiture as president. The verbal support for the franc offered by the Germans and their acceptance of relatively large mark revaluations, in addition to the Socialist government's own rhetoric regarding European solidarity versus the Americans, encouraged the maintenance of the franc within the ERM. The potential diplomatic impact of removing the franc from the ERM was also greater because, although the economic reasons for the departure of the franc from the Snake and from the ERM were similar, the governments were perceived differently. A decision by the Socialist government to leave the ERM would have been seen as considerably more economically and politically portentous than the same decision by a UDF–RPR government.

Those who supported continued reflation emphasized the limitation that the EMS placed on the expression of French negative European monetary power. The opposition of the CERES faction to the EMS was overtly nationalist, as it was based partially on opposition to 'German economic and ideological imperialism' (*Projet Socialiste*, 1979, p. 191). The EMS was perceived as a means to consolidate German economic and then political control within the Community, which turned Giscard's perspective on its head. The fact that the EMS had been initiated by Schmidt, who showed great unease regarding the Socialist Party's economic policies and its links with the Communists, and supported the Giscard candidacy in the 1981 presidential elections, exacerbated a certain anti-German sentiment throughout the Party.

Choosing *'rigueur'* over *'l'autre politique'*

As during the previous period, the debate on desirable economic policy largely shaped the French approach to European monetary co-operation. Each decision to devalue the franc within the ERM was made in parallel to a change in Socialist economic policy: moving gradually from demand-stimulus and some supply-oriented reflationary policies to deflationary measures. The two policy developments were closely inter-linked. Continued EMS membership was considered inherently deflationary both because of the asymmetry of the system and also because the Germans insisted upon the adoption of tighter economic measures in exchange for large mark revaluations in the context of joint realignments. The decisions to keep the franc in the ERM were affected by the larger debate on the economy, but this debate was also shaped by decisions on European monetary policy. The ERM constraint forced the more rapid transformation of Socialist economic and budgetary policies than would have been the case in the context of a managed float, in which the government would have spent fewer reserves attempting to defend the parity of the franc. In theory, there were more options open to the government than continued participation in the ERM and deflation, on the one hand, and floating and reflation, on the other. The Socialist government could have continued for some time devaluing within the ERM while pursuing half-hearted deflationary measures, not unlike Italy during most of the 1980s. However, the Germans would have likely become less flexible on the issue of mutual realignments. Moreover, floating could have been accompanied by the adoption of greater austerity. However, political pressures within the Socialist Party and government made difficult the pursuit of this policy combination.

There were two main ideological factions within the Socialist Party and government which have often been labelled the Left and the 'Social Democrats'. In spite of strong differences on economic and social policies, all of those on the Left and most of the 'Social Democrats' supported the removal of the franc from the ERM in order to increase the government's margin of manoeuvre in economic policymaking. Only a handful of leading Socialists, notably Delors, argued for more moderate economic policies – called the 'third way' – which would enable the government to keep the franc in the ERM, which in turn was seen as a useful external constraint on the danger of excessive reflation. These policies sought to find a compromise between economic expansion, redistribution and a firm control over inflation. Most of Prime Minister

Mauroy's and the President's economic advisers argued in favour of similar policies. The majority of the French financial administrative élite in the Treasury and the Bank of France argued in favour of deflationary economic measures to bring France into line with its major trading partners.

Neither the Left nor the 'Social Democrats' can be considered victors in their struggle over economic policy. It might be argued that the real victory went to Jacques Delors who was the only leading Socialist politician to argue consistently in favour of keeping the franc in the ERM. However, even his idea of a 'third way' was effectively abandoned. Indeed, it can be argued that the decision of March 1983 signified the defeat of all the former economic policies recommended by the different Party faction leaders. *The true victor was the financial administrative élite* which, following the 1983 decision, successfully managed to have its anti-inflationary bias adopted as the official Socialist government economic, monetary and industrial policy, subsequently labelled 'competitive disinflation'. This in turn permitted a policy strongly in favour of the continued participation of the franc in the ERM.[70]

Most Socialist politicians focused their attention upon economic growth and redistributive economic measures. However, the Party spent little time prior to its 1981 election victory considering the economic implications of its policy and, indeed, little time elaborating the details of the measures to be pursued (Bell and Criddle, 1988). Pre-victory Socialist economic policies were normally grounded in a statist version of Keynesianism, uneasily combined with a strong dose of Marxist analysis and rhetoric: a mistrust of the market, active government intervention in the economy, and a strong commitment to egalitarianism and redistributive social justice. To the majority of Socialists, as to public opinion more generally, inflation was not a serious concern.

CERES, on the left-wing of the Party, presented the most thought-out opposition to anti-inflationary financial orthodoxy. To this group, a preoccupation with inflation and financial equilibrium was seen as part of liberal economic thought, manipulated to block the implementation of egalitarian economic measures. Growth was crucial, even if this required pursuing economic policies at odds with those adopted by France's neighbours and autarchy. Indeed, a central focus of this group was for State intervention to enable French industry to 'recapture the domestic French market' which in the context of reflation meant necessary protectionist measures (Favier and Martin-Roland, 1990, p. 442). Prior to the 1981 elections, CERES dominated the preparation of official Socialist policy, as reflected in the *Projet Socialiste* of 1979, and pulled

Mitterrand's own rhetoric on economic issues to the left. CERES and other leading left-wing Socialist politicians such as Pierre Joxe and Jean Poperen had previously rejected the Schmidt–Giscard Bremen accords as either an electoral bluff or a calculated political manoeuvre designed to facilitate the implementation of the Barre austerity plan.[71]

The label 'Social Democrats' applies generally to those Socialist politicians with somewhat more moderate views on economic policy.[72] They also supported reflationary economic measures and most argued in favour of floating if only to increase the margin of manoeuvre in economic policymaking. However, they were less ideologically opposed to the market, more willing to accept its constraints and to bring about a gradual transformation of society. Their opposition to the EMS was consequently less deeply rooted than those on the Left.

The 'Social Democrats' included Pierre Mauroy; Michel Rocard, the minister of agriculture and former candidate for the Party leadership; Pierre Bérégovoy, the secretary general at the Elysée in 1981 and then minister for social affairs; and many of the advisers to Mauroy and Mitterrand on non-economic affairs, including initially, Jacques Attali. Fabius' idea of a '*Nouvel élan*' and Rocard's 'economic realism' encouraged a large devaluation of the franc as a boost to French industry. Rocard claimed that he preferred to keep the franc in the ERM but only if the European partners were sufficiently flexible to permit its substantial devaluation, which in reality meant that he lent towards a departure from the mechanism (Favier and Martin-Roland, 1990, p. 57).

Despite this label, Fabius did not represent any particularly strong economic tradition in the Party. Although minister responsible for the budget, his principal objective was to tackle unemployment effectively – even if this meant financial sacrifices: higher inflation, financial disequilibria and the large devaluation of the franc outside the ERM (interview, 7 June 1994). The modification of his position, after a discussion with Treasury Director, Michel Camdessus, demonstrates his pragmatism on economic policy. Pierre Mauroy had no strong views on the economy and, as prime minister, set about co-ordinating the policies agreed upon by his ministers. However, he came to oppose continued reflation during spring 1982, largely because of the efforts of his economic advisers who convinced him of the negative impact of government policies (interviews with advisers; Favier and Martin-Roland, 1990, p. 432). Bérégovoy argued in favour of a large devaluation outside the ERM coupled with austerity. His focus was on lowering interest rates, improving the competitive position of French industry via competitive devaluations, and 'reconquering' the domestic market (Favier and

Martin-Roland, 1990, p. 482). He argued for this policy combination at the time of both the second and third devaluations.

Some influential advisers on the staffs of Mauroy and Mitterrand supported reflation and removing the franc from the ERM. They tended to lack the knowledge to present clearly thought out arguments on the matter, and few argued consistently and forcefully in favour of a float. Robert Lion, the director of Mauroy's cabinet in 1981–82, opposed the imposition of greater austerity that participation in the ERM required, principally because of his political sensitivity to the demands from other Socialist ministers, deputies and advisers in favour of a float. However, he lacked the financial knowledge and the conviction to counter the more determined influence of the financial and economic advisers on Mauroy's staff (interviews with Mauroy and Delors staff members). One notable and well-informed opponent of the ERM at the Elysée was Alain Boublil, Mitterrand's adviser on industrial questions (Favier and Martin-Roland, 1990, p. 442).

Most of the more determined advisers in favour of a float came from outside government. During the months prior to the third devaluation, Mitterrand met in the evening with numerous opponents to the ERM, who Mauroy labelled 'the night visitors'. They were of varied ideological stripe, but they shared both a belief in the need for an active industrial policy and a nationalist refusal to accept the economic diktats of Washington, Bonn and Brussels. The most influential was the French industrialist, Jean Riboud, the president of the Schlumberger industrial group, and a close Mitterrand associate since the war. His influence stemmed from his economic standing as one of France's most successful industrialists, his strong commitment to the Socialist Party and the President, and his effective presentation of ideas which were well thought out and far from radical – thanks largely to the intellectual support of the economist Jean Denizet.[73] Riboud and Denizet sought one large devaluation outside the ERM to improve the competitive position of French industry and permit the substantial lowering of interest rates. Their plan involved the temporary raising of tariff barriers against American, Japanese and even some European industrial products in order to improve the French share of their own market. However, they also argued that this should coincide with the imposition of determined anti-inflationary policies in order to avoid future devaluations, in addition to measures to strengthen the efficiency of French industry (Favier and Martin-Roland, 1990, p. 441).

Delors and leading economic advisers advocated some kind of 'third way' which was an attempt to bridge Socialist demands for expansion

with the Treasury's anti-inflationary bias – objectives which were probably inherently contradictory.[74] This 'third way' stressed both a challenge to social inequality through supply-side economic measures and
job creation, but also a tight control over money supply to prevent
higher inflation. Delors was the only leading Socialist politician consistently in favour of pursuing less reflationary economic policies and
keeping the franc in the ERM. His efforts were, therefore, crucial to
ensure devaluations within the ERM during the first two years of Socialist government. His preference for economic moderation was rooted in
his 17-year experience at the Bank of France and was demonstrated
repeatedly, even prior to the 1981 election victories, when moderation
was rare in the Socialist Party, notably when he refused to support the
Projet Socialiste. As minister, he made numerous public statements –
unique for a French Socialist politician at the time – connecting economic growth and low inflation.[75] Following the October 1981 devaluation, he called publicly for a pause in Socialist reforms and refused to
countersign the 1982 budget.[76] Moreover, he threatened to resign on at
least three occasions if further anti-inflationary and other austerity
measures were not implemented by the government and if the franc
were removed from the ERM (Attali, 1993; Favier and Martin-Roland,
1990, p. 453).

The economic advisers on the staffs of Delors, Mauroy and Mitterrand
were prone to support Delors' position. They had nearly all previously
worked in the Treasury (Mauroy's economic adviser Jean Peyrelevade
was the one exception). Although financially cautious, all described
themselves as Socialist supporters and thus in favour of redistributive
measures and some demand stimulus. Their support for moderate reflation was rooted in the widespread belief that there would be a world
economic recovery in 1982 and 1983. They were not, however, in favour
of prolonged reflation when this led to excessively high levels of inflation and a large trade deficit, and they were not willing to remove the
franc from the ERM.[77]

The economic advisers played a crucial role in convincing both
Mauroy and Mitterrand to pursue more moderate economic policies
and to keep the franc in the ERM. In the spring of 1982, these advisers
organised a series of joint meetings between the Prime Minister and the
President at which they argued for greater austerity, and then further
meetings also with Delors, Fabius and Yvon Gattaz, the CNPF President.
The development of another version of '*Nouvel élan*', by Mitterrand's
special adviser Jacques Attali and economic advisers, was a means to
challenge the President's sentiment that a departure from the ERM was

necessary to bring about the necessary support and restructuring of French industry. Advisers argued that this version of the 'third way' ensured greater control over government expenditure, slowed down reflation, yet provided the necessary support for industry. It was presented as an ideologically more acceptable and politically less damaging alternative to austerity, while bringing the financial situation under control.

Treasury and Bank of France officials had a strong bias against reflation and in favour of anti-inflationary economic policies, even if this meant lower economic growth in the short and medium term. For these officials the principal economic motivations to keep the franc in the ERM were the same as those to create the EMS: to control the inflationary tendencies in the French economy; to maintain financial equilibrium or to avoid too great a disequilibrium – termed 'financial orthodoxy'; and to force industry to become more efficient via the use of higher interest rates.

The March 1983 decision to keep the franc in the ERM was rooted in large part in the perceived financial difficulties attached to a float. These difficulties were crucial to changing Fabius' and Defferre's position on floating, which in turn shaped Mitterrand's final decision. France had few remaining currency reserves with which to defend the franc in the context of a float, was burdened with a 330 billion franc foreign debt and faced the near exhaustion of international loan possibilities.[78] Attempts to maintain a managed float would likely have led to excessively high interest rates. To have let the franc float freely would have led to a dramatic drop in its value. This would have increased France's foreign debt burden which would have forced the Socialist government either to suspend repayment and/or adopt serious austerity measures to compensate for the loss. Temporary competitive gains from the devaluation would have come too late to help cover the costs.

Again, what mattered were the economic attitudes of leading officials and the manner in which they perceived the financial situation, not the economic validity of the arguments for and against floating. Such arguments would not have convinced the more entrenched opponents of the EMS. Moreover, the difficulty of floating the franc would have depended very much on the size of the initial devaluation and the accompanying economic policies. While political pressure resulted in the association of removing the ERM constraint and continued reflationary economic policies, it is not impossible that the Socialist government would have adopted a moderate strategy – recommended by

Riboud and Denizet – embracing more severe deflationary measures. Indeed, both the managed floats of the 1970s were the result of the refusal of governments to accept deflationary economic measures, but were both soon followed by such policies in order to redress increasingly difficult economic conditions.

What further complicated the matter was that knowledge of the current amount of foreign exchange reserves was considered a State secret and limited to approximately 20 people (the president, prime minister, minister of finance, a few of their advisers and concerned Bank of France and Treasury officials). This information was not available to those who supported floating the franc. With the exception of the President, all of those who knew the state of French reserves were opposed to leaving the ERM.[79] However, it is problematic to claim that this knowledge *necessarily* led to opposition to floating.

The attitudes of the financial administrative élite towards the possible use of gold reserves to defend the franc in the context of a float provides a good example of their financial conservatism and caution.[80] Most Treasury officials and advisers of the period claim that the use of gold reserves was not presented as an option because it was inherently unworkable. They argue that this would have encouraged further speculation and forced the government to accept an even larger devaluation, which in turn was considered unacceptable because of the resulting rise in inflation and the value of foreign-held debt. Left-wing critics claim that the possible use of gold reserves was not presented by Treasury officials because they did not want supporters of a float to use this to defend their position (Grjebine, interview, 10 April 1994).

While Mitterrand's decisions on ERM participation were not based on economic attitudes, it is clear that in spite of a strong reflationary rhetoric prior to, and after, his May 1981 victory, he was cautious on economic matters. As noted above, much of his pre-1981 rhetoric on the need for reflation was due to political considerations.[81] However, immediately following his election victory, several of Mitterrand's statements and actions also indicated caution in his approach. First, the decision not to devalue the franc in May 1981 effectively stemmed speculation. Moreover, the President made several statements which placed firm limits around his support for reflationary growth. In July 1981, for example, he publicly insisted that the budget deficit must not exceed 3 per cent of GNP (*Le Monde*, 25 July 1981). His appointment of Jacques Delors as minister of finance was also clearly motivated by a desire to demonstrate caution, as there were few political reasons to choose

Delors, given his marginal position in the Party. Mitterrand's refusal to accept Delors' resignation on several occasions suggests his full awareness that his minister of finance performed a valuable role within the government. Furthermore, the President's willingness to take the political risk of introducing austerity measures following the June 1982 devaluation demonstrates his acceptance that reflation was not sustainable without the previously expected world economic recovery. At this point, he began to emphasize the goal of controlling inflation as much as that of lowering unemployment. Nonetheless, Mitterrand's hesitation on the appropriate economic path to choose following the renewed speculation against the franc in August 1982, demonstrates his lack of commitment to the half-hearted austerity measures already adopted. As for the President's policy on ERM participation, his lack of a determined position was demonstrated by rather foolish comments to the international and French press, which worked to feed speculation against the franc (see above).

Mitterrand admitted to lacking the sufficient economic knowledge to decide between the different arguments in favour and against the participation of the franc in the mechanism on economic grounds alone.[82] He claimed that he did not wish to leave the ERM – principally due to a concern regarding France's position in Europe – and that he had hoped to be presented with economic arguments sufficiently convincing not to do so. However, he also admitted to having been very much tempted by the industrial arguments presented by Riboud and Denizet (Favier and Martin-Roland, 1990, p. 462). The President's hesitation on desirable policy during the autumn of 1982 and spring of 1983 centred around the problem of industrial modernisation in the context of severe financial constraints.

Following the March 1983 decision, Mitterrand adopted a stronger position in favour of the EMS and the austerity measures adopted by Delors. While the debate on appropriate economic policy within the Socialist Party continued, the public expression of opposition to government policy was largely contained. It is important to exclude from this analysis of economic attitudes, the post-March 1983 reformulation of official Socialist government policy on EMS membership and anti-inflationary measures. The attempt was made to justify monetary and economic policies in terms with which Socialist Party activists and voters could identify: notably the stabilisation of the level of unemployment. It was argued that this goal could only be realized within the context of relative monetary stability and low inflationary growth.[83]

'Choosing Europe'

Attitudes on European integration within the Socialist Party both encouraged and discouraged support for keeping the franc in the ERM. On the Party's Left, the European Community was perceived as a device for imposing capitalism upon member states, of which the EMS was seen as the latest example. However, unlike orthodox Gaullist opinion, left-wing Socialists did not oppose in principle the transfer of national powers to the Community, although they argued that it was first necessary to arrange substantial reforms. The 'Social Democrats' tended to stress a more positive attitude towards the Community, although they also recommended reforms. Mitterrand's support for limited further European integration was of some importance in encouraging his March 1983 decision to keep the franc in the ERM.

The vast majority of the Socialist Party did not consider the Community and limited further integration to be a priority. The CERES-dominated Left of the Party perceived the Community as inherently linked to a liberal conception of the economy and thus incapable of adequately serving the interests of European workers. It was, therefore, necessary either to reform substantially the objectives of the Community in order to serve socialist objectives or end French participation altogether. Several policies advocated by CERES ran against the basic principles of the Common Market. The economic nationalism – the 'reconquest of the domestic market' – involved limiting international trade to 20 per cent of GNP, which would have required protectionist measures against both non-European and European goods (*Projet Socialiste*, 1979). The *Projet* also argued for the significant reform of virtually all Community policies, placed a new emphasis upon the social provisions of the Rome Treaty, including an enhanced regional policy, and insisted upon the development of common industrial policies of particular interest to France.

The 'Social Democratic' wing of the Party can be described as generally more favourable towards European integration and more cautious regarding the establishment of policies which might have placed France in direct conflict with its neighbours. Specific attitudes varied considerably. Because their vision of economic change was generally more flexible than that of the Party's Left, the European Community and the degree of economic interdependence posed less of a threat, although most noted the contradiction between a European economic identity and socialist economic objectives. There was a hard core of pro-Europeans in the Socialist Party, who attempted to counter the isolationist tendencies on the left. To this end, more moderate Party journals stressed that isolationism was not the answer to the economic crisis and that a rupture of French relations with the Community 'could only lead to a formidable economic and social regression, for which the workers would be the first to pay'.[84] The anti-Germanism of CERES was balanced by the more general Socialist view that a strong Franco-German partnership was crucial for French economic and security interests. Moderate Socialist policy on the Community as presented in the *101 Propositions* and the *Créteil Manifesto* stressed the idea of Europe as a third international force, independent of the United States and the Soviet Union. In the *Manifesto*, under the heading 'France', the Socialists presented a pragmatic approach on how the Community could serve French interests. 'Social Democrats' generally stressed the need for European economic co-operation, especially in those fields in which individual member states could not hope to compete with American and Asian competitors. Within government, however, positive attitudes on Europe did not dissuade many 'Social Democrats' from supporting a float, because many believed that it would not seriously damage relations with France's European partners.

All of Mitterrand's advisers claim that the most important factor encouraging his decision in favour of the ERM was a long-standing commitment to the European Community, especially given that his knowledge of economics was extremely limited. The President himself had a long record of strong rhetorical support for European integration – albeit never precisely defined. Still, his wavering on the issue suggests the qualified importance of this commitment. There is no reason to believe, as some have claimed, that Mitterrand's decision in favour of the ERM provided him with the opportunity to change government policy on the Community along lines that he had always wanted but could never develop as the leader of the Socialist Party. The President's support for limited further integration and selected initiatives following 1983 does not prove a positive pre-1983 position. Indeed, the change might have been due to the need to develop a new policy line to justify the economic decisions made in 1982 and 1983 and to make the best of the new situation, rather than any previous commitment to European integration. Whatever the case, even if Mitterrand maintained a generally positive attitude towards the Community, it is clear that his public commitment was highly pragmatic, influenced at any point in time by pressing political concerns.

One indication of Mitterrand's recognition of the crucial importance of the Community to French interests was his appointment of pro-European politicians to the cabinet posts most concerned with European policymaking: finance, foreign affairs and European affairs. Jacques Delors, Claude Cheysson and André Chandernagor had all had extensive experience in the institutions of the Community. Prior to May 1981, Delors, an MEP, was chairman of the European Parliament's economic and monetary affairs Committee, while Cheysson was the European Commissioner responsible for development. Mitterrand also decided to upgrade the post of secretary of state for european affairs to junior minister.

Domestic political motives

Domestic political motives both encouraged leading socialists to keep the franc in the ERM and discouraged them from doing so. First, the population generally supported the idea of a strong currency and the EMS, although not necessarily the corresponding economic policies.[85] Moreover, diverse political considerations help to explain the timing of all three devaluations. For example, the municipal elections of March 1983 encouraged Mitterrand to delay the third devaluation, although they do not explain the motives behind the decision to devalue within the ERM.

It was also necessary to establish the image of the Socialists as responsible economic managers, as much for domestic political reasons as to challenge international speculation against the franc. Mitterrand sought to overcome the legacy of socialist devaluations – as in 1924 with the arrival in office of the *Cartel des Gauches* and in 1936 following the victory of the Popular Front – even though this could have been blamed on the previous government (Halimi, 1996; Mauroy, 1982, p. 19). He had portrayed himself as '*la force tranquille*' during the election campaign, with calm in the money markets as an important campaign point. In avoiding the devaluation of the franc, Mitterrand also wanted to succeed where de Gaulle, Pompidou and Giscard had failed.[86] Some claim that his decision also stemmed from a desire to emulate the Gaullist precedent of a strong franc in order to build a powerful an image of himself as President (Simonnot, 1993). For Mitterrand – as for many others on all sides of the political spectrum – a strong franc was a symbol of national pride and managerial competence. A devaluation would have been psychologically disastrous because it would have given the appearance of surrendering to speculative pressures – precisely what the twentieth proposal of Mitterrand's *101* promised not to do – especially as these pressures were in large part due to a belief that the new government did not intend to defend the franc.[87] The May 1981

decision was meant as a strong statement to counter the sceptical attitude towards the Socialists in French and international financial circles.[88] Likewise, while the October 1981 devaluation could be blamed
on the previous government, the June 1982 and March 1983 devaluations were both perceived as embarrassing failures by the President. This
was even more so, as they were followed by austerity measures
demanded by the Germans. Finally, a devaluation in May 1981 might
have damaged Socialist National Assembly election prospects.

The policies of the Socialist Party prior to the 1981 elections and the
rhetoric of its leadership created considerable expectation within the
Party's rank and file, the new government and the trade unions of
the pursuit of social and economic policies which would transform
French society. This expectation increased opposition to the ERM, as
the most obvious manifestation of the 'international capitalist' constraint which prevented the fulfilment of Socialist goals. Much of Mitterrand's rhetorical commitment to growth-oriented policies, under-
emphasis of austerity, and his statements suggesting the possibility of
a franc devaluation outside the ERM stemmed from the need to mollify
this demand. In the negotiations with the Germans prior to the first and
second devaluations, Delors had to be careful in order to avoid the
imposition of excessive austerity which would promote a backlash
within the Socialist Party. Moreover, there were important political
reasons for ignoring and down-playing Delors' calls in October 1981
for a 'pause' in Socialist reforms in order to stabilise the economy. The
mention of a 'pause' immediately brought to mind the 1937 decision of
the Blum government to delay the implementation of reforms which
effectively brought an end to the fulfilment of the Socialist dream
promised in 1936. In order to respond to the left-wing Socialist and
communist criticism of the new austerity measures adopted following
the second devaluation, Mitterrand invoked the possibility of a departure from the ERM and a move to a 'third phase' if the austerity measures of the 'second phase' 'failed'.[89] Moreover, the failure of the
Socialists to outline a clear position on the EMS prior to 1983, was due
to the opposition to the system on the Party's left.

The decisions to devalue within the ERM of June 1982 and March
1983 were made in spite of the considerable political difficulties these
created for Mitterrand within the Socialist Party. The President had to
engage in serious political damage control following the March 1983
decision and maintain a determined stance on the pursuit of austerity. It
was necessary to establish an acceptable ideological defence of anti-
inflationary economic measures. The new policy threatened to cost

Mitterrand's faction control over the Party leadership at the October 1983 Lille conference and required the President's active intervention in defence of his minister of finance.[90]

Cameron (1996) points to the importance of another domestic political factor: the relative influence of different economic interests.[91] He claims that groups which had an interest in removing the franc from the ERM had insufficient influence in the policymaking process. Both communist and socialist trade unions were kept at arms length from the government and the export lobby was poorly organised. The efforts of Riboud – although the head of a large exporting company, he was acting in a personal capacity – were unique for the potential anti-EMS lobby. Although the CNPF and other business organisations preferred caution on economic and monetary policies, they did not campaign actively for a pro-ERM policy. As Cameron claims, the financial sector, in favour of the EMS, proved to be the most influential economic interest group. However, it is also important to note that this sector did not need to organise any campaign. It was largely publicly owned and its interests were defended by the financial administrative élite in the Treasury and, by extension, the financial policy advisers on the staffs of Mitterrand, Mauroy and Delors.

Conclusion

During the 1981–83 period, the battle in the Socialist government over the EMS was shaped by different perceptions of monetary power which, in turn, were structured by economic attitudes. Those who supported reflation argued that the existing EMS imposed both American and German economic preferences upon France. As it was unlikely that the French could change these preferences, it was necessary to remove the monetary constraint in order to increase French negative power. For these actors, the best way to increase this power was to float the franc rather than pursue intra-European monetary stability. Those who accepted deflation and the continued imposition of the ERM constraint also tended to focus on the need for monetary stability in Europe and the desirability of maximising the possibility of positive French monetary power. Moderate economic attitudes also led erstwhile opponents of the ERM constraint, notably Fabius, to reject what were perceived to be financially hazardous alternatives. French demands for EMS reform, to the extent that they were made during this period, demonstrate both the persistence of core French power motives from the pre-1981 period as well as the limited degree to which they were satisfied by the new monetary system. Reform of the EMS was, however, not high on the list of Socialist government priorities, as the central issue was desirable and feasible economic policies.

More general attitudes on European integration were secondary to those on desirable economic policy. Nonetheless, they were of some importance in determining Mitterrand's position and thus the final decision to keep the franc in the ERM, especially given his ignorance on economic matters. As during the previous period, domestic political motives – here, the demands of most of the Socialist Party for reflation – weighed in favour of a float. However, certain groups whose perceived interests were most likely damaged by a decision to keep the franc in the ERM – notably workers – failed to mount any significant campaign against membership. The opposition of the large majority of the Socialist Party and government to the ERM constraint and the tenuous nature of Mitterrand's support for the continued participation of the franc in the mechanism, should be contrasted with the determined support of the financial administrative élite and a handful of financial staff members. In the face of strong political pressure, this small group proved crucial to the direction of French policymaking during this period. Their economic attitudes and corresponding interpretation of power motives ensured the continuity in French policy on European monetary co-operation in spite of political change.

4
The French Challenge to German Monetary Dominance: Demands for EMS Reform, March 1983 to May 1988

Introduction

French policymaking on monetary co-operation between March 1983 and May 1988 differed from that of the Socialist government 's first two years principally in that continued membership in the EMS was no longer seriously in question. Core French demands on EMS reform remained the same although they were now made more assiduously. Moreover, the defeat of the Fabius Socialist government in the March 1986 elections and the arrival to power of the RPR–UDF government led by Jacques Chirac did not modify the general thrust of French policy, even though the rhetoric in favour of reform became decidedly more vitriolic. In *cohabitation* with the Chirac government , President Mitterrand chose not to interfere in the formulation of French policy, even though some aspects of EMS reform – principally institutional matters – fell within the reserved domain of presidential powers guaranteed in the Constitution. The boundaries of this period are marked by the March 1983 decision to tie the franc definitively into the EMS and the May 1988 presidential elections which renewed President Mitterrand's mandate and enabled him to pursue a policy in favour of a more rapid move to Economic and Monetary Union. The paucity of academic coverage is easily explained: the period lacks the ideological and political interest of the first two years of Socialist government and the European policymaking interest of the negotiations leading up to the Maastricht European Council.[92]

Nonetheless, the developments between March 1983 and May 1988 were of central importance to the development of French policy on European monetary integration. Government demands for reform did not extend to full Economic and Monetary Union. Few French policymakers were ready to accept the implied loss of *de jure* autonomous control. However, the failure of French reform efforts to fundamentally alter the asymmetry of the EMS demonstrated to key policymakers that their core European monetary power motives could not be served in the context of the existing system. On 8 January 1988, RPR Finance Minister Edouard Balladur presented a memorandum to Ecofin in which he called for 'the rapid pursuit of the monetary construction of Europe' – although he provided few details as to the manner in which this could be achieved – and accepted the logic behind the creation of a 'single currency zone'. On 26 February 1988, to the surprise of most observers, the German Minister of Foreign Affairs Hans-Dietrich Genscher proposed the creation of a system of European central banks and the strengthening of the ECU (Genscher, 1988).

Monetary policy developments

Following the 21 March 1983 realignment, the Mauroy and Fabius governments succeeded in avoiding a further realignment of the franc–mark parity in spite of repeated speculative attacks. Pressure against the franc, due to both the accumulated inflation differential between the French and German economies and the fall of the dollar, increased prior to the March 1986 elections. In order to stem speculation, the Fabius government maintained real interest rates at record high levels. Under internal political pressure to lower rates – there was no speculative pressure thanks to the decision to maintain high rates for two weeks following the elections – the Chirac government arranged a realignment within the ERM. On 6 April 1986, the franc was devalued by 2 per cent and the mark revalued by 3 per cent.

Speculative pressure, due to the continued fall of the dollar and the flow of capital from the dollar to the mark, increased again in September 1986. This was stemmed by the 5 November 1986 decision to raise interest rates, the first time that the RPR–UDF government did so. However, speculation began again at the end of the year. The government let the franc drop to its parity fluctuation floor against the mark, which forced the Germans to intervene by purchasing francs in order to ease the attack. The French refused to devalue on the grounds that economic fundamentals did not require them to do so. This led to the 12 January 1987 revaluation of the mark and guilder by 3 per cent and the Belgian franc by 2 per cent, as a means of decreasing pressure on the weak currencies of the ERM. This was the first realignment within the ERM that was not required on the grounds of the inflation differential between the countries involved.

Following from the agreements at Basle and Nyborg to improve economic policy co-ordination, speculative pressure on the franc was successfully alleviated for the first time by a co-ordinated change of interest rates by the Bank of France and the Bundesbank, on 5 November 1987. Two of the leading French rates increased each by 0.75 percentage points and two of the leading German rates decreased over a six day period by 0.30 and 0.50 percentage points. Bundesbank loans for intramarginal interventions – another product of the Basle–Nyborg accords – were likely crucial to the stabilisation of the EMS and the success in avoiding any realignments during the mid October 1987 to mid January 1988 wave of speculation against the weaker European currencies, due to the October 1987 stock market crash and the continued fall of the dollar. Over these three months, the Bundesbank lent partner central banks 21.5 billion marks for intramarginal interventions (*Financial Times*, 20 May 1988).

During this period there was also a rapid expansion in the public and private use of the ECU in spite of the limited nature of European agreements. By the end of 1983, it was the third largest currency used to denominate Eurobond issues thanks to the issues of the French and other governments – although not the German – the Commission and the European Investment Bank (EIB).[93] By the end of 1984, the ECU had moved into fourth place as a non-dollar vehicle for bank lending – well ahead of both sterling and the franc. Several factors explain its rise: demand by French and Italian borrowers eager to avoid the capital controls imposed on the franc and the lira; active promotion by Delors and his replacement as minister of finance, Pierre Bérégovoy; the instability of the dollar and the stability of the EMS following the 1983 realignment. Public and private banks also increased the use of the ECU in interbank transitions.[94] Several factors placed clear limits on its rise: notably, the German government blocked its expanded public and private use,[95] while central banks, led by the Bundesbank, were reluctant to provide holders of ECU with the automatic right to demand its exchange for national currencies. To reduce the risk, a system of compensation was established and managed by the Bank for International Settlements (BIS) in Basle. Nonetheless, the expanded use of the ECU slowed in 1985, and by 1986 the volume of ECU issues dropped by 20 per cent to reach 7.1 billion, or 3 per cent of total international issues (Bundesbank report on the ECU, 18 August 1987).

Challenging EMS asymmetry

While French governments accepted the need for anti-inflationary measures and were reluctant to devalue, they considered the German standard on inflation too constraining for the French economy and inhibitive of the adoption of policies that would help to alleviate the worsening French unemployment problem. French efforts to reform the EMS thus stemmed from similar – although clearly modified – objectives to those which the French pursued in the EMU negotiations in the early 1970s: increased monetary stability without unacceptable economic and monetary convergence. In the early 1970s they opposed any form of convergence; in the 1980s they opposed full convergence to the German standard. More specifically, they sought to improve EMS support mechanisms, establish the principle of German responsibility through the reinforcement of the 'divergence indicator', and ensure German participation in intramarginal interventions and interest rate co-ordination. By increasing the co-ordination of policies and the mutual obligations within the system – thereby decreasing the *de facto* autonomy of policymaking but increasing positive monetary power – French governments sought to increase their room to manoeuvre in economic policymaking.

Improving EMS support mechanisms

The first objective stemming from European monetary power motives involved expanding the funds available to weak currency countries to defend their currencies against speculation and requiring strong currency countries to accept intramarginal intervention which might ease speculative pressure earlier on and therefore save weak currency countries considerable reserves. In more general terms, this would contribute to the perceived stability of the fixed exchange rates in the EMS and the ability of member states to defend them. The first objective also encouraged French governments to call for the Europeanisation of EMS central bank reserve holdings. It was argued that this would help to stabilise the franc–mark parity, principally by selling dollars and buying weaker European currencies. The French, in particular, wanted the Germans and Dutch to purchase francs in exchange for dollars, which would help to maintain the strength of the franc despite the continued fall of the dollar (Fabra, *Le Monde*, 27 October 1987). Moreover, the French argued that each time the Bundesbank or the Dutch central bank intervened on the market to support the franc, they should conserve a certain portion of the purchased francs as this would help strengthen the French currency. According to the existing rules of the operation of the VSTF (Ortoli facility), weak currency central banks were obliged, within two months, to repurchase their currencies that the strong currency central banks had accumulated in their defence. This helped to ensure the perfect neutrality of the EMS with regard to inflation. French governments argued that the strong currency central banks could use these holdings to subscribe to French Treasury bonds and other short term debt (Fabra, *ibid.*). The franc would thus be promoted to the rank of a true reserve currency and strengthened as a result. It was argued that this would in turn help to strengthen 'the European monetary zone' and better protect European currencies from the fluctuation of the dollar.

As early as May 1984, Delors had achieved some progress with regard to the first objective, with an agreement of the ministers of finance to enlarge the VSTF, and thus increase the limit on Community loans available to those member state governments whose currencies had reached the floor of their permitted margin of fluctuation.[96] A more significant reinforcement of the VSTF was agreed upon at Nyborg and Basle in September 1987. This involved three measures: first, the reimbursement of credits via this facility – both to the EMCF and the other member states – could be stretched over a three-and-a-half month period instead of the previous two-and-a-half months; second, in future the reimbursement of loans could be completely in ECU rather than the 50 per cent maximum to date; and third, for loans borrowed through the VSTF, member states could delay repayment of twice the debtor quota ratio for three to six months as opposed to the single debtor quota ratio, which eased the financial burden of loans. Regarding the second measure, the previous requirement that 50 per cent of any loan had to be repaid in the creditor country's currency raised the problem that when the debtor central bank raised the funds in the market, the initial purpose of the intervention may have been vitiated – because the purchase of this currency in the market would in effect strengthen it again. At Nyborg, it was agreed that up to 100 per cent of the loan from strong currency central banks via the VSTF could be repaid in ECUs, or in currencies which suited the debtor's central bank, as long as the creditor agreed. The Germans agreed to do this for an experimental period of two years.

Achieving a balanced convergence

Since the 1978 EMS negotiations, the French had sought to establish some sort of binding 'divergence indicator' to determine the divergence of member state economic and monetary results from the Community average (Ludlow, 1982). The principle behind the establishment of the indicator was that the economic and monetary policies pursued by strong currency countries could be as responsible for speculation against weak currencies as those pursued in weak currency countries themselves and that strong currency countries should as a result modify their policies. The instrument established in 1979 was the first example of an objective indicator ever adopted for international policy co-ordination. However, this was non-binding and largely ignored due to German – principally Bundesbank – opposition.

The French and Commission sought, therefore, to introduce other measures to entrench the underlying principle of strong currency country responsibility in order to convince the Germans to modify their policies. The first clearly successful application of this principle was in January 1987 when the Germans and other strong currency countries agreed for the first time to revalue unilaterally in order to stabilise the EMS. French demands also led to the Nyborg agreement to increase the collective surveillance of economic and monetary policies through a monthly examination of a battery of indicators that would encourage co-ordinated decisions in the case of discovered anomalies and thus contribute to EMS stability. This was in essence a reinforcement of the non-mandatory version of the divergence indicator. Thus, the Germans *appeared* to concede on an important point: that strong currency countries could be as much to blame for EMS instability as weak currency countries.

Ensuring intramarginal interventions

The French and the Commission also sought the establishment of rules on intramarginal interventions which would force strong currency countries to support weaker currencies prior to their reaching the floor of their parity fluctuation margins and thus help discourage speculation against the weaker currencies. During the January 1987 realignment negotiations, the finance ministers agreed to call upon EMS Central Bank Governors and the EEC Monetary Committee to examine ways of strengthening the operating mechanisms of the EMS, notably through the possible introduction of intramarginal interventions. After a series of French and Commission initiatives during the first

half of 1987, the Germans accepted the principle of intramarginal interventions in June. An agreement was reached to permit governments
access to EMCF funds through the conditions of the VSTF before their
currencies reached the floor of the ERM system, from the moment their
currency had been attacked.

At the September 1987 Nyborg Ecofin Council, the Germans finally
agreed to the principle of strong currency country participation in
intramarginal interventions: that these countries should open lines of
limited credit according to the rules of the VSTF to their partners with
weak currencies, so that they could more easily defend these currencies
from the moment they were first attacked. This meant that France would
be able to benefit from a supplementary line of defence, from all the
intervening countries combined, of twice its debtor quota ratio to
the EMCF, or 6.8 billion ECU (at the time 41 billion francs). The
French and Commission officials claimed that this commitment was
'quasi-automatic' (*Le Monde*, 14 September 1987). However, the Germans made their full participation in the 'spirit' of the agreement and
their fulfilment of the obligations enumerated for strong currency countries, conditional upon the removal of capital controls. With French
controls still in place, the developments over the following months
demonstrated that there was no automaticity. Nonetheless, the agreement was successful in weakening Bundesbank resistance to German
intervention on behalf of the franc and there was a reversal of the
responsibility for justifying action or inaction. If a strong currency
central bank – principally the Bundesbank – decided not to help to
defend a particular currency, it would have to justify publicly why it
refused to do so.

Limited German commitment to intramarginal interventions
was demonstrated shortly after the Basle–Nyborg accords. From mid-
October 1987 to mid-January 1988, the Bundesbank lent partner central
banks DM21.5 billion for intramarginal interventions, most of which
went to support the franc (*Financial Times*, 20 May 1988). However, on
other agreed reforms, the Bundesbank was less co-operative. The commitment to accept reimbursements in ECUs for loans made in marks was
circumscribed by its decision to treat this provision on a case-by-case
basis. Nonetheless, interest rate co-ordination and German intramarginal intervention helped to stabilise the system. They were crucial in
helping the French avoid another devaluation until 1993. However, as
noted above, they only alleviated the economic impact of the asymmetric operation of the EMS: they did not address the underlying causes
for this asymmetry.

Improving interest rate co-ordination

An important element of increasing German responsibility for EMS stability was interest rate co-ordination – with the Germans lowering their interest rates to help decrease the degree to which the French would have to raise their rates. The French made little progress on this objective. Pressure created by capital flowing from the declining dollar to the strong mark, from the end of 1986 into January 1987, made necessary either an ERM realignment or appropriate interest rate changes. For the first time since the creation of the EMS, the Chirac government refused to accept the devaluation of the franc, arguing that this was not justified on grounds of an inflation differential between France and Germany.[97] It was argued that pressure on the franc was due principally to high German rates. Moreover, it was argued that if the French were expected to maintain high interest rates in spite of the elimination of the inflation differential, then the Germans should also be prepared to make certain sacrifices. The Chirac government and the Commission placed unprecedented pressure on the Germans to lower their interest rates (see, for example, *Le Monde*, 7 January 1987). However, the Bundesbank refused to do so.

The commitment to improve interest rate co-ordination was first tested in November 1987. On 5 November, after two days of secret bilateral negotiations between French and German bankers and bureaucrats, the Bundesbank and the Bank of France each announced a change in leading interest rates – the Germans lowering two of their leading rates, the French raising two of theirs – in order to discourage speculation and remove for the moment the risk of a realignment of ERM parities. To strengthen this co-ordinated effort, Balladur and Stoltenberg, the German finance minister, publicised a Franco-German communiqué explaining the manoeuvre (*Le Monde*, 7 November 1987). This had the desired impact and the franc soon rose against the mark. The agreement to co-ordinate rates marked a significant victory for the French, as this was the first time that the German government had agreed to overcome the reticence of the Bundesbank regarding the lowering of rates in order to ease speculative pressure against another currency. The decision of the Bundesbank to lower its rates encouraged the Dutch, British and Swiss to follow this lead, which helped redirect even more currency flows and ease pressure on the franc. However, it is clear that the Bundesbank remained reluctant on the issue of interest rate co-ordination, which explains why it refused to lower its leading interest rate – the discount rate – and why the French had to accept a considerably larger increase of their two leading rates than the German decrease.

In November 1987, the French succeeded in convincing the Germans to accept the creation of the Franco-German Economic Council consisting of national treasury officials. French interest in this council was sparked by a reaction to what was perceived as the inadequate consultation on the mark–guilder revaluation of January 1987. More generally, the French sought to re-emphasize the centrality of the Franco-German relationship in all areas of monetary and economic co-operation in the EC, and thus increase French influence over German economic policy-making.

Financial markets were not impressed by the reforms agreed at Basle and Nyborg, which appeared as minor technical adjustments and not a substantial alteration of the different attractiveness of the EMS currencies. Speculation against the franc continued unabated. So too did French insistence upon a more fundamental reform of the EMS. In an 8 January 1988 memorandum to the other Community finance ministers, Balladur for the first time presented demands – rather than a 'proposal for consideration', as his February 1987 memorandum was worded – that went well beyond the non-institutional reform of the ERM. He argued that:

> the various credit mechanisms could only temporarily spread the costs of intervention: ultimately it was the central bank whose currency was at the lower end of the permitted range which had to bear the cost. However, it was not necessarily the currency at the lower end of the range which was the source of the tension. The discipline imposed by the exchange-rate mechanism may, for its part, have had good effects when it served to put a constraint on economic and monetary policies which were insufficiently rigorous. It produced an abnormal situation when its effect was to exempt any countries whose policies were too restrictive from the necessary adjustment. Thus the fact that some countries piled up current account surpluses for several years equal to between 2 and 3 per cent of their GDPs constituted a grave anomaly. The asymmetry was one of the reasons for the tendency of European currencies to rise against the dollar and the currencies tied to it. This rise was contrary to the fundamental interest of Europe and its constituent economies. [It was therefore necessary] to find a new system under which this problem could not arise.[98]

French reluctance to remove capital controls

At Basle and Nyborg, the Germans established the condition that their commitment to intramarginal interventions and interest rate co-ordination depended upon French agreement to the removal of remaining capital controls. In terms of the expression of monetary power motives, the French were placed in a difficult situation. On the one hand, they wanted to increase their positive monetary power by ensuring German intervention. On the other, their reluctance to liberalise capital flows reflected negative European monetary power motives: to diminish the impact of EMS asymmetry. This explains Balladur's hesitation to remove controls.

As during previous periods, most European governments were able to exploit certain loopholes in Community law and maintain certain forms of capital controls, while some governments occasionally flouted the law, often with the Commission turning a blind eye.[99] Several economists have argued that given the lack of adequate convergence in the early to mid-1980s, the EMS would have collapsed if all capital controls in the Community had been removed.[100] Moreover, the continued speculation against the franc following the April 1986 realignment indicated that French policy efforts to converge to the German standard would fail to ease pressure on the franc. French governments also argued that full capital liberalisation would substantially increase the cost of defending weak currencies in the system. They sought in exchange guaranteed intramarginal interventions and increased access to foreign bank loans. The Germans, in the meantime, were unwilling to provide the degree of support that would ensure stability following the removal of controls.

Nonetheless, the Fabius government accepted the principle of financial integration during the negotiations leading to the Single European Act (SEA). It appears contradictory that the Socialists accepted this principle, yet were consistently reluctant to remove capital controls. However, capital liberalisation was a German condition for their acceptance of the Single Market Programme. Moreover, Bérégovoy believed that the position of the franc in the ERM could eventually be strengthened sufficiently to withstand liberalised capital flows. Indeed, the Socialists might well have begun removing capital controls if they had not lost the March 1986 elections. One observer of the SEA negotiations notes that the French poorly understood the full implications of financial integration for the formation of French monetary policy (Wyplosz, interview, 9 June 1994).[101] Principally, the French had not yet conceived the 'triangle of incompatibility'. This postulate, which had only recently been reformulated in 1985,[102] stated that no country, with the exception of that with the dominant currency, could maintain all three sides of the monetary policy triangle: fixed exchange-rates, an independent monetary policy, and liberalised capital flows. The next chapter explores the manner in which this 'triangle of incompatibility' created a situation in which certain French policymakers believed that they had little choice but to demand further monetary integration.

The election of the Chirac government in March 1986 ended any possibility that the French might begin to remove capital controls. The Germans attempted to coax the Chirac government into promising their removal by manipulating this point as a condition for increased German flexibility on EMS reform measures advocated by the French and the revaluations of the mark during ERM realignments. If the French wanted to increase their positive European monetary power, then they had to accept a decline in their negative monetary power. In late 1986 there was a formal agreement to remove controls on a wide variety of capital movements within the Community – the first such EC accord in nearly a quarter century.[103] However, the Chirac government did not put this agreement into effect.

The French position on capital controls was becoming more malleable principally due to new economic realities. In addition to German demands, there was growing domestic pressure to remove the remaining controls. Industrial leaders, for example, argued that restrictions on capital outflows resulted in the restriction of capital inflows and thus hindered foreign investment in the French economy. Given high French interest rates, the significant decline in parastatal institutionalised credit facilities, and the drop in French government financial assistance for industry, foreign investment was an increasingly important source of capital.[104] Following the 15 March 1985 removal of certain controls on the movement of ECUs, French and foreign proponents of liberalised capital flows would have to wait until the commitment of the Rocard government in June 1988 to remove all controls by 1 July 1990.

The ECU against the mark

European power motives also prompted increased French interest in expanding the public and private use of the ECU as a 'parallel' or 'common' currency – although they normally did not use these terms – that would circulate freely in each EMS member state with the existing national currency. There were important economic motives that encouraged both the French government and private groups to use the ECU.

Principally, it was a relatively stable currency in comparison to the weak franc, and bond offers in ECU provided the French government with another means to raise capital. However, such financial motives do not explain why the French and certain other Community governments so actively promoted the expanded use of the currency. European monetary power motives were the most important here. As the value of the ECU was determined by the values of the EMS currencies weighted according to the economic size of their economies, it would be a weaker currency than the mark and – if sufficiently attractive to speculative capital – permit the relaxation of economic and monetary policies throughout the Community. There was a significant gap between the ECU as a dominant parallel currency – that is, an additional European currency used more than any of the other national currencies – and a single currency. The latter would involve the permanently fixed exchange rates of all participating member state currencies and the loss of *de jure* monetary autonomy which was not required by the former. As in the 1970s, few French policymakers believed in the possibility or desirability of a rapid move to a single currency.

Some French Treasury and Bank officials had conceived of the creation of a dominant European parallel currency prior to the creation of the ECU in 1979. Roy Jenkins and other Commission officials had publicly stated that it was their intention that the ECU eventually become the 'dominant' European currency (Ludlow, 1982). Although official Socialist government reticence prevented the active promotion of the ECU prior to the March 1983 decision, it is clear that Delors was interested in developing the currency, which explains the speed at which he began to do so following the decision.[105] At the national level, progress was particularly rapid. At the Community level, the first small step in the promotion of the ECU was taken at the June 1984 Fontainebleau Summit, when Mitterrand convinced the heads of government to include a feasibility study on minting the European currency in the guidelines for the 'Adonnino ad hoc committee on a Citizens' Europe' (*Bulletin*, EC 6–1984, p. 11). As Commission President, Delors presented his first set of proposals on the expanded use of the ECU to the Community ministers of finance at a May 1985 extraordinary meeting (*Le Monde*, 15 May 1984).[106]

French efforts to promote the ECU

There were four principal ways in which the French promoted the expanded use of the ECU: first, by encouraging its use in the accounting, financial and lending transactions of the Community and internationally; second, by encouraging the privileged access to the ECU market for residents of countries with exchange controls – notably France and Italy; third, by endowing the ECU with the characteristics of a real reserve asset; and fourth, by arguing for the transformation of the EMCF into an institution which could both manage the ECU and encourage its use, and eventually regulate its issue. During this period, progress was limited due principally to German opposition. The French achieved unconditional success only with regard to the second way, mainly because this did not require the agreement of the Germans.

First, the French sought to increase the use of the ECU in the repayment of loans and the intervention of strong currency countries. Efforts in this regard had another economic motive: if weak currency countries could repay loans from the strong currency countries in ECU rather than the appropriate strong currencies, this would avoid further strengthening these currencies. Success in this one area was relatively rapid, with an agreement reached on the basis of French and Commission proposals at the 13/14 April 1985 Ecofin meeting in Palermo. At this meeting, generally non-binding agreements were reached on four points: first, the possibility for EMS central banks to mobilise ECUs as opposed to dollars in payments to and interventions by member states through the intermediary of the EMCF; second, the repayment of debts incurred through the VSTF up to 100 per cent *in ECU* rather than 50 per cent that had hitherto been the case; third, the possibility for the central banks of non-Community member states to hold ECU; and fourth, the increase in the interest rates paid on the net creditor and debtor positions in ECU: in order to make the currency more attractive – the rates previously being calculated on the weighted average of the official discount rates of the EMS currencies, which was lower than real market rates. The Bundesbank refused to accept the second point, which forced member state governments to agree on a somewhat more binding measure at the September 1987 Nyborg meeting.

At the national level, the French government permitted the introduction of the ECU on the exchange market of the Paris stock exchange, which took place on 4 June 1984. Moreover, the French Treasury emitted more bonds in ECU than any other Community Treasury. The ECU was considered both more stable and more popular than the franc in international financial circles. As of February 1985, French bond issues in ECU accounted for 24 per cent of the world total, or ECU 1477.2 million, more than seven times greater than any other Community member state. Given German reluctance to promote the ECU, it could be argued that the French efforts to expand its use may well have weakened the franc further by redirecting international capital that might otherwise have gone to the French currency. Nonetheless, this possibility did not apparently decrease French efforts to promote the ECU.

The second way in which the French government promoted the use of the ECU required the least effort. In March 1985, Bérégovoy decided to relax exchange control measures on importers' terms of payments if they were billed in ECU and allowed ECU-bond issues by the Community institutions on the French financial market. This measure also provided the Germans with some proof of the French intention to remove capital controls. The third way – endowing the ECU with the characteristics of a real reserve asset – led the Fabius government to advocate the establishment of a separate interest rate for the ECU, independent of the discount rates of the EMS participating currencies. French demands on this resulted in the fourth element of the April 1985 Palermo agreement, although nothing of a more far reaching character.

The expanded role of the EMCF – the creation of an EMI or European Central Bank (ECB) to manage the ECU – was the fourth path to a strengthened European currency. The Socialists supported the immediate creation of an EMI with the responsibility to expand the use of the ECU as a 'parallel' currency. RPR–UDF policy – to the extent that it can be determined through speeches, interviews and articles – was considerably less straightforward. The Chirac government did not persist with Socialist efforts to reinforce the EMCF. However, on a few occasions in 1987, in newspaper interviews and speeches in France, Balladur speculated on the possible eventual creation of an EMI, anticipating the most important issues discussed in the Delors Committee and during the intergovernmental negotiations on EMU in 1990 and 1991.[107] The questions that he posed – in place of specific proposals for the establishment of an EMI – suggest that he, or at least his advisers, had actively considered the transformation of the EMCF, but that this was not a high priority for the moment. Starting in 1988, the frequency of this speculation increased considerably. In his 8 January memorandum to Ecofin, following his comments on the need for 'the rapid pursuit of the monetary construction', Balladur speculated on the creation of a 'common central institution'. Domestically, he and Chirac presented a far more gradualist vision and insisted that the creation of an EMI was a long term issue, not of immediate importance, and refused to give details of their vision (Balleix-Banerjee, 1993, 1997, 1999). Acting independently of the government, former president Giscard d'Estaing joined former West German chancellor Schmidt to lead the campaign for the establishment of an ECB. On 24 February 1988, they presented a statute for an independent central bank (*Le Monde*, 25 February 1988).

In an attempt to overcome German intransigence on the ECU and EMS reform more generally, French and Commission officials frequently linked progress on the Single European Market and economic convergence to progress in monetary matters.[108] Moreover, during the negotiations leading to the SEA, Delors and Bérégovoy attempted to include a mention of the ECU 'as the foundation' of the EMS within Article 107 of the Treaty of Rome. However, this was seen by some as an attempt to 'constitutionalise' the promotion of the ECU as a way of forcing the removal of German restrictions on its private use (*Le Monde*, 20 November 1985). Indeed, this perhaps explains German opposition to this wording and the large debate over the issue. Article 107 was therefore amended to describe the ECU as simply 'the European currency'.

The Germans – both the government and the Bundesbank – argued that there were numerous economic factors which worked against the successful promotion of a European parallel currency.[109] Crucially, they opposed the expanded use of the ECU on the grounds that it was inherently inflationary. Nonetheless, the Germans attempted to use the possibility of their increased flexibility on the ECU to win concessions from the French and the other Europeans on related matters: notably, the continued convergence of European economic and monetary policies towards those in Germany; and the liberalisation of capital movements.

French reluctance to remove capital controls – in spite of favourable rhetoric and the potentially legal commitments to financial integration in the SEA – thus perhaps hindered the expanded private use of the ECU. As with other French reform demands, the German counter-demand placed French governments in the difficult situation of having to determine the most favourable balance between expressions of positive and negative monetary power. They sought the creation of the ECU as a means of decreasing German economic hegemony in the Community. However, to achieve this, French governments would have to accept the removal of capital controls which provided the last protection against forced convergence within the EMS. Moreover, the French fully recognized that the rapid expansion of the private use of the ECU during the 1981 to 1985 period was due largely to the efforts of French and Italian citizens to circumvent existing controls placed on the movement of the lira and the franc but relaxed for the ECU. It was possible that the removal of these controls would involve the dramatic decline of the private use of the ECU – which was likely an important consideration behind German thinking on liberalisation. Between 1983 and 1988 many positive declarations were made on both sides with little real progress.

No French policymaker during this period argued in favour of a single currency – that is, implying the elimination of national currencies. In his January 1988 memorandum, Balladur argued that 'a single currency zone' followed logically from European economic integration through the Single Market Programme and the liberalisation of capital movements. However, it is important to stress that he did not propose the creation of a single currency *per se*. Rather he explicitly defined 'a single currency zone' as one 'in which a single monetary "device" (*signe*) could circulate freely', which was a restatement of French policy that all obstacles to the circulation of the ECU should be removed. Balladur only speculated on the possibility of a single currency and how it might be defined. He repeatedly stressed the *eventual* 'creation' of a 'common' European currency which could be either a parallel or a single currency. He posed several important questions on the future of the ECU.[110] However, he refused to provide any answers.

Ongoing attempts to contain dollar instability

As during previous periods, international monetary instability, particularly the dramatic rise and fall of the American dollar, was the source of considerable speculative pressure against the franc during this period. During the period of the dollar's rapid fall, the Germans maintained relatively high rates to avoid the rapid expansion of the domestic monetary supply. Thus, lower American interest rates did not contribute to lower French rates. International monetary power motives – intensified because of this growing instability – encouraged the French to embrace four European monetary policy responses: EMS reform; the Europeanisation of EMS central bank reserve holdings; the promotion of the ECU as an international reserve currency; and the development of a common European position on IMS reform. The first is outlined in the preceding section because the essential motives behind French demands for EMS reform were rooted in considerations of European power. International monetary instability provided a catalyst for French action by increasing the cost of maintaining the exchange rate of the franc. It did not, however, create the problem of EMS asymmetry. The second policy response is also outlined in the European power section because the Europeanisation of reserves had more to do with increasing the responsibility of strong currency countries for the stability of weak currencies than as a direct response to international monetary instability.

As during the previous period, the French reacted to international monetary instability by promoting the ECU as the third international reserve currency to rival the dollar and the yen and decrease the impact of American monetary policy on European economic policies. French ministers of finance argued that it was economically impossible for the mark to rival the dollar effectively, given the relatively small size of the German financial market and reserve holdings.[111] Moreover, it was argued that the mark-centric EMS resulted in complete submission to the dollar system. To increase the international role of the mark – because it could never come close to rivalling the dollar as an international reserve currency – would fail to diminish the influence of American monetary policies upon European currencies (Fabra, *Le Monde*, 27 October 1987).

As during previous periods, there were negative international power motives to decrease the use of the dollar. The French were concerned with the economic implications of the looming problem of the American debt which encouraged them to avoid issuing bonds denominated in dollars and to replace gradually Bank of France dollar reserve holdings (Aglietta, interview, 13 June 1994; *Le Monde*, 27 October 1987). It was argued that to accomplish this, it was necessary to promote the ECU and yen as currencies of international financing. Moreover, from the point of view of financial equilibria, an ECU made sense. A common currency would provide Europeans with their own settlement unit in which to denominate oil and commodity transactions and finance export credits.

IMS reform

As during previous periods, the French were the most active promoters of IMS reform. Their efforts were motivated both by international and European monetary power motives and should be considered here because they were a direct reinforcement of French efforts for EMS reform. French governments during this period drew a direct link between IMS, EMS and, more generally, European Community reform. In September 1983, Jacques Delors (as part of the run-up to both the Socialist Party Congress and the French EC Council Presidency) published an article advocating an increased role for the EMS and the ECU, which made clear the link between an enhanced EMS and the IMS reform called for by Mitterrand. For Delors, it went without saying that monetary co-operation in turn required the revitalisation of the Community: a strong Community could then get to grips with the US and Japan over world debt, diversification of reserve measures (SDR, ECU, yen) and interest rates (Delors, *Le Monde*, 9 September 1983). The principal change from previous periods was that the ideologically inspired opposition of successive American administrations to international monetary co-operation diminished substantially during the mid-1980s, which made possible certain limited initiatives to decrease international monetary instability.[112] However, the limited nature of these initiatives demonstrated to French governments that EMS reforms were the only possible route to improved European stability.

In May 1983, Mitterrand and Delors failed to convince either the Americans or the Germans to support their new proposals for reform. However, within a year, the Americans demonstrated greater responsiveness to international monetary targeting, largely because of the surprise created by the rapid drop in the value of the dollar. German flexibility on the matter increased due to this responsiveness and French efforts to present IMS reforms in the context of larger economic reforms including the strengthening of the common market. This resulted in the Plaza Accord of March 1985, in which the Americans agreed to relax their tight monetary policy. The French also engineered the Louvre accords of 23 February 1987 which – for the first time since the collapse of the tunnel that enclosed the Snake mechanism – applied the idea of a target zone for the dollar in order to diminish its excessive fluctuation. The American and German commitment to this zone was, however, limited, which explains why it was kept secret and why the dollar soon fluctuated outside it. The French commitment to the Louvre accords was far greater.[113]

French international efforts also reflect a failure to convince the Germans to co-ordinate the adjustment of European monetary policies to follow the dollar. The effort of member states to keep the dollar within a certain target zone had initially been agreed upon by the Community ministers of finance at the September 1986 Gleneagles meeting. The Bundesbank, however, refused to decrease its interest rates in order to slow the dollar's fall and alleviate the speculative pressure on the franc during the December 1986 to January 1987 period. It preferred instead to accept a unilateral revaluation of the mark. Moreover, Balladur claimed that the Basle–Nyborg reforms brought the international effort of monetary stabilisation to the European level (*Le Monde*, 14 September 1987). He also recommended the application to the EMS of ideas for monetary stabilisation developed at the international level. His February 1987 proposals for EMS reform drew on the ideas regarding the creation of a system of collective surveillance of a range of monetary and economic indicators presented at the June 1986 Tokyo G-7 summit (*Le Monde*, 14 February 1987).

An important aspect of French efforts to establish a target zone for the dollar was to increase the responsibility of both German and American central banks to intervene to control the level of the dollar and, ideally, co-ordinate interest rate changes to stem speculation. This effort, supported by several other G-7 countries, reinforced French efforts at the European level. The French also knew that the responsibility to intervene to prevent the fall of the dollar lay principally with the Germans and Japanese and would increase German flexibility on interest rate changes. Therefore, the 4 November 1987 co-ordination of Franco-German rates was due not only to agreements reached at Basle and Nyborg but also to the commitment to defend the dollar within its target zone previously agreed at the Louvre summit. In this way, target zones potentially decreased the economic cost of defending the franc. The Germans, led by the Bundesbank, continued to challenge the idea of international exchange-rate targetry.[114] However, the French succeeded in 'internationalising' the pressure upon them to be more flexible. American proposals for improved economic policy co-ordination to decrease international monetary instability – notably through the reflation of the German and Japanese economies – directly served French interests. The French, therefore, attempted to manipulate co-operation at both the European and international levels to their advantage. They joined the Americans in placing pressure on the German government to adopt more reflationary economic policies, which would permit the other Europeans to do so and diminish the large French trade deficit. In the meantime, the French joined the Germans in creating a European consensus on encouraging the Americans to adopt more responsible monetary policies, lower their enormous external trade deficit and decrease the federal budget deficit.[115]

During his last months in office as minister of finance in 1988, Balladur presented numerous specifically formulated proposals on IMS reform, which echoed his simultaneous demands regarding the EMS (see, for example, *Le Monde*, 20 January 1988; *Wall Street Journal*, 23 January 1988). The failure of the Louvre accords to prevent instability in the money markets in late 1987 encouraged the G-7 governments to publish a common declaration of 23 December regarding the need to progress with economic policy co-ordination. Balladur argued that the commitment regarding interventions and changes to economic policy to avoid disequilibria in the Louvre accords lacked the automaticity and discipline which would effectively curtail speculative pressure.[116] Balladur also advocated the creation of a small supranational body to manage a new international standard which could be an international version of the ECU.

German opposition was due to the fundamental difference between German and French conceptions of progress in international monetary co-ordination, which was also at the root of German reluctance on EMS reform. The Germans believed that international exchange rate stability would only follow from economic discipline – which corresponded to the German refusal to relax tight monetary policies. The French government emphasized that only the creation of a stable international currency framework with a certain automatic discipline could force governments to act in conformity with co-ordinated economic policies. The French also recommended increased economic policy co-ordination, independent of monetary efforts, hoping that both the Germans and Americans would be forced to alter their policies. The French argued that without this framework there would be little incentive or discipline to converge. In reality, they sought to play the Americans and Germans off against one another in order to achieve a more balanced policy convergence that would serve French interests.

'Competitive disinflation' as a conceptual framework

The period between March 1983 and May 1988 marked an intellectual and political consolidation of the supply-oriented policies of the financial administrative élite – involving a strong currency within the EMS and low inflation – which came to be labelled 'competitive disinflation'.[117] Critics of the imposed support for these ideas and the ferocious attack directed against heretics have since deemed this period as the start of *la Pensée Unique* (roughly translated as the Thatcherite argument that 'There Is No Alternative' policy or TINA) which was further entrenched following the return of the Socialists to government in 1988.

At the intellectual level, the extensive influence of the State in the area of economic research, through the studies produced in the Treasury, the forecasting division of the Ministry of Finance and the National Institute of Statistics and Economic Studies (INSEE), facilitated the rapid extension of these ideas into the academic economic community and then their dominance. Starting in 1982, these organs of the State produced a series of reports confirming the limited short term competitive gain of devaluations and their long term negative impact. This was part of a larger series of studies which stressed that the weakening competitive position of French exports was due to structural problems which could not be resolved through competitive devaluations. A 1986 study of the *Observatoire français des conjonctures économiques* (OFCE) challenged the effectiveness of competitive devaluations by stressing a structural disequilibrium with West Germany and by challenging the idea that the French competitive position was damaged principally by the inflation differential (*Le Monde*, 27 March 1986). Two INSEE studies (1985 and 1987) further supported this claim.[118]

The ideological shift was reinforced by the modernisation and liberalisation of the French financial markets, including the creation of the MATIF, as part of the drive to reform the 'overdraft' economy (Mamou, 1988; Loriaux, 1991). While the objective of opening access to foreign capital to finance French debt was to lower interest rates, the increased reliance on foreign capital made both attractive rates and a strong currency more necessary than previously. The French sought to address the growing imbalance in international payments by the second method discussed in Chapter 1. This involved altering the course of the domestic economy to address the imbalance indirectly: to decrease domestic consumption and keep inflation down, to decrease imports and increase the competitiveness of exports. French business and industrial groups increasingly accepted this economic logic.[119] The period also saw the first of several official and independent academic reports proclaiming the success of the EMS in achieving monetary stability and encouraging convergence.[120]

Some opponents of the policy of competitive disinflation produced their own studies, although these tended to be less well researched and less convincing.[121] Some studies – while generally favourable to the policy of competitive disinflation – argued in favour of a more relaxed monetary policy and further large devaluations, both to eliminate the accumulated inflation differential but also – still in the logic of competitive devaluations – to improve the competitiveness of French industry.[122] Moreover, although mainstream French economic opinion generally opposed floating, there remained several liberal and left-wing academics and journalists who continued to support the free float of the franc.[123]

The Single European Market programme – made possible by the SEA of 1986 – reduced the government's room to manoeuvre even further and thus reinforced the policy of competitive disinflation. An agreement in principle on the liberalisation of capital flows in Europe was made in the compromise deal leading to the SEA. Both Bérégovoy and Balladur accepted, and indeed argued, that it was impossible to establish the single market without also liberalising capital controls. They also recognized that greater economic policy convergence was both necessary to make the single market work and the necessary implication of liberalised capital flows (Bauchard, 1994; Balladur, *Financial Times*, 17 June 1987).

The Single Market programme also increased the logic behind the expanded use of the ECU in order to minimise currency transaction costs and cross-border investment disincentives. Even prior to the adoption of the SEA, French governments presented these kinds of economic arguments as part of their promotion of the ECU.[124] They were joined by a few French banks and companies.[125] However, that these arguments did not form the most important logic behind French government support for the European currency is clearly demonstrated by the absence of government studies on the economic impact of the expanded use of the ECU. Given the extent to which these economic arguments figured in the public – although far from convincing – justification for EMU presented by Socialist governments from 1988, this issue is further explored in the Chapter 5.

The 1983–88 period also marked progress in the consolidation of cross-party political support for competitive disinflation. The Mauroy and Fabius governments attached themselves to a strong franc and an anti-inflationary policy, in spite of the continued opposition from the CERES-dominated Left in the Socialist Party. Mauroy, Delors, Fabius and Bérégovoy were all determined to demonstrate the capacity of the Socialists to be good economic managers. Socialist governments refused to devalue the franc after March 1983. While many Socialists were reluctant to support the kinds of structural reforms that reinforced the policy of competitive disinflation, Bérégovoy was determined to avoid the devaluation of the franc – however debilitating in terms of real interest rates and despite the growing accumulated inflation differential with West Germany.[126]

There was considerably more criticism of the EMS constraint and support for devaluation within the RPR while in opposition. However, in government, the RPR–UDF coalition only devalued once, shortly after the March 1986 election. Balladur was – like Bérégovoy – opposed in principle to devaluation and fully supported the policy of 'competitive disinflation'. He accepted devaluation principally to satisfy pressure from within the RPR – including the Prime Minister – for more reflationary economic policies and to give the new government more room to manoeuvre in its liberalisation of the economy (Bauchard, 1994). The 5 November 1986 decision to raise French interest rates to defend the franc against the renewed speculative attack was very important, as it demonstrated for the first time that the RPR–UDF government was determined to pursue a strong franc policy even though this made the failure of the government's credit policy certain. This decision was, for the RPR–UDF government , the equivalent of the Socialist government's March 1983 decision, although it appears to have been considerably less controversial and less debated within the new government.

The entrenched commitment to competitive disinflation did not signify the complete abandonment of French policy to the German standard, which was generally seen as requiring far more austerity than was either desired or necessary. This explains the Fabius government's active pursuit of a more balanced convergence of European economic policies. However, the Socialists were not yet in a position to make particularly strong demands on the Germans, as they were still attempting to demonstrate their effective commitment to anti-inflationary measures. The general attitude was that if the franc had to be kept in the ERM for power and economic reasons, then the EMS should be reformed to serve French economic needs better. Therefore, there was a contradiction between the insistence of French governments upon the need to reduce inflation and their demands for a more balanced economic convergence which would in effect weaken the anti-inflationary constraint of the EMS.

The political commitment to deflationary policies, given the rapid increase of unemployment after 1982, remained fragile despite the best efforts of Treasury officials. Still, the political leadership increasingly accepted that unilateral reflation would create more economic problems than it solved. The objective was, therefore, to encourage a joint European reflation principally via the lowering of German interest rates. French political leadership could in fact accept higher levels of inflation – despite all the official claims to the contrary – but only if the increase in French inflation was matched by a corresponding increase in German inflation. The demands of French governments to create a more balanced convergence suggest that their principal worry was not inflation *per se* but rather the inflation differential and trade imbalance with France's major trading partners. The label 'competitive disinflation' is thus quite revealing because disinflation was required principally to the extent that it improved the French competitive position *vis-à-vis* the Federal Republic. The distinction is important because it demonstrates the shallowness of anti-inflationary sentiment in French political circles, beyond a small hard core including Barre, Giscard and Bérégovoy. Moreover, it introduces a different angle on the economic logic behind French support for the EMS constraint. The purpose of this constraint for many leading French politicians was not to reduce the level of

French inflation as an objective in itself, but rather to reduce the level of inflation in order to improve the French competitive position. Treasury officials and ministers of finance accepted – more or less – the need to lower inflation as an economic goal in itself. However, for a political class historically obsessed with the trade balance – and notably in relation to West Germany – the competitive element of the policy had much greater resonance.

Relaunching European integration

Attitudes on European integration infused French monetary policy in three ways. First, the general acceptance on both the mainstream Left and Right of the *acquis communautaire*, including the basic structure of the EMS, limited French governments to proposals to reform the System rather than overhaul it entirely. Second, the tone of President Mitterrand and the Socialist government on further European economic and political integration became much more positive after the March 1983 decision, which increased the possibility of developments in other areas. Third, although the RPR leadership was hostile to further European integration while in opposition and did not propose or accept any further political integration once in government, it dropped its demands to renegotiate the SEA. Sentiment in the party against supranational developments likely explains the paucity of the Chirac government's demands on the expanded use of the ECU and the reinforcement of the EMCF.

Following the March 1983 devaluation, the official Socialist government line became considerably more positive on revitalising the Community and more pragmatic on the issues hindering progress at the European level.[127] At the June 1984 European Council at Fontainebleau, Mitterrand accepted a compromise on the British budget rebate problem as a means of encouraging the British to be more flexible on other issues, most importantly the increase of the Community's own resources. This was not inspired by any idealism – Mitterrand's increased efforts to revitalise the Community were directly concerned with the pursuit of French interests on budget and CAP reform and other new policies, and he was quick to block German proposals to accelerate the negotiating process on Iberian accession in order to ensure an agreement to protect Midi farmers from cheaper Iberian food products. Mitterrand's interest in the Single Market Programme – actively encouraged by major French business groups – stemmed principally from his concern for the strengthening and the modernisation of French industry. On political integration, Mitterrand accepted the introduction of qualified majority voting to facilitate the adoption of Single Market legislation. He was also willing to meet part way German demands to increase the powers of the European Parliament.

The reluctance on both the mainstream Left and Right to the loss of *de jure* autonomy in policymaking in most areas did not prevent the active support of Socialist governments for the creation of an EMI, or the vaguer and more cautious public statements of the RPR–UDF leadership on the eventual creation of a European monetary institution. However, this was normally presented as a supranational institution which did not supplant national powers, designed to promote and manage the ECU as a parallel currency. Few politicians of the period would countenance the creation of a single currency except as part of a very long term strategy. Likewise, the French decision to accept the inclusion of the EMU goal within the SEA – providing it with a treaty basis for the first time – could only be seen as an indication of Socialist government acceptance of the goal as a long term prospect.[128]

The promotion of the ECU, unlike monetary union, could be – and was – easily presented in nationalistic terms. RPR neo-Gaullists, left-wing Socialists, Communists and the National Front, were most likely to oppose the supranational implications of a parallel currency and the inevitable decreased importance of the franc. However, the promotion of the ECU also appealed to their traditional ambivalence towards what they saw as irresponsible American hegemony in the management of world economic affairs and the menace of growing German economic power.[129] Moreover, in France, the ECU was always referred to as the 'écu', a mediaeval French currency which helped to make it more palatable to nationalist opinion.

The approach of the Socialist and RPR–UDF governments differed more on the promotion of the ECU and the reinforcement of the EMCF than the other areas of EMS reform. The paucity of Chirac government statements on the ECU and the EMI until January 1988 – and then their speculative and gradualist nature – was likely due in large part to nationalist sentiment within the RPR. The attitudes of the RPR leadership regarding a European monetary institution had been traditionally mixed (Balleix-Banerjee, 1993). During the 1978 parliamentary debate on the ratification of the EMS, several leading RPR politicians, including Michel Debré, with the support of a majority of the RPR deputies in the National Assembly, opposed the abandonment of one-fifth of French gold and foreign currency reserves to the EMCF in exchange for ECUs, and any future transfer of decision making powers to the fund. In 1986, in spite of the asymmetric operation of the EMS and the strategic logic behind strengthening the ECU, there remained a large minority within the RPR firmly opposed to the creation of a more powerful European monetary institution.

The decision to speculate positively on the ECU and a 'common central [European] institution' marked an apparent shift in government policy. The precise reasons for this shift and its timing are difficult to determine. Balladur, himself, was at odds with the nationalist majority in the RPR. As finance minister he made repeated comments on the misunderstanding of those who rallied to support national 'sovereignty' regarding the nature of the integrated international economy and the restrictions that this placed on national policymaking (see, for example, *Le Monde*, 18 May 1987). He was less ideologically opposed to limited further European integration. However, this does not mean that he was necessarily in favour of EMU. Rather his comments on the ECU and the EMI came in the context of strongly worded criticism of continued EMS asymmetry. In effect, Balladur was attempting to bully the Germans to the negotiating table to pursue more fundamental EMS reform. As in the EMU negotiations of the early 1970s, plans for the long term could be made to help bring the Germans to the negotiating table, although immediate reforms were the French priority. Domestic political considerations also likely encouraged Balladur's pragmatism.

Containing opposition to *rigueur*

During this period, party opposition to the EMS and limited further European integration was generally outmanoeuvred by both the Socialist and RPR leadership. Nonetheless, widespread lingering opposition within parties and governments forced political leadership to avoid excessively positive pro-European rhetoric. Many on both the Left and the Right could not understand why such emphasis was placed on maintaining the parity of the franc, while low economic growth and the worsening problem of unemployment suggested the need for lower interest rates.

Opposition in the Socialist Party to the austerity package and EMS constraint was particularly strong immediately after the March 1983 devaluation.[130] The last major attempt by the CERES faction to reverse Party policy took place at the Bourg-en-Bresse Party conference later that year.[131] However, buoyed by the improved international economic environment, Mitterrand succeeded in gathering the support of a clear majority of the Party in favour of the new economic line. From 1983–86, the mood in the Party also became more favourable to limited further European integration. Communist withdrawal from the government, which seemed inevitable by the start of 1984, also freed Socialist ministers to make more pro-European proposals and act upon them (Haywood, 1989, p. 250).

The majority of deputies of the dominant party within the new conservative government coalition, the RPR, had consistently opposed the anti-inflationary policies embraced by the Barre, Mauroy and Fabius governments. However, populist conservative opposition to these policies rarely translated into support for removing the franc from the ERM, as it had on the Socialist Left. Nevertheless, prior to 1986, many on the Right argued in favour of a large devaluation of the franc within the ERM, demonstrating their refusal to accept the logic of competitive disinflation and the problematic nature of competitive devaluations. The decision to devalue the franc shortly after the March 1986 RPR–UDF National Assembly election victory – despite the lack of speculative pressure – demonstrated the new government's reluctance to accept the high interest rates required to defend the parity of the franc. Similar to the Socialists in 1981, the new conservative government faced considerable pressure, particularly from RPR deputies, to reflate the economy and increase policymaking flexibility. The demands within the RPR for a more expansionist economic policy partly explain the increasingly vitriolic rhetoric from Chirac and Balladur on the need to create a more symmetric system.[132]

Electoral considerations help to explain Balladur's call for 'the rapid pursuit of the monetary construction of Europe' during the first two months of 1988 and his positive yet vague response to the 26 February Genscher memorandum on the creation of a system of European central banks and the strengthening of the ECU. Chirac also spoke along these lines, albeit even more vaguely (Balleix-Banerjee, 1993, 1997, 1999). Some observers have suggested that Chirac and Balladur aimed their message strategically at pro-Community centrists in order to attract support from Barre to the Chirac candidacy in the presidential elections (Balleix-Banerjee, *ibid.*; Goldey, interview, 1998). Indeed, both Barre and Mitterrand called explicitly for the creation of an ECB in their election campaign documents, although their projects were as ambiguous as that of Chirac. This positive rhetoric was part of the more generalised effort of the mainstream presidential candidates and other politicians to tap into the widespread, although rather vague, public support for 'Europe' during the period (Benoit, 1997, p. 7). However, it has been claimed that neither Chirac nor Balladur used the term 'European Central Bank' because of their sensitivity to neo-Gaullist opinion (Balleix-Banerjee, *op. cit.*).

Conclusion

The major European monetary policy initiatives of French governments during the 1983 to 1988 period corresponded largely to those made during previous periods. They were rooted principally in European power motives. International motives remained important but they were clearly secondary. The French had five major European monetary policy objectives: to reform the EMS in order to increase the obligation of strong currency countries to support weak currencies in the system, via intramarginal interventions, against speculation; to increase economic and monetary policy convergence around standards agreed upon by all EMS member states, as opposed to the German standard; to improve European policy co-ordination as a means to shield European currencies from the impact of American monetary policy; to expand the use of the European Currency Unit (ECU) in order to decrease the dominance of the mark in Europe, with the long term objective of challenging the international position of the dollar; and to develop a single European monetary stance *vis-à-vis* third countries, particularly on the issue of IMS reform. None of these objectives was met satisfactorily.

First, the Basle–Nyborg accords of September 1987 introduced the principle of intramarginal interventions, although the Germans insisted upon its conservative interpretation. More substantially, the accords also increased the size of funds available for the defence of weaker currencies and the flexibility on the repayment of these funds. Second, with regard to convergence, the negligible progress achieved was due largely to the failure of joint French and American efforts to convince the Germans to reflate their economy. The Germans only very briefly lowered their interest rates and no more than slightly decreased income taxes on just one occasion. Third, French and American pressure on the Germans to co-ordinate interest rates had some success late in the period, when the French and German central banks agreed in November 1987 to a co-ordinated change of interest rates to stem speculative pressure on the franc. Fourth, the use of the ECU increased throughout the period. This was principally due to its active promotion by the French and Italian treasuries and central banks and the Commission, as well as the clear financial interest of French and Italian individuals to avoid capital controls on the franc and the lira. However, French governments failed to convince the Germans to increase their public use of the ECU and remove legal obstacles to its private use.

Fifth, French governments successfully convinced their European partners, including the Germans, of the need to adopt a common position regarding the dollar. However, with the exception of demands for the Americans to decrease their budget and trade deficits, there was little agreement as to what this position should be. The relaxation of the Reagan administration's commitment to free floating was more crucial to progress on IMS reform than any joint European demands. Indeed, secret target zones for the dollar were agreed upon in February 1987 in spite of German opposition to such zones. The lack of sufficient American commitment also effectively destroyed all attempts at regulating the dollar. Nonetheless, the efforts of the French government were principally responsible for the building of international support for increased monetary and economic policy co-ordination at the international level and the restructuring of the IMS.

The attitudes of the leadership of the three main parties on suitable economic policies and on European integration remained important. This was because – while reticence on the economic desirability of the EMS constraint and European integration was widespread – hostility was never sufficiently great to menace the end of French participation and to lead to a reappraisal of European power motives. An increasingly entrenched consensus on desirable economic policy reinforced French commitment to the EMS. This involved the policy of 'competitive disinflation', and the corresponding maintenance of a strong franc and convergence to the German economic standard. Likewise, French support for the Single Market programme and increased acceptance of the liberalisation of capital flows within Europe reinforced the commitment to low inflation and economic convergence. However, economic attitudes did not shape the details of French policy demands. Relatively favourable (or insufficiently negative) attitudes on European integration encouraged (or permitted) support for EMS membership, the expanded use of the ECU at the expense of the franc and cautious speculation on the creation of a full-fledged 'common' currency run by a European Central Bank.

The basic power motives and policy objectives of the Socialist (Mauroy and Fabius) and the Conservative (Chirac) governments were largely the same. The most important difference was the intensity with which they were pursued, largely due to differences of conviction as to the necessity of reform. Domestic political developments shaped government rhetoric on European monetary co-operation, encouraged certain policy positions which otherwise might not have been adopted and affected the timing of particular decisions. However, they did not determine overall French policy.

The five major European monetary reform demands were made by Jacques Delors as Minister of Finance, prior to March 1983. However, given the inadequate commitment of the Socialist government to adopt appropriate economic policies, these demands lacked both the intensity of later efforts and met with complete German intransigence. As Commission President he directly intervened in the preparation of Commission proposals on EMS reform to support French objectives. Bérégovoy could pursue reform more confidently given his success in lowering French inflation. However, some advisers have suggested that Bérégovoy was less insistent on EMS reform than the Chirac government was subsequently, because he was confident that if French inflation could be brought down to German levels and if the franc–mark parity could be firmly defended, this would end speculation against the franc.[133] Balladur adopted both a more determined position on EMS reform. In addition to the intensely nationalist sentiment in the RPR, this was also due partly to the continued speculative attacks against the franc in spite of the French success at lowering inflation to German levels. The basic objectives of these three finance ministers were nonetheless the same, which reflects the increasingly entrenched consensus on economic policy.

On 26 February 1988, the German Foreign Minister Genscher presented his memorandum. Chirac and Balladur responded favourably but only vaguely. A more detailed French response would have to wait until after the May presidential elections. Genscher was principally motivated by his own 'Euro-federalist' objectives, a full exploration of which goes beyond the scope of this analysis (Genscher, 1998). He used the opportunity both to address French concerns regarding the asymmetrical operation of the EMS and circumvent Bundesbank and Ministry of Finance opposition to EMS reform and further monetary integration. Genscher's initiative was thus an attempt to defuse a deepening crisis in the Community over the EMS. As such, it gained the full support of the previously sceptical German Chancellor. Given the importance of this increased German flexibility to subsequent developments, it can be claimed that persistent French demands were largely responsible for the start of talks on the EMU project.[134]

5
Negotiating the EMU Project, May 1988 to December 1991: the Victory of European Power Motives over National Policymaking Tradition

Introduction

The decision to embrace the EMU project was the logical expression of European power motives, given the German refusal to accept French demands on EMS reform and the expanded use of the ECU. However, French support for the project was neither inevitable nor acceptable to many key policymakers. During all periods of policymaking on European monetary co-operation there was a clear division within the government, normally based on the economic policy implications of European monetary co-operation. During this period leading to the Maastricht European Council of December 1991, the division both intensified and extended into the administration. The reluctance can be explained by both the stakes – the loss of national monetary policymaking power – and the conditions imposed by the Germans.[135]

French policymaking during this period reflected both the willingness of Mitterrand and Bank of France Governor Jacques de Larosière to accept German conditions on EMU, but also the strong reluctance of Minister of Finance Bérégovoy and the Treasury. Contradictory and apparently negative policy statements have led numerous analyses of French motives and attitudes astray. During most of the period, both Mitterrand and Bérégovoy publicly opposed national and European central bank independence or argued in favour of its limitation (Bérégovoy for longer than Mitterrand). However, Mitterrand's positioning in public should not be confused with the strategic pursuit of his objectives. Understanding completely German demands and their institutional implications, Mitterrand decided at the start of his second term in office to pursue EMU. He argued against central bank independence and permitted Bérégovoy and Treasury officials to do likewise, in order to push the Germans as much as possible towards a compromise. He was not, however, willing to allow the intransigence of his Minister of Finance and the Treasury to block the project.

Monetary developments

There were five important monetary developments during this period from mid-1988 to the end of 1991. First, the asymmetrical operation of the EMS did not alter and thus there was no reason for the French to modify their demands for the system's reform. The mark remained the anchor of the system in spite of French success at lowering inflation below German levels following reunification.

Second, during the entire period, a major economic objective of the Socialist government was to lower interest rates, in order to narrow the rate differential with Germany. Meeting campaign promises, Bérégovoy managed to lower rates by 1 per cent between May and July 1988, significantly narrowing the differential with German rates. However, the growing strength of the dollar and the rise of German rates forced Bérégovoy to raise French rates by mid July. In spite of the negligible Franco-German inflation differential, the mark rose substantially against the franc – from 3.36 in June 1988 to 3.41 by mid October – largely due to concerns about the growing French trade deficit. However, for most of the period the tendency was towards lowering the interest rate differential between the two countries, with brief periods of increases in French rates during large scale capital movements to and from the dollar. A combination of good French economic indicators, lower French inflation and a rise of German inflation following reunification to above French levels, enabled the French to diminish the Franco-German interest rate differential to a post-1979 low and to lower short term rates to German levels by mid-1991. In October 1991, they lowered rates to a quarter of a point below German rates, but after this sparked off much speculation, Bérégovoy was forced to raise rates by half a point.[136]

Third, the Socialist government insisted that the EMS be seen as a system of fixed rates, and thus refused German demands to revalue the mark. The French objective was to reinforce the stability of the ERM and bolster confidence in the franc. They also argued that the revaluation of the mark in relation to the franc was not justified on economic grounds, especially in that French inflation rates largely corresponded to those in Germany. Prior to reunification, the Germans argued that revaluation was necessary due to their accumulated trade surplus. Following reunification, they argued that revaluation would help stem inflationary pressures in Germany and discourage speculation against ERM parities.

Fourth, for most of the period from mid-1988 to the end of 1990, instability in the ERM was caused principally by dollar fluctuations and large scale international capital movements. The target zone established for the dollar in the Louvre accords was shown to be an inadequate restraining device upon American monetary authorities. Fifth, starting in late 1990, the Bundesbank began to raise interest rates in order to stem rising inflation, due to the fiscal and monetary decisions of the German government preceding reunification and the subsequent transfer payments. The rise in German rates provoked considerable hostility on the part of the other member states which were forced to follow suit. They sought to lower their rates, given the general decline in economic growth and the opportunity created by the drop in American rates.

A summary of European level negotiations on EMU and related developments

At the Franco-German bilateral summit at Evian on 2 June 1988, President Mitterrand and Chancellor Kohl agreed to proceed with discussions on EMU and to establish the Delors Committee. This agreement relied upon Mitterrand's support for a precise timetable for capital liberalisation. On 13 June, Ecofin ministers adopted the directive calling for the removal of all remaining obstacles to capital movements by 30 June 1990 for eight countries and the end of 1992 for the poorer four member states.[137] This would mark the start of Stage One of the EMU project. The Heads of State and Government meeting at the 27–28 June 1988 European Council in Hanover stated that their objective remained monetary union as conceived in the Werner report. On the basis of a Commission proposal, they agreed to the creation of the Delors Committee, consisting of the heads of European central banks and some outside experts, charged with looking at the progressive evolution towards a System of European Central Banks (ESCB). The Heads of State and Government also agreed in principle to the final stage of complete capital liberalisation in Europe. The conclusions of the Delors Committee (the Delors Report) included: (1) a brief overview of the past record of economic and monetary integration in the Community;

(2) a more detailed analysis of the implications of Stage Three of the EMU project, including institutional arrangements; and (3) proposals for the approach by stages.[138] More specifically, the Report insisted upon convergence criteria, defined monetary union, outlined the ESCB, including the relative roles of the ECB and national central banks, and the role of the ECU in the transition to Stage Three. Committee members failed to reach agreement on several points: the inclusion of a specific budget deficit criterion, the transition by stages – notably, the timetable and the powers of the fledging ECB during Stage Two – and the development of the role of the ECU. At the June 1989 Madrid Council, the Heads of State and Government adopted the Report. The peseta and escudo entered the ECU basket and the ERM with expanded fluctuation margins in September 1989.

Under the French EC Council presidency, the High Level (Guigou) Group for the preparation of the IGC met in September and October of 1989. On 27 October, it submitted a ten page list of questions to which the IGC would have to respond. According to this group, the four issues that needed to be overcome in the context of the IGC were (1) the parallelism between monetary and economic policies: the need to define what is meant by Economic Union; (2) the role to be allocated to the Community budget; (3) economic and social cohesion; and (4) institutions. Consisting of mostly Treasury officials, the Group was more reticent than had been the Delors Committee on the principle of independent central banks and the separation of monetary from other economic policymaking (Balleix-Banerjee, 1997, pp. 192–6).

Bérégovoy stressed the need for binding agreements on economic convergence and monetary co-operation prior to the start of the EMU project. At a mid November 1989 Ecofin meeting in Brussels, the finance ministers agreed to submit their economic policies to the judgement of their peers in closed Council meetings. They also agreed to prohibit all monetary financing of public deficits, which the Monetary Committee was to define precisely. In a step forward for monetary co-ordination, five countries (Germany, France, Italy, Spain and Denmark) announced a project in May 1990 (to be elaborated by a group of experts of the Committee of Governors) to control their money supply collectively (*Agence Europe*, 5 May 1990, 5248). This involved the announcement before the end of 1990 of the objective for the common growth of the money supply based on M3 with the aim to reduce inflation as much as possible (to 2 per cent in 1991 from 5 per cent in 1989). The method of using M3 approximated German methods, whereas the French had used M2. Statements by Roland Dumas, the French Minister of Foreign

Affairs, to 'synchronise' German monetary union and EMU, had been opposed by Chancellor Kohl (*Agence Europe*, 3 January 1990, 5206). However, conscious of the problems created by German unification, Finance Minister Waigel, announced in late September 1991 that he would present to the Ecofin a 'detailed programme of convergence' (*Agence Europe*, 23/24 September 1991, 5573).

At Basle on 11 June 1990, the governors of the Community central banks agreed upon the structures that were to prepare for EMU. The Monetary Committee presented its report on the stages for moving towards EMU to the Council on 23 July 1990 (*Agence Europe*, 25 July 1990, 5302). The report recommended that the second stage should be kept short and called for the ESCB – to be put in place at the start of the second stage – to be given real powers. John Major subsequently toured the Southern European capitals to argue for the necessity of a long transition phase. In October 1990, the British government announced its intention for the pound to enter the ERM. On 12 December 1990, the governors of the twelve European central banks agreed to ask the German government to reduce its budget deficit, noting that it weighed too heavily on monetary policy and created tensions within the EMS (*Agence Europe*, 13 December 1990, 5390).

At the Rome II European Council on 14 and 15 December 1990, the Heads of State and Government agreed upon the basic objectives of the two parallel IGCs on EMU and PU.[139] The Heads of State and Government agreed to establish an EMI by 1 January 1994. The final objective of the IGC, to adopt a programme leading towards EMU, was approved by eleven of the twelve member states (Britain abstaining) and the parallel conferences began on 15 January 1991. On 16 January 1991, the French delegation to the IGC presented a draft treaty on EMU prepared principally by the French Treasury. This incorporated both the objectives approved at the Rome summit and certain elements of the British proposals but maintained the three stages. The Germans presented the elements of a draft treaty at the 26 February 1991 Ecofin meeting in Luxembourg (their 'Luxembourg non-paper'). The governors of the central banks presented their project of a statute of the ECB on 9 April 1991 (*Agence Europe*, 10 April 1991, 5468). On 23 September, the ministers of finance agreed upon minimal institutional developments during Stage Two. On 29 October 1991, the Dutch Council Presidency distributed its draft treaty to the other Heads of State and Government (*Agence Europe*, 30 October 1991, 5599; *Europe Documents*, 1740/1741). This presented statutes of the ESCB, ECB and EMI; the specific criteria for the transition towards the third stage; the principle of noncoercion for moving to the third stage; the development of sanctions on excessive budget deficits; mechanisms of financial assistance; and transition measures for the ECB. The role of the European Parliament remained unclear, the Commission was to lose its exclusive right of initiative in specific domains, while the ECB was to gain the right of initiative on exchange rate policy.

Ending Bundesbank dominance

European power motives, combined with German reluctance to reform the EMS in order to create a more symmetric system and unwillingness to expand the use of the ECU, encouraged French policymakers to embrace the goal of EMU. Also of importance was the growing awareness that the German refusal to reform the EMS would increase the friction within the Franco-German relationship. The geopolitical developments in Eastern Europe during the late 1980s and early 1990s reinforced the importance of power motives. The French reaction to these developments should not, however, be considered as part of an explanation of why the French initially supported the project, although it helps to explain the conversion of certain policymakers in favour of EMU.

Power motives translated into the goal of ending the dominance of the Bundesbank over monetary policymaking by pooling control over monetary policy at the European level. EMU provided a means to redress partially the imbalance in the Franco-German relationship created by German economic power. In this respect, French policy during this period reflected an old concern. As German economic power became all too evident, given the asymmetric operation of the EMS, the French motivation became all the more pressing. This was the most important factor in explaining French interest in EMU and the extent to which the French were willing to compromise on the details of the project in order to satisfy German demands.[140]

The French also sought to share monetary policymaking power with the Germans in order to set interest rates collectively at levels which better suited the needs of the French economy, notably lower rates. Putting this goal into practice required its considerable dilution. In addition to sharing control over monetary policy with the other participating countries, power over this policy was to be held by the governors of independent national central banks and was to be exercised within economic guidelines to be entrenched in the EMU Treaty. These conditions were accepted more by certain officials than by others. The Governor of the Bank of France supported the EMU project from

1988. Bérégovoy and Treasury officials supported the goal of EMU but were considerably more reluctant to accept all the German conditions to be included in the project. In the post-reunification period, with the frustration of French monetary policymakers regarding the German policy mix and rising interest rates, this goal took on new significance. The sharing of monetary power became a means to prevent the Germans from pursuing what were perceived as 'irresponsible' policies.

The French did not come automatically to the conclusion that decreasing German monetary power in the context of EMU was the necessary solution to the asymmetry of the EMS. In the last chapter it was argued that Chirac and Balladur's statements on the ECU and EMI in early 1988 do not indicate that they were seriously contemplating EMU. Moreover, Mitterrand also gave no indication prior to the 1988 presidential elections of any support for opening discussions on EMU. His statements conformed to those made by the Socialists since 1981. In his presidential campaign document *Lettre à tous les Français* of 7 April 1988, Mitterrand called for 'the transformation of the ECU into a true reserve currency capable of competing with other international currencies' which would be managed 'eventually' by an ECB (p. 8, author's translation).

The impact of German reunification

The support of key French policymakers for EMU did not depend upon German reunification.[141] From the German perspective, reunification encouraged support for EMU to allay fears in the rest of Europe of the political and economic power of Germany. French policymakers were also clearly concerned about the end to any disguised balance (political/economic) that existed between the two countries and the potential impact that the end of the Cold War would have on Franco-German relations with the expansion of German economic and political influence in Central and Eastern Europe (Garcin, 1993; Hoffmann, 1992; Sur, 1993; and Anonymous, 1993). Mitterrand's visit with Gorbachev in Kiev in December 1989 was an ill-conceived attempt to slow down the reunification process.

The principal impact of reunification on the EMU project was to reinforce the obsession in France over growing German economic and political power (Frisch, 1993; Vernet, 1992). For many politicians, academics and the larger public this was due to geopolitical developments. For monetary policy officials this was due to frustration with the German policy mix and the consequent rise of interest rates throughout Europe. Larger geopolitical considerations about German dominance were well aired during the 1992 referendum campaign. However, prior to the Maastricht Treaty, monetary power motives were of much greater relevance. The economic effects of reunification and German interest rate policy strongly reinforced French European power motives.

It is more difficult to determine the precise political impact of reunification upon French policy on EMU. Some officials suggest Bérégovoy and other Socialist politicians became less reluctant to accept central bank independence and other undesirable elements demanded by the Germans because of the new political dynamic created by reunification (or rather the perception of this dynamic). It is clear that many French officials continued to seek German concessions on these points right up to the Maastricht summit. However, reunification provided Mitterrand additional reasons to impose the project and suppress opposition. Some analyses have also suggested that the President became more flexible on Political Union than he would otherwise have been. This is also questionable for the following reasons. First, the French already sought or accepted certain policy developments and minor changes to European institutions prior to reunification. Second, reunification likely made the Germans more, not less, open to EMU as a political gesture and PU became less important as a point of compromise. Third, the French never saw PU as a means of containing German power in Europe: EMU was the principal means of doing so.

The ECU

The French recognized that the German government would continue to oppose the expanded use of the ECU in the context of the EMS. The Germans had claimed that their willingness to emit bond issues in the European currency and to modify national legislation to permit the expanded private use of the ECU, depended upon the removal of capital controls in the other member states. Subsequent developments demonstrated that this was not the case. The French and the other reluctant member states agreed in June 1988 to remove remaining capital controls within two years. However, the Germans failed to introduce concomitant measures to increase the use of the ECU in Germany, short of the creation of a single currency in Stage Three of the EMU project. It was also agreed in the Delors Report that there should be no discrimination against, or administrative obstacles to, the private use of the ECU. However, the Germans succeeded in keeping all such provisions out of the final text of the Maastricht Treaty.

Opposed to German EMU proposals and de Larosière's preference for the single currency approach, Bérégovoy and Treasury officials continued to argue in favour of the parallel currency approach. They sought the immediate creation of an ECB to emit and manage the ECU. Their efforts were undermined by de Larosière and the other central bank governors who agreed in the Delors Report that a parallel currency strategy for the expanded use of the ECU was economically problematic. Given the demands of the German government and the Bundesbank, the failure of the French to conform would have blocked all progress in the negotiations. During the course of the IGC negotiations on EMU in January 1991, Mitterrand suppressed internal opposition to the approach advocated by bank governors.

Nonetheless, Bérégovoy and the Treasury did not reject the parallel currency, but rather incorporated the approach into their January 1991 draft treaty. The logic remained to ensure the most rapid expansion of the use of the ECU, diminish the economic importance of the mark and prolong Stage Two of EMU as long as possible. They never used the term 'parallel currency' but rather argued, albeit vaguely, in favour of the promotion of a '*"strong and stable"* currency which would be a factor of acceleration towards the adoption of a single currency' (article 5–6 of the draft treaty, italics added). Moreover, they sought the creation of the ECB from the start of Stage Two (1 January 1994) (article 5–4.1) which would have the power to promote the use of the ECU.

Bérégovoy and the Treasury presented several arguments in favour of this approach. First, they claimed that it was preferable to expand gradually the use of the ECU than to introduce it rapidly in Stage Three of the project, although they failed to present developed economic arguments to defend this claim. Second, they argued that German inflationary concerns were less valid in the context of the EMU project, given the necessity of national governments to adopt economic policies in order to ensure respect of the convergence criteria. The ECU would be an increasingly stable currency because *all* the European currencies would become increasingly stable. Third, the French argued that the adoption of a *de facto* parallel currency approach during the first two stages of the EMU project would encourage the British government – which supported this approach rather than monetary union – to participate. In the face of continued German opposition to the expanded use of the ECU in Stage Two, Mitterrand insisted that the French had no choice but to accept its creation as a hard currency only in Stage Three of the project.

Despite setbacks in negotiations with the Germans, the French continued to issue more loans in ECU. As previously, they sought to accentuate the credibility of the European currency progressively. At the start of September 1988, Bérégovoy asked the Treasury to prepare a study on the possibility for the French State to emit bond issues in ECU. Italy had already done so once and the United Kingdom twice in October and November 1988. The Community's May 1983 bond issue of ECU 4 billion on behalf of France was reimbursed in dollars. The objective, therefore, was to emit a bond issue which would have to be repaid in the European currency. The details of this issue were announced on 11 April 1989. France and several other member states subsequently made additional ECU bond issues.

French policy on the details of the EMU project

French policy changed substantially during 1991 due to the German refusal to accept several key French demands, concessions made during the negotiation process and Mitterrand's decision to assume control of all elements of French policy in the weeks prior to the Maastricht summit in order to arrange a deal on EMU. The French draft treaty of January 1991 was prepared by Bérégovoy and the Treasury and largely represents their vision of desirable progress.[142] However, they had little choice but to conform to the draft to the Conclusions of Heads of Government and State at the December 1990 Rome II European Council. These Conclusions largely upheld the recommendations of the Delors Report – and thus the central bankers' and German bias against the parallel currency approach to EMU and in favour of independent central banks. While necessarily incorporating these points, the draft treaty nonetheless reasserts Bérégovoy and the Treasury's vision of desirable developments. On the matter of central bank independence, therefore, the draft treaty is inherently contradictory: it both recognizes independence and attempts to reassert a political control at the European level over the formation of monetary policy.

The draft treaty advocates substantial institutional developments in Stage Two. The Germans had sought to place conditions on the participation of member states in this transitory stage – notably respect for the convergence criteria. The French argued that the move from Stage One to Stage Two was to be automatic at the start of January 1994 and should exclude none of the member states. The draft treaty also calls for a potentially long period of transition to EMU: article 5–9 requires the Heads of Government and State to meet prior to the end of 1996 to determine by *unanimity* the length of a subsequent transition period prior to the final decision on the move to Stage Three.[143] As noted in the above section on the ECU, Bérégovoy and the Treasury could no longer explicitly advocate a parallel currency approach. However, they sought a lengthy – if not indefinite – Stage Two: thus the emphasis placed upon unanimous voting to decide if and when the member states would move to Stage Three. The draft treaty advocates an ECB with substantial powers to be established at the start of Stage Two. This was to promote the use of the ECU and manage a pool of exchange reserves with which it could intervene *vis-à-vis* third currencies (article 5–5.1 of the draft treaty).

The first major concession that Mitterrand imposed upon Bérégovoy and the Treasury was on the creation of the ECB at the start of Stage Two. The Germans refused to accept an ECB with any significant power prior to the move to Stage Three. At the Ecofin Apeldoorn meeting on 23 September 1991, they agreed to French demands on the automaticity of Stage Two, but they only allowed the creation of an EMI with minimal powers – indeed, few beyond those already granted to the existing Committee of Central Bank Governors. The EMI would only be allowed to submit opinions and recommendations to the Council on certain matters – including the use and development of the ECU – while the pooling of reserves would remain voluntary.[144]

This concession effectively blocked the French parallel currency approach. In the meantime, Bérégovoy remained reluctant to advance beyond Stage Two and continued to insist upon unanimous voting prior to moving to Stage Three. Moreover, the Germans continued to insist upon the rigorous application of the convergence criteria to determine entry into Stage Three. The prospect therefore loomed of the adoption of an EMU project which would either stall at the time of the vote on Stage Three or lead to the creation of an EMU hard core consisting of Germany and its monetary satellites. Moreover, the poorer European member states and Italy sought to block any attempt to create a two-speed monetary Europe and insisted that the member states proceed together or not at all.

On 28 November 1991, Mitterrand presided over the only interministerial committee meeting on the subject of EMU, at which he imposed an alternative French policy on the move to Stage Three which would simultaneously satisfy the Germans and the poorer member states. This necessarily involved meeting German demands on the convergence criteria, but also sought to involve as many member states as possible while preventing the less rigorous member states from blocking the progress of those that wished to proceed to Stage Three. Previously, during the month of October 1991, the Minister for European Affairs, Elisabeth Guigou, and a negotiator from the Ministry of Foreign Affairs, Pierre de Boissieu, proposed a two step voting procedure to move to Stage Three. The first step was similar to the proposal in the French draft treaty: with the Heads of Government and State voting by *qualified majority* prior to the end of 1996 to determine if a majority of the member states met the convergence criteria and to decide upon a future date on which the final decision – also by qualified majority voting – on the move to Stage Three would take place (TEU 109J.3). By replacing unanimity with qualified majority voting, this proposal decreased the likelihood of blocking votes. Like the draft treaty provisions, it created the possibility of a prolonged transition period. However, Guigou and de Boissieu anticipated that this deadline would not be respected. They, therefore proposed a second step, prior to the end of 1998, at which the Heads of Government and State would be required to determine by *qualified majority vote* the member states which met the convergence criteria and could proceed automatically to Stage Three of the EMU project (TEU 109J.4).[145] In addition to ensuring irreversibility, this two stage voting procedure had the merits of meeting German demands but also helping member states to prepare themselves to respect the criteria. Kohl's decision at the Maastricht summit to accept this irreversibility was the major German compromise during the negotiations.

Although French negotiators accepted criteria sufficiently rigorous to quash German opposition, they also sought to ensure Italian and Spanish participation. The southern European countries were worried that they would not be able to fulfil the criteria and that a two-tiered monetary Europe would result. For their part, the French did not want the adoption of unreasonable criteria which the southern European member states would be unable to satisfy. The participation of the Italians and the Spanish was crucial to the French aim of preventing an EMU consisting of only the mark, mark zone currencies and the franc – especially given British non-participation – which would continue the excessive influence of the Bundesbank.

Consequently, Mitterrand made several high profile interventions on the issue of the criteria, including his October 1990 meeting with the Italian Prime Minister at which they agreed on a list of precise criteria considerably more flexible than those demanded by the Germans (*Agence Europe*, 19 October 1991, 5592). Mitterrand and the French negotiators were careful not to allow these efforts to undermine the successful conclusion of their negotiations with the Germans. They were, nonetheless, important in bolstering Belgian demands for the inclusion of escape clauses in the application of the convergence criteria. These clauses, added into the body of the Treaty (article 104c), allowed the possible participation of countries which did not respect the deficit and debt criteria but were judged (by the Council) *either* to be making sufficient progress in the right direction (for both the excessive deficit and the debt) or to be in an 'exceptional and temporary' situation (for the excessive deficit).[146] Likewise, the judgement of a qualified majority in the Council on the progress made by the recalcitrant member states towards respecting the criteria (article 109j, 2, 3 and 4) would ensure that Germany would not be able to veto unilaterally the participation of insufficiently rigorous countries.

The French and other EC partners succeeded in encouraging German flexibility on budgetary policies. The Germans had attempted to apply the conclusions of the 1970 Werner Group on the matter. These included common decisions to be taken on the size of deficits and their financing, but also the main elements of budgets such as revenue and expenditure and the distribution of the latter between investment and consumption. The French and other partners insisted that such a far reaching control was politically unacceptable and economically unnecessary. The Delors Report called only for binding rules on budget deficits and their financing. The Treaty does not impose binding rules on fiscal policy, but it contains fairly strict provisions which aim at responsible fiscal policies: no bail-out (article 104b); no central bank financing of budget deficits (article 104.1); the convergence criteria on deficits and debts (article 104c, 1 and 2); and the possible application of gradually more severe sanctions (article 104c, 11).

While seeking to include as many member states as possible in Stage Three, Guigou and de Boissieu incorporated qualified majority voting rules into their proposal in order to prevent any country – notably the less rigorous – from blocking passage to the single currency. During the Maastricht Summit negotiations, Mitterrand and Dumas agreed to give Britain and Denmark optional opt-outs, in the context of a protocol attached to the Treaty. However, the French insisted that if they chose to exercise their opt-outs, they should not be allowed to block the progress of the other member states and should not be allowed to participate in voting.[147] Mitterrand and Dumas also sought to minimise the number of countries choosing to opt-out of Stage Three. They opposed, therefore, Dutch, Danish and British proposals that the optional opt-out be extended to all the member states. The French were concerned that extended opt-outs would undermine the project and would render it irrelevant were the Germans to exercise the right. Countries could not be forced to participate in Stage Three, especially given the precedent if the Danish and British chose to exercise their opt-outs. However, the French sought to discourage this as much as possible: thus the inclusion of a clause in the Maastricht Treaty which requires member states meeting the criteria yet choosing not to participate in Stage Three to justify their decision.

The compromise on the deadlines was one the most diplomatically controversial elements of the EMU provisions of the Maastricht Treaty, as it entrenched the possibility, indeed likelihood, of a two speed Europe. The French thus accepted the necessity to place diplomatic objectives ahead of European solidarity, although all the member states were entitled to join subsequently. On the optional opt-outs, the French also placed strategic objectives ahead of European solidarity by refusing to extend the right to all the member states. However, by recognizing the Danish right to submit participation in Stage Three to the possible constitutional requirement of a referendum, the member states explicitly accepted a precedent which some of them would subsequently insist also applied to their participation in the final stage. For Germany this meant the necessary approval of the Bundestag, which significantly weakened the automaticity that the French sought to entrench in the EMU treaty.[148]

The German government and the Bundesbank also insisted that all Community currencies be present in the ERM in order to move to Stage Two. This was established as a condition in the Delors Report. The Germans claimed that as the pound sterling was a component value of the ECU but not stabilised within the rules of the ERM, it was a source of potential instability. Consequently, the non-participation of the pound presented an obstacle to the EMU project. The French, therefore, focused considerable diplomatic attention upon the British government to bring the pound into the ERM. French efforts also reflect Bérégovoy's concern that the British be kept on board, as part of his general aim to balance German power in Europe and more specifically counterbalance German monetary influence in the future ECB.[149] This also explains, in part, his support for the parallel currency approach: to encourage continued British participation. French comments on a two-speed monetary Europe were principally designed to encourage British action on the issue.[150] Mitterrand, however, did not share Bérégovoy's opinion on necessary British participation.

International power motives

Continued international monetary instability – the failure of previous agreements to impose stability and conflicts over international mutual surveillance – provided further incentives to establish a zone of stability in Europe. The Louvre accords did not achieve their objective of keeping the dollar from fluctuating excessively, and by mid-1989 it had been pushed out of the established secret limits.[151] This does not explain initial French interest in the EMU project because in mid-1988 the Louvre accords had not yet been infringed. However, French policy-makers lacked confidence in American commitment to the accords and placed little hope in the development of more constraining international agreements in the short to medium term.

Nonetheless, after the departure of the dollar from the target zone, French policymakers continued their efforts to encourage international monetary stabilisation. They recognized that international monetary instability could also impinge upon progress to EMU, particularly in the context of a lengthy Stage Two. At the June 1989 G-7 Summit, Mitterrand proposed a plan for monetary stabilisation and in September of that year, the Americans agreed on the objective to lower the dollar, although the Bush administration refused to accept the establishment of new target zones. By late 1990, the French sought to halt the decline of the dollar and requested the organisation of a special G-7 meeting to discuss the problem. However, they lacked American and German support to establish new zones.

The French motive to establish the ECU as an international reserve currency is presented in the preceding chapters and requires little elaboration here. It remained part of the strategy behind French moves to expand the use of the ECU, although European power motives were predominant.

Attitudes and EMU

Attitudes on economic policy – notably opposition to floating and support for anti-inflationary monetary and economic policies – made it possible for the French to pursue the EMU project. Political attitudes generally discouraged support for EMU. The opposition of Bérégovoy and Treasury officials to the independence of the Bank of France and to the ECB controlling monetary policy without a framework of economic policy established by elected officials, both discouraged their support for the project and hindered progress in the negotiations. The ambivalent attitudes of most leading Socialist politicians on European political integration did not affect support for monetary integration *per se*, but potentially hindered progress towards EMU given German insistence on parallel progress towards PU.

In considering the diverse attitudes and their impact upon French policy on monetary integration, it is important to distinguish between the attitudes of the four principal policymakers (individuals and institutions) involved: Mitterrand, Bérégovoy, the Head of the French Treasury, Jean-Claude Trichet, and his division of the Ministry of Finance, de Larosière and the Bank of France. These differences existed during the periods considered in the previous chapters. However, they became more important in terms of shaping the details of French policy during this period given the extent and the nature of monetary integration.

President Mitterrand's precise attitudes are impossible to determine. Few former advisers and policymakers grant him any significant awareness as to the economic merits and demerits of the EMU project. His support was based principally upon European power motives, although his attitudes on European integration were of some importance. For Pierre Bérégovoy and leading Treasury officials, ideology provided more reason to oppose the project than to support it. As a general goal, Monetary Union conformed to most of the basic economic principles upheld by the Treasury. However, the EMU project clashed with at least one of these principles: notably the indivisibility of economic and monetary policy. Bérégovoy and Treasury officials opposed the project also on political grounds: namely, that it required the removal of all political control over monetary policy. The anti-inflationary focus of de Larosière and Bank of France officials encouraged their support for the project.

The entrenchment of 'sound money' ideas

French academic economic thinking provided few obstacles and considerable support for the move to EMU. However, few academics were proactive on monetary union and none had campaigned on the matter prior to 1988.[152] There were three core economic policy ideas which encouraged support for EMU yet none provided compelling reasons to do so. First, with the re-election of a Socialist government, 'competitive disinflation' became fully entrenched as unquestionable government economic doctrine opposed only in fringe political and academic circles. The pursuit of 'competitive disinflation' made it easier for French officials to accept the inclusion of the convergence criteria in the TEU which would constitutionalise the goal of price stability.[153] However, there was considerable disagreement as to the extent to which EMU was necessary to achieve this goal. It was advocated as a necessary step only by Bank of France officials and a few academics who saw the project as the ultimate guarantee of entrenching anti-inflationary monetary policies in a country, the politicians and public of which were still reticent and prone to excess (de Larosière, interview, 26 August 1996).

Second, by 1988 many French academic economists, Treasury officials and politicians had begun to perceive the EMS as a system of fixed rates and publicly insisted upon this in order to discourage speculation. This was justified by the convergence of French and German inflation rates, although it ignored the higher inflation in certain other member states. This perception, combined with the policy of 'competitive disinflation', led Bérégovoy to refuse to accept German demands following reunification for the realignment of parities within the ERM in order to permit the revaluation of the mark *vis-à-vis* the franc and certain other currencies. The move from a system of fixed rates to EMU is not an intellectually necessary one. However, the move to monetary union was less difficult to accept and could be seen – and, more importantly, presented – as a logical step in the progress of European monetary integration.

Third, the links between a fixed exchange rate system, the single market, the liberalisation of capital flows and EMU, were not publicly presented prior to the political initiatives of 1988. The 'triangle of incompatibility', which would subsequently become a major economic justification for EMU, circulated in limited academic circles during the period. However, all policymakers were well aware of the potential instability created by liberalised capital flows and the dramatic growth of speculative capital. There were firm suspicions that fixed exchange rates could not be maintained *regardless* of the degree of economic and monetary policy convergence (Wyplosz and Begg, 1992). Despite the unprecedented stability in the ERM during this period, even after the removal of exchange controls in 1990, French officials continued to argue for the immediate reform of the EMS. They sought increased strong currency country obligations and the reinforcement of the EMCF to ensure the stability of EMS intermarginal parities in the context of liberalised capital flows (*Le Monde*, 17 December 1988). Barring the establishment of a truly symmetric EMS, EMU was the only way to guarantee the maintenance of fixed rates.

French monetary policymakers and politicians have, with near uniformity, argued *publicly* that the economic merit of EMU has been the principal factor explaining their support for the project. They have presented the full range of economic arguments that have been elaborated in favour of EMU. These included the end of speculation costs for weak currency countries, and the removal of transaction costs and of the

exchange rate uncertainty which discouraged both cross-border investment and trade. Moreover, French support for the single currency was
bolstered partially by the belief that a single European interest rate
would drop to American levels because an international reserve currency is inherently more stable than smaller national currencies. This
belief provided a counterweight to the imposition of the convergence
criteria and the priority of price stability. However, the extent to which
French authorities actually believed that EMU would permit lower interest rates is unclear. In the post-reunification period, when the French
were forced to follow the Germans in raising rates despite the lowering
of American rates and the economic slow-down in France, power
motives reinforced the attraction of a potentially lower European interest rate. Moreover, in the context of EMU, the Germans would be prevented from pursuing what were seen as inappropriate economic
policies which imposed rate increases on their European partners.[154]

Academic economists, principally Anglo-American, demonstrated
during the period that the economic arguments in favour of EMU were
poorly conceived or exaggerated.[155] However, it is wrong to claim, as
some analyses have done, that these economic reasons are of no value in
explaining support for the project (see, for example, Connolly (1995)).
Many French monetary policymakers firmly embraced these arguments
irrespective of their validity and, in many minds, they helped to justify a
very political project. EMU was imposed from the top down: there was
no *sui generis* economically-based support for the project emanating
from the Bank of France and the Treasury. Prior to Genscher's ESCB
initiative, neither the Bank of France nor the Treasury had recommended the project and neither had produced studies on EMU since
the mid-1970s. Economic reasons were formulated to justify a project
conceived due to the interplay of other motives.[156]

While the economic gains from EMU were likely exaggerated, the
economic losses for France were perceived to be minimal. It is unlikely
that a monetary union would have been supported by French officials if
there were strong economic arguments against it. Again, most French
monetary officials were convinced that the manipulation of exchange
rates was an unnecessary economic mechanism. Its suppression at the
national level was, therefore, not seen to be economically problematic.
The principal potential economic loss was the restraint placed on
demand in order to respect German insistence upon economic convergence. However, the French had already succeeded in lowering inflation
to near German levels and the other indicators of French economic
performance (on the deficit and the debt) corresponded to the kinds of

criteria the Germans sought to impose. Therefore, little additional French effort would be necessary to meet German demands. The impact of the convergence criteria on the other, principally southern European member states would be considerable, and the suppression of demand in these countries would impact upon French exports. The other costs of EMU were poorly understood and, in any event, caused little concern among French policymakers during the period. The concerns expressed by Anglo-American economists that the EC is not an optimal currency zone sparked surprisingly little public or even academic debate in France and had negligible impact on French support for the project.

Defending the 'republican ideal'

The EMU project put into question two central elements of the French State: its independence and the republican tradition. The first involved the loss of an important symbol of statehood: the replacement of the franc by the ECU. The second involved severing the link between democratically elected officials and an important element of economic policy by rendering the Bank of France independent and transferring power over monetary policy to an independent ECB. The loss of the franc was not an important factor discouraging support for EMU among most important policymakers. The issue was manipulated somewhat by the RPR in opposition: Chirac and Balladur claimed to support the parallel currency approach because the French population was not yet prepared to see the franc disappear. However, the public debate, in which the loss of the franc would excite greater opposition, was minimal until the referendum campaign on the Maastricht Treaty in 1992.

Most of the French political class and administrative officials were opposed to national central bank and ECB independence.[157] This opposition was rooted in three beliefs: that all policy should be ultimately controlled by the republican State; that monetary policy should not be managed separately from other areas of economic policy; and that the maintenance of low inflationary policies did not rely upon independent central banks. First, independence ran against the postwar French tradition that the levers of economic, indeed all, policy should be ultimately controlled by the republican State and democratically elected officials, not bureaucrats or bankers. Chirac, who had briefly supported independence in 1985, appealed to republicanism to justify his change of policy upon returning to government in 1986 (Bouvier, 1988; Fabra, *Le Monde*, 27 October 1987). In a September 1992 article, Treasury Director, Christian Noyer, stated publicly that independence was incompatible with the French tradition of the 'one and indivisible' republic.

The Bank of France had never been entirely 'independent' from the State. Its margin of autonomy had never been clarified precisely by its statutes but rather depended largely upon the political and economic situation of the day and the personalities of both the governor and the minister of finance (Bouvier, 1988; Prate, 1987). Certain factors always limited the autonomy of the Bank: notably, the tendency to appoint as governor financial inspectors with close ties to the Treasury, as well as the dependence of the Bank upon the Ministry of Finance for statistical information and expertise. Bank of France 'independence' was generally associated with its public display of autonomy during the interwar years when it repeatedly challenged government economic and monetary policy decisions. This expression of autonomy was in turn negatively associated with the Laval Deflation of the mid-1930s and the political difficulties that followed. On the Left, the Bank's activities during the interwar period were associated with the pre-war '*mur d'argent*', the oligopoly of private capital which was widely blamed for the mismanagement of the economy, its relative backwardness and the military defeat of 1940. The Bank's nationalisation by de Gaulle in 1945 was designed to direct investment capital more effectively to ensure the country's economic development in the postwar period. The deregulation of the French financial sector, starting in 1984, and the modification of State financial procedures which had involved the Bank of France, had severely limited the investment role of the State. Nonetheless, the move to complete central bank independence remained difficult to accept.

Opposition to central bank independence was also rooted in the widespread belief in political and administrative circles that monetary policy should not be completely separated from economic policy: the former should be seen as a tool of the latter. These two beliefs were not necessarily linked: the central bank could be given 'independence' but political officials should still retain complete control over the establishment of the economic framework in which monetary policy would be made, including exchange rate policy. There were different degrees of 'independence' (autonomy).

Beneath the different German and French attitudes on central bank independence, there lay two different conceptions of the role of money. According to the German conception, monetary stability was considered to be a categorical imperative of economic and democratic order linked to the maintenance of the rule of law (inflation is a non voted tax). According to this tradition – rooted in the German experience of hyperinflation during the 1920s – citizens have as much right to a stable currency, as they have a right to the security of their person and their property. In consequence, macroeconomic policy should involve as little manipulation as possible of credit, which explains the decision to transfer control over monetary policy to an independent central bank. Most leading French politicians and the Treasury were opposed to the idea that the stability of the currency be considered as an imperative separate from other economic goals.[158] Low inflation was valuable but not as a goal regardless of its impact. Other factors had also to be considered.

Furthermore, Treasury officials did not accept the principle that an independent central bank was necessary to ensure price stability, especially given the widespread political commitment to this goal in the late 1980s. Having struggled to build and then maintain government support for 'sound money' economic policies over the previous two decades, Treasury officials were opposed to the principle that they should surrender their control in order to ensure the continuation of these policies. On the economic justification for central bank independence, there was a split in the opinion of French academic economists, with a bias against independence. Anglo-American thinking on the subject, driven by developments in economic theory, increasingly stressed the correlation between independence and success in controlling inflation and the corollary of the harmful influence which elected policymakers could exercise on monetary, and more generally economic, policy (Goodman, 1991, 1992). Such arguments found sympathy with certain French economists, most Bank of France officials and several politicians.[159] However, many leading French monetary economists found German demands for an independent central bank misplaced or unacceptable. Michel Aglietta, for example, stresses the reform of a country's financial structure – which took place in France during the 1980s – as a sufficient guarantee against inflation.[160]

Genscher's proposal on the creation of a European System of Central Banks (ESCB) stated clearly that central banks would have to be made independent. In May 1988, Kohl and Delors decided together that the German Council presidency would propose to convene central bankers in the Delors Committee for the initial examination of the project. This would help to diminish Bundesbank reluctance, side-step the inevitable opposition of certain member state governments and treasuries to central bank independence and accustom these governments to this independence via the decisions reached by their own central bankers, acting in a personal capacity.[161] The deliberations of the Committee imposed a central banker's bias on the project and shaped future discussions. The Delors Report recommended both the independence of all the national and the European central banks and precise measures on the manner in which this development should be ensured. Bérégovoy conceded defeat on the matter, after a much publicised and prolonged outcry, only when the President forced his acquiescence (Fabra, *Le Monde*, 4 July 1989).

   When it became clear that the central bank governors were going to propose independent central banks, Bérégovoy and Treasury officials first introduced the idea of *'gouvernement économique'* – or the establishment of some form of political counterweight at European level to the ECB's control over monetary policy.[162] With little elaboration, the French draft treaty notes: 'Everywhere in the world, central banks in charge of monetary policy are in dialogue with the governments in charge of the rest of economic policy. Ignore the parallelism between economic and monetary matters...and this could lead to failure.' It recommends (article 4–1) that the European Council, on the basis of Ecofin reports, define the broad orientations for EMU and the economic policy of the Community. Within these orientations, Ecofin would co-ordinate the policies of member states and make recommendations to individual governments and the ECB would manage European monetary policy. Bérégovoy and Treasury officials also argued in favour of giving the ministers of economics and finance control over exchange rate policy. Bérégovoy claimed that the draft treaty did not seek to challenge the independence of the ECB and the pursuit of the goal of price stability – which the Germans would have refused to accept. However, it clearly presents a vision of EMU that limits the European bank's margin of manoeuvre as much as possible.

   The French draft treaty had to respect the basic conclusions of the Rome II European Council which granted complete independence to the ESCB. Its article 2–3.2 therefore states that the ESCB will neither solicit nor receive the instructions of the Council, the Commission, the European Parliament or the member states. However, this list omits mention of the European Council. In addition to appearing self-contradictory, the French project thus seemed to be in direct contradiction with the conclusion of the Rome II summit. The draft treaty also very much reflects Treasury attitudes regarding the goal of price stability and French monetary policy tradition. It maintains a double language in favour of both the primacy of monetary stability (article 2–3.1) while giving the European Council and Ecofin the means to challenge this primacy. The Germans opposed the establishment of any political counterweight beyond ensuring that the member states respect the specific convergence criteria they sought to place in the EMU treaty. Several unsuccessful attempts were made to reconcile the French and German approaches to the link between Community institutions and the ECB.[163]

On parliamentary control, Bérégovoy proposed a combined sitting of European and national parliamentary members to confirm the monetary policies pursued by the ECB (*Agence Europe*, 13 April 1991, 5471). However, he did not elaborate in any detail on this control and nothing was included in the draft treaty on the matter. There is reason to doubt Bérégovoy's democratic motives. Rather it is more likely that he sought allies for his efforts to establish a political control over the ECB (*Agence Europe*, 26 October 1989, 5119). On the Commission's participation in the economic affairs of the Union, the French draft treaty proposal went further than any previous French document in advocating 'an active role' of proposal and recommendation. Given French reluctance to increase Commission control in any policymaking areas, this reflected Bérégovoy's attempt to balance the powers of the ECB.

The French succeeded in establishing a certain role for Ecofin, but had to accept German demands that this role be contained within a tight framework which respected price stability. First, Ecofin was granted power over the establishment of agreements for exchange rate systems with non-Community countries (by unanimous vote) and over the setting of parities between the ECU and their currencies (by qualified majority) (article 109.1). Second, the Council was granted the power to formulate general orientations for exchange rate policy in relation to other non-Community currencies with which exchange rate systems have not been established (by qualified majority) (article 109.2). Both these powers involve necessary prior consultation with the ECB 'in an endeavour to reach a consensus consistent with the objective of price stability' (article 109.3). The Council was given no further powers over the ECB, not even to submit motions on monetary policy for discussion by the Governing Council of the ESCB. Article 107 states that 'neither the ECB, nor a national central bank, nor any member of their decision-making bodies shall seek or take instructions from Community institutions or bodies, from any government of a member state or from any other body.' In all, the future ECB was guaranteed a greater independence than that already enjoyed by the German Bundesbank.

The unease regarding the lack of political control over monetary policy was demonstrated on several occasions during the 1992 campaign preceding the French referendum on the Maastricht Treaty, as Socialist politicians sought to avoid the issue or made deliberately misleading statements. On one significant occasion, during a televised debate on the Treaty, President Mitterrand misleadingly claimed that elected officials would establish the economic policy framework for the formation of monetary policy: an interpretation of the Treaty inconsistent with its actual provisions (*Libération*, 4 September 1992).

French policy on the convergence criteria

There is an apparent contradiction between Bérégovoy's demands for setting monetary policy within an economic policy framework established by elected politicians, on the one hand, and his acceptance of Treaty based economic convergence criteria, on the other, given that the imposition of these criteria would severely constrain the economic policymaking powers of national officials. In other words, Bérégovoy appears to have been more concerned with the elements of formal control than the details of permissible economic policy. The logic of this apparent contradiction can be explained principally in terms of the degree of the loss of the government's control over policymaking. In principle, the independence of central banks ended virtually all government control over monetary policy, whereas the convergence criteria only provided limits not to be exceeded by national policymakers.

French acceptance of and support for the criteria was based on four considerations reflecting negotiating necessities as well as economic and ideological concerns. First, and most importantly, the French realized that the incorporation of the criteria into the Treaty was a *sine qua non* of progress, given the German insistence upon a large degree of economic convergence. Second, as France was one of the few European countries which respected the criteria there was no reason to oppose them on economic grounds.[164] Third, the French agreed with the German argument on the dangers of importing inflation from other, notably southern European, member states. Fourth, the criteria conformed to the policy of competitive disinflation.

Although EMU was seen as the best way to lower interest rates in Europe, the French had no intention of permitting lax budgetary policies. The major obstacle to the achievement of EMU in the 1970s was, therefore, no longer a source of conflict between the French and the Germans, because of the considerable change in French economic attitudes. *Indeed, the French were willing to impose more restrictive convergence criteria than those demanded by the Germans.* On the deficit, French negotiators proposed a specific percentage figure, while the Germans had already demonstrated their willingness to accept a more flexible calculation of this criterion.[165] If they subsequently sought a more flexible application of the criteria, this was to reassure the less rigorous member states.[166]

EMU as part of a Euro-federalist goal

President Mitterrand was perhaps the only key French policymaker – apart from Delors in the Commission – who perceived the project as a means to a federal European state, even though a single European currency was a potent symbol of a shared political destiny. On this point, Mitterrand was considerably more ambiguous than French Euro-federalists. Although he publicly stated that he supported the long term objective of a federal Europe, he did not actively support the adoption of policies to make substantial progress towards this objective in the short term.[167] Two principal claims have been made which fully demonstrate the ambiguity of the President's position on further political integration. First, he supported further European integration and, given the widespread opposition in France to political integration, knew that the best way to achieve this was to pursue EMU. Second, he did not want further European integration *per se*, but supported EMU for purely European power reasons, and then accepted limited further political integration given German demands and the geostrategic difficulties posed by reunification. Dyson (1999) suggests that Mitterrand was motivated by larger historical considerations which he felt able to bring to fruition in the context of a second presidential term.

Moreover, few leading members of the Socialist Party expressed support for federalism. The Socialist government's reluctance was demonstrated by its ambivalent position on PU and its refusal to support significant advances in this area, and most clearly by its opposition to the explicit mention of federalist goals in the Maastricht Treaty – although here the French could always rely on the British to block progress. The inclusion of a social protocol in the TEU helped bolster support in the Socialist Party for limited further integration. However, the numerous, albeit vague, public statements of Mitterrand and other Socialist government leaders in favour of PU should be seen as part of the overall French strategy to convince the Germans to support monetary integration. Moreover, Bérégovoy's focus on political integration was principally directed towards the establishment of some form of political counterweight to the ECB – which in no way corresponded to the German vision.[168]

The Germans, both the government and the Bundesbank, argued that EMU required PU, which necessitated some French flexibility on the issue.[169] This did not prevent the French from expressing considerable reticence on political integration. French willingness to support limited further political integration also corresponds to German reunification, which suggests both the increased urgency that the French attached to EMU and a reconsideration of geostrategic motives. Discussions on PU began in late 1989, and Kohl and Mitterrand presented their joint initiative on PU in a 19 April 1990 letter to the Irish Council President. This was followed by the decision of the Dublin European Council on 28 April 1990 to convene an Intergovernmental Conference (IGC) on PU, to proceed in parallel with the IGC on EMU. In the context of the parallel negotiations, the Germans moderated their demands on PU considerably. Some observers have also suggested that the French accepted developments on a common foreign and security policy and military integration as part of a German compromise on EMU. Such claims are, however, problematic, as they ignore French objectives in pursuing some progress in these areas.[170]

Jacques Delors, as President of the European Commission, was officially in favour of the establishment of a federal European state. His direct link to Mitterrand clearly had some impact on shaping the President's attitudes towards European integration, although it is impossible to determine how much. At the very least, this link ensured the President's support for Delors' strategy to advance the EMU negotiations, notably through the assignment of central bank governors to examine the project. However, Delors himself claimed that it was a bad idea to deal with both EMU and PU at the same time, principally because difficult negotiations on the latter would damage progress on the former.[171] His official approach to integration followed the functionalist tradition of economic to political spill-over: that EMU was a necessary development in the move towards PU. However, it is impossible to determine the extent to which his approach was infused first and foremost with the pursuit of French interests and a French bias, rather than a strategic approach to the progression of European integration.[172] In any event, his opposition to the establishment of an IGC on PU is surprising. Did he not recognize, as did Mitterrand, that some progress on political integration was necessary in order to increase German flexibility on the EMU project?

Domestic political motives

The Rocard government had considerable room to manoeuvre in the domestic sphere on the issue of monetary integration. Members of both the Socialist Party and the government who were hostile to the

European Community and limited further integration were largely marginalised. The political opposition was divided and insufficiently focused. Economic interests (business and trade unions) were either passively supportive or indifferent. Moreover, the favourable economic climate of the period ensured less potential public opposition to integration and the economic constraints imposed by the EMU project. In terms of interinstitutional politics, the support of the Bank of France, for both the goal of EMU and project details acceptable to the Germans, was crucial to negotiating success. The central role of Mitterrand in ensuring French support for the project also requires further elaboration.

The political opposition, with the exception of some component parties of the UDF, either opposed EMU or the details of the project. However, the division of the mainstream political opposition (the UDF and the RPR) made the development of a strong movement against EMU difficult (*Agence Europe*, 6 December 1990, 5385).[173] The National Front and the Communists were united as parties in their opposition to the project. Most of the UDF was in favour of EMU, although officially it opposed particular elements of the project principally on technical grounds. The RPR leadership opposed monetary union as a short or medium term goal, on political rather than economic grounds. Chirac and Balladur argued that the French population would not accept the end of the franc, the creation of independent central banks and the degree of political integration required to make EMU work.[174] They advocated the parallel currency approach and EMS reform along the lines of the demands in the January 1988 Balladur memorandum.[175] It is surprising that the position of the RPR group in the National Assembly Finance Committee was more closely aligned to the positions outlined in the French draft treaty which, at least in principle, accepted the final goal of a single currency. The group also recommended the creation of a 'uniform common European currency' at the start of Stage Two and criticised the insufficient democratic control over monetary policy (*Commission des Finances*, 1991, pp. 49–51). Opposition in French political circles to the independence of the Bank of France was widespread although not unanimous. Many members of the UDF were in favour although the party confederation chose officially not to embrace independence (Balleix-Banerjee, 1995).

Claims that the formation of a European monetary union was promoted by interest groups with an economic interest in fixed rates misinterpret reality.[176] It is unlikely that any economic interests actively encouraged Mitterrand and the Socialist government to support the project initially and there was no domestic political pressure on the issue.[177] Policy was led by a political and technocratic élite, not societal actors. Nonetheless, consistently high levels of business support provided a useful justificatory weapon for those in favour of EMU which could be wielded against those who opposed the project. Polls gauging the attitudes of the owners and managers of large French businesses towards EMU since 1988 indicated consistently high levels of support. According to a January 1989 poll, 97 per cent of French employers supported the project (*Quotidien de Paris*, 20 January 1989). In spite of these results, the leading organisation of large French employers (CNPF) did not argue in favour of the project during most of this period. The CNPF produced its opinion on the matter only just prior to the Maastricht Treaty (November 1991). At the European level, UNICE announced officially only in December 1990 that it supported a single currency (*Agence Europe*, 1 December 1990, 5382). French banks and financial houses also tended to support the project but, again, did not do so actively.

In 1986, Giscard and Schmidt established their Committee for European Monetary Union, the membership of which included several leading French bankers (both private and national), politicians and academics. This led to the creation in 1987 of the Association for Monetary Union in Europe, which also included the membership of the directors of several large French industrial companies. The goals of the Committee and Association were to encourage public awareness, mobilise support for EMU and propose ways forward in order to ensure progress (Committee for European Monetary Union, 1988). It is difficult to gauge the nature of their influence, although this was likely limited. In April 1988, the Committee published a fairly detailed blueprint for monetary union and a ECB. As one of two such blueprints in circulation, it was considered by Bérégovoy and Treasury officials and by the members of the Delors Committee. However, many of the Giscard–Schmidt Committee's major proposals – for example, a parallel currency by Stage One and the immediate establishment of a reserve fund to ensure systemic stability until Stage Three – did not adequately take into consideration Bundesbank sensitivities to be regarded as serious a contributor on to the negotiating process.

Public opinion did not prevent progress on the issue. Polls throughout the period demonstrated high levels of support in France for both further European integration and EMU. In part, this was linked to the relatively favourable economic situation of the late 1980s. However, given the issues at stake – notably the loss of an important symbol of statehood – the limited public debate is surprising. This was due principally to the often vague public statements of government officials as to

French policy, the different positions of the different French actors and the complex, normally secret, negotiations, the final outcome of which was far from certain prior to Maastricht. It was only after the Summit, well into the referendum campaign, that the public became more familiar with the contents of the Treaty and popular discontent increased. The change in public attitudes by 1992 also corresponded to the serious downturn in the economy.

Interinstitutional politics: the Bank of France versus the Treasury

In terms of interinstitutional politics, the support of de Larosière for the EMU project was crucial to the success of intergovernmental negotiations. In June 1988, he was the only key policymaker that accepted the German condition on independent central banks. It was de Larosière who convinced President Mitterrand of the necessity of accepting this condition, who then imposed it upon a reluctant Minister of Finance and Treasury.[178] De Larosière's support for the project was based on a combination of the different motivating factors outlined above and an institutional dynamic to extend the control powers of the Bank of France.

Since World War II, but notably since the departure of de Gaulle, the Bank of France had attempted on several occasions to assert its autonomy and even to move towards statutory independence (Bouvier, 1988; Prate, 1987). Three former Bank governors, Wormser, de La Genière and Camdessus all advocated developments in this direction. Following his retirement, de La Genière encouraged the RPR minister Charles Pasqua to introduce his April 1985 bill on independence and helped to convince Chirac to support the measure (Mamou, 1987, chapter 10). Following the 1986 election, Camdessus attempted again. Treasury opposition – on the grounds of 'the technical complexities of the issue' – largely explains the decision by Chirac and Balladur to block further discussion on the matter. The change in dominant French economic thinking on inflation, the strength of the German model and Anglo-American studies on the low inflationary bias of independent central banks, bolstered Bank of France arguments in favour of independence. However, given institutional power considerations, academic arguments repeatedly failed to modify government policy. Only German demands in the context of the EMU negotiations provided the Bank with the necessary political leverage to ensure the President's support.[179]

The Mitterrand factor

Given that Mitterrand alone was able to impose German conditions upon reluctant Socialist politicians and Treasury officials, his role was determinant in the formation of French policy on EMU. Given his efforts to overcome the differences between the member states, he was central to the successful conclusion of a deal at the Maastricht summit. Without delving further into his motives, it is useful to present the specific ways in which Mitterrand demonstrated political leadership in shaping French policy on the EMU project.[180] EMU fell clearly into the 'reserved domain' of the President, both as a subject of Community affairs and as a key agenda issue for Franco-German summits. He was assisted by two close advisers, Roland Dumas, the Minister of Foreign Affairs, and Elisabeth Guigou, the Head of the SGCI, member of the President's staff, and then Junior Minister for European Affairs. The Prime Minister, Michel Rocard, initially hostile to the project and mistrusted by the President, was largely excluded from policymaking on the matter and his public opposition suppressed.

In order to advance the discussions and negotiations on EMU, Mitterrand took several key decisions and initiatives, often in the face of strong domestic and foreign political and technocratic opposition. First, in June 1988, at the Evian Franco-German summit, he accepted freedom of EC capital movements – despite Bérégovoy's reluctance on the issue – in order to avoid any obstacles to the relaunch of EMU negotiations at the Hanover Council. Second, prior to the start of the Delors Committee, he accepted de Larosière's arguments that ECB independence would eventually have to be adopted into the French position as a necessary development to ensure progress in the negotiations. Third, during the French Council presidency, Mitterrand appointed Guigou to chair the High Level Group created to progress the discussions on EMU and accustom national Treasury officials to the Delors Report. Fourth, the President pushed Kohl to establish clarifying dates for the IGC – set at the Strasbourg summit in December 1989. Fifth, Mitterrand convinced Kohl to accept the automatic move of all the member states to Stage Two at the start of 1994. Sixth, Mitterrand actively supported Andreotti's efforts to push for a more flexible interpretation of the convergence criteria in order to ensure that the southern European member states would not block the project. Seventh, at the 28 November 1991 interministerial committee, Mitterrand imposed support upon reluctant ministers for an irreversible move to Stage Three for those member states which fulfilled the convergence criteria. He joined with Andreotti at Maastricht to insist upon this irreversibility. Eighth, he ensured that the final decision on the start of Stage Three would be taken in the European Council, not in Ecofin, in order to ensure continuing political direction.

Finally, Mitterrand imposed French support for independent central banks and rejection of the parallel currency approach. The President first publicly stated his position when agreeing to the conclusions of the Rome II European Council. He insisted upon Bérégovoy's acquiescence at a 26 January 1991 meeting at the Elysée and imposed French support for the minimalist German vision of the elements of Stage Two prior to the 23 September 1991 Apeldoorn meeting of the Ecofin Council (Aeschimann and Riché, 1996, p. 227). Throughout the discussions and negotiations on EMU, Mitterrand advocated the concept of *'gouvernement économique'*. However, on this point – as on most – his precise objectives were ambiguous. The extent to which he was committed to the principle of a political counterweight to the ECB is unclear. The issue also provided a useful bargaining chip in the negotiations with the Germans, only conceding complete central bank independence at the Maastricht Summit.

Conclusion

European power motives encouraged all leading French policymakers to support the EMU project. However, it is important to avoid generalisation. The precise character of these motives differed depending on the institutional perspective of the actors. Mitterrand, Elysée and Ministry of Foreign Affairs officials were more preoccupied – especially in the post- reunification period – with more general geostrategic motives: the European and international implications of German economic power. Concerned above all with the successful conclusion to the negotiations, Mitterrand and de Larosière were willing to accept the German design for EMU in exchange for guarantees of the irreversibility of the transition period. Central bankers were concerned specifically with enhancing French monetary power in relation to the Bundesbank. The Minister of Finance and Treasury officials were concerned with the preservation of their economic power *as well as* the extension of French monetary power and thus were reluctant to accept independent central banks.

Furthermore, the different approaches to the project and the often contradictory French policy positions can only be explained through an examination of the attitudes of these actors on economic policy and on the role of the State, in addition to their institutional power considerations. Mitterrand, Elysée and Ministry of Foreign Affairs prioritised geostrategic considerations to the extent that their attitudes on economic policy and on the role of the State – potentially in conflict with the EMU project – did not lead them to reject the conditions imposed by the Germans. French central bankers sought principally to entrench anti-inflationary policies in France and increase their control over domestic monetary policy in relation to the Treasury. Bérégovoy and Treasury officials sought other routes to EMU which would avoid the separation of monetary and economic policy and avoid central bank independence, thus maintaining their control over policymaking. Although Mitterrand probably shared these concerns, or at least allowed their public expression to win concessions from the Germans, he did not allow them to prevent the successful conclusion to the EMU negotiations. These different approaches – Mitterrand's insistence that EMU proceed combined with public demands that the details of the project be qualified – continued to inform the development of French policy-making during the post-Maastricht period.

6
After Maastricht, December 1991 to January 1999: Keeping the EMU Project on Track and Challenging German Monetary Dominance

Introduction

European power motives ensured the general continuity of French government policy on the ERM and EMU during the seven years following the Maastricht summit to the start of Stage Three of the project on 1 January 1999. This was despite considerable economic and domestic political pressures to abandon, or at least significantly modify, the project and the frequently ambiguous rhetoric of leading politicians. Political developments encouraged speculation on a change in French policy: a close result in the 20 September 1992 French referendum on the Maastricht Treaty, two changes in government – the overwhelming victory of the RPR–UDF in March 1993 and the surprise victory of the Socialist-led 'Plural Left' in June 1997 – and the election of a neo-Gaullist president, Jacques Chirac, in May 1995. The strength of these motives was such that in spite of the economic and political difficulties associated with the project, few formerly pro-EMU politicians switched camp during this period. First and foremost, French governments sought to keep the project on track in order to ensure the end of Bundesbank dominance by 1999 at the latest and, ideally, earlier if possible.[181]

Monetary developments

By the end of 1992, low inflation began to develop into the menace of deflation. French inflation dropped from 3.1 per cent in April 1992 at an annual rate – well below the 4.6 per cent in Germany – to near 2 per cent at the end of 1993, 1.6 per cent in 1994 and below 2 per cent throughout the rest of the period.[182] Real interest rates reached 5 per cent in 1993 and started to drop substantially only at the start of 1996. This recalled the difficult period of the 1930s when France adhered to the Gold Standard. From the end of 1995 with the relaxation of German interest rates and increased confidence in the Juppé government's commitment to lowering the deficit, French rates started dropping. Economic growth remained generally low until 1997 (1991–96 average of 1.5 per cent) when it began to rise moderately. Unemployment remained persistently high and rose to record levels (12.8 per cent by 1997) although it started to fall in 1998. On the positive side, the yield differential in long term interest rates between France and Germany continued to decrease and in August 1993 their rates reached the same level, the lowest in France since 1966. This was a major indication of the confidence of international financial markets in the capacity of French governments to maintain low inflationary policies. Moreover, in 1992, the competitive element of the policy of 'competitive disinflation' finally bore fruit – helped by German government spending to finance reunification – and France enjoyed a trade surplus for the first time since 1978. This surplus continued to grow, reaching record levels from the mid-1990s.

From June 1992 to August 1993, massive periodic speculation against the franc and most of the ERM currencies, triggered by inappropriate exchange rates and the growing lack of confidence in the commitment of European leaders to EMU. Speculation was initially set off by the negative vote in the June 1992 Danish referendum. It was encouraged further by the close French referendum result (only 51.05 per cent in favour) and further still by the various comments against the current ERM parities and the EMU project emanating from members of the Bundesbank Council, French and other leading European politicians.[183] The worsening economic climate across Europe, rising unemployment, budget deficits and debt combined with a stubborn refusal to allow realignment, made increased speculation inevitable.[184] The removal of capital controls in the early 1990s made EMS currencies even more vulnerable. Pound sterling and the lira were forced out of the ERM on 16 September 1992. The punt was devalued within the mechanism at the end of January 1993, despite having previously been its strongest currency, as was the peseta in mid May. The speculative attack against the franc in July 1993 was the largest to date.[185]

The Bundesbank helped the Bank of France to maintain the franc–mark parity. This consisted of two joint declarations on 23 September

1992 and 5 January 1993 and numerous public statements in favour of the parity by Bundesbank Council members and German government officials. In practical terms, this meant the active intervention of the Bundesbank on the exchange markets: creating and selling marks in exchange for francs. The Bundesbank intervened to support other currencies but publicly declared its determination only with regard to the parity of the franc. The largest interventions came in September 1992 and July 1993, but intervention between these two large waves of speculation was repeatedly necessary. In December 1992 alone, the Bundesbank intervened three times to defend the franc. Bundesbank intervention was not unlimited, however, as the speculation attack at the end of July 1993 was to demonstrate. Moreover, Bundesbank intervention in support of the franc did not extend to substantial decreases in German interest rates. Two cuts were made during the speculation crisis at the end of July, but not sufficiently large to discourage speculation and stem the mark's appreciation. The only interest rate cut which likely had an impact on the mark–franc parity was managed on 3 August 1993, after the decision to widen the fluctuation margins.[186]

The Ecofin Brussels compromise of 1–2 August 1993, consisted of an agreement to save the ERM by expanding its margins of fluctuation to ±15 per cent. On 31 July, the EC Monetary Committee failed to agree on a plan to save the ERM, accepting only the principle that the mechanism had to be preserved. The French were determined to resist a large devaluation of the franc. They, therefore, maintained high interest rates and allowed the franc to devalue to just below its previous floor. Several of the other member states pursued similar policies. Periodic speculation continued against the franc, which continued to slide to as low as 3.55 marks by the early autumn, or a fall of more than 5 per cent from its ERM central rate. However, speculation soon subsided and the franc subsequently rose against the mark, surpassing by December its previous ERM floor. There was little speculation from the autumn of 1993 until November 1994, when Chirac announced that as president he would organise another referendum on EMU. To stem the run on the franc, he subsequently insisted that he fully supported the EMU goal and the existing convergence criteria. However, his ambiguous comments continued, feeding speculation against the franc throughout the campaign. His victory led to further attacks. The announcement of the 1996 budget – which the markets perceived as a demonstration of the Juppé government's inadequate commitment to deficit cutting – sparked a great deal of speculation, stemmed only by the substantial increase in French interest rates and Chirac's announcement of his firm support for the necessary cutbacks to maintain the strong franc policy pursued by the Bank of France. This renewed commitment succeeded in preventing speculation against the franc during the worst civil unrest since May 1968 sparked off by the announcement of the Juppé Plan on 15 November 1995. Indeed, by January 1996, the Bank of France had succeeded in lowering rates to levels below those prior to the announcement of the 1996 Budget, without speculation. Even the surprise election victory of the Plural Left – which promised an end to deficit cutting and increased uncertainty about the start of EMU – failed to trigger off significant speculation.

This period also witnessed the steep decline in the ECU bond market followed eventually by its dramatic rise. The results of the Danish and French referendums, doubts about the future of the EMU project, the September speculation crisis and the economic downturn in Europe seriously undermined international financial confidence in the ECU. By October 1992, ECU bonds were barely traded and yielded more than 50 basis points above their theoretical value, based on the yields of component currencies. Although committed to the expanded use of the European currency, the French Treasury refused to issue ECU-denominated bonds if no one was prepared to purchase them. Therefore, while it had announced at the start of 1992 that it would hold an ECU auction once a quarter, the Treasury failed to issue from the third quarter of the year. All European governments postponed indefinitely plans for further auctions of ECU bonds. However, by the start of July 1993, the French Treasury cautiously restarted the regular issue of ECU bonds. Over the next two years several other governments also continued their issues and confidence in the ECU began to rise. However, the private use of the European currency remained limited. A substantial expansion of the ECU market required the strong commitment of European governments to the irreversibility of the EMU project. This was finally provided at the Madrid European Council in December 1995.

European policy developments

Despite the difficulties in the ERM, the member states agreed in October 1993 to move to Stage Two of the EMU project at the start of 1994 (as arranged in the TEU). According to the Maastricht Treaty, this stage was to consist of the adoption of necessary measures to enable the member states to meet the convergence criteria and the creation of the European Monetary Institute (EMI). In December 1991, the Heads of State and Government had only reached a minimal agreement as to the precise institutional implications of the move to Stage Two,[187] given German opposition. In 1993, the Germans still refused to go beyond this minimum, despite French and Belgian efforts (the Maystadt Plan) to strengthen the EMI. The provisions of the Maastricht Treaty ensured the creation of the Institute with a legal personality and to be directed and managed by a Council, consisting of a President and the governors of the member state central banks (article 109f.1). The EMI was assigned the responsibility to strengthen co-operation and co-ordination between the member state central banks with the aim of ensuring price stability, to assume the responsibilities previously assigned to the EMCF (the management of the VSTF), to facilitate the use of the ECU and oversee its development, and to prepare for Stage Three (article 109f.2 and 3). The EMI was granted minimal powers to formulate and submit opinions and recommendations on monetary policy matters (article 109f.4 and 5). At the October 1993 extraordinary European Council in Brussels, the Heads of State and Government agreed to locate the EMI – and thus the future ECB – in Frankfurt in preference to Lyon.

At the December 1995 Madrid European Council, the Heads of State and government agreed to delay the start of Stage Three until 1999 and, at German insistence, to replace the ECU label with the euro. They also adopted the German and central bankers' gradual approach to the removal of national currencies following the start of Stage Three. Euro banknotes and coins would be introduced from 1 January 2002 and member state currencies would gradually be withdrawn by 1 June 2002. At the Dublin European Council of December 1996, the Heads of State and Government agreed to adopt the 'Growth and Stability Pact', also at German insistence. The right of the Council to agree upon and impose specific fines on countries not respecting the criteria following the start of Stage Three was established in the Maastricht Treaty (article 108a.3). The pact established these fines with the possibility of partial or complete derogation for countries suffering from a shrinking GDP. It was signed at the June 1997 Amsterdam European Council as a resolution partnered with another on 'Growth and Employment' and topped with a common preamble which ostensibly gave equal weight to both resolutions. In October 1997, EU ministers of finance reached an agreement on the Euro-X Council, consisting of the ministers of finance from those countries participating in the eurozone, which would assume the powers granted to the Council (Ecofin) in the Maastricht Treaty.

At the May 1998 extraordinary European Council in Brussels, the Heads of State and Government met to decide which member states could participate in Stage Three. Eleven were admitted on the grounds that they met most of the convergence criteria or were moving in the right direction. Of the countries that sought to join, only Greece was not allowed to do so. Britain, Denmark and Sweden chose not to participate. At this meeting, the final conversion rates of European currencies were officially established and the first president of the ECB selected. On 1 June 1998, the ECB and the ESCB were officially established. Stage Three of EMU started on 1 January 1999.

European power motives

The core power motive underlying French policymaking during this period was to keep the EMU project on track in order to ensure the end of Bundesbank dominance by the start of 1999 at the latest. This involved five specific objectives: to approve the Treaty in a national referendum; to ensure that it would be approved in the other member states or that difficulties in these countries would not block the progress of a hardcore including France; to move to EMU on schedule and ideally as quickly as possible; to keep the ERM intact in the face of speculative attacks; and to meet the convergence criteria. European power motives informed two other French policy demands which focused upon lowering the economic cost of moving to EMU: to lower excessively high French interest rates by either forcing the Germans to lower their rates or lowering French rates below those in Germany; and to require the Bundesbank to intervene to support the franc in the ERM. Both demands were linked to French efforts to keep the EMU project on track, by making French participation less economically and politically difficult. However, they went beyond this objective as they sought to increase French power *vis-à-vis* the Germans prior to the start of Stage Three.

During the referendum campaign, general European strategic objectives formed the central focus of the government's argumentation in favour of the EMU project, far more than economic objectives and to the near exclusion of other goals. EMU was most often presented as the best way to bind a reunified Germany to the European Union and prevent the independent expression of its potential political and economic power. Frequently, this motive was presented in the form of crude Germanophobia. By 1992, the containment of German power had become the most compelling public justification for the project, the economic logic of which was being increasingly challenged. The parallel justification of sharing monetary policymaking power with the

Bundesbank was, perhaps surprisingly, a secondary argument during the referendum campaign.

Keeping the EMU project on track

The fulfilment of the five specific objectives to keep the project on track proved extremely arduous, both politically and economically. First, the hotly contested referendum campaign and the 48.95 per cent 'no' vote promised further domestic political difficulties on the issue and spurred on speculation. Meeting the second objective proved awkward. The Danish voted 'no' in their first referendum, which threatened to unravel the entire process. This was resolved by the December 1992 Edinburgh compromise which enabled a second successful referendum to be held in Denmark, in May 1993. The British and the Germans also imposed conditions upon their ratification of the Treaty. The Major government's approval depended upon a 'yes' vote in the second Danish referendum, while in October 1993 the German constitutional court ruled that a Bundestag vote would be necessary prior to the move to Stage Three.

The third objective was to move to Stage Three as quickly as possible. Its delay for at least five, perhaps seven, years created considerable risk, given free capital movements which made the defence of ERM parities inherently difficult. This was one of the few points on which nearly all economists agreed. The Germans had sought a lengthy Stage Two because of their insistence upon economic convergence and an evolutionary approach, and their preference to exclude those countries that did not respect the convergence criteria (in addition to the secret hope of many Germans that the project would collapse). The onslaught of speculative attacks, the costs involved in defending the franc, the risk of the destruction of the ERM, and the increasingly apparent difficulty in meeting the convergence criteria encouraged the French to argue in favour of a more rapid move to Stage Three for a hardcore of the most economically and monetarily stable countries. They obtained the very tentative support of the German government for a rapid move, but were opposed firmly by the Bundesbank which argued that economic conditions in Germany prevented this. Bundesbank President Schlesinger insisted upon a change in the wording of the Maastricht ratification law in Germany to rule out any non-Maastricht monetary union. Shortly after the September 1992 crisis, at the January 1993 celebration of the thirtieth anniversary of the Franco-German Treaty of Friendship, Mitterrand and Kohl issued a joint statement which vaguely promoted the idea of speeding up EMU. However, in February 1993, French and Belgian proposals for an acceleration of the project were rejected by the

Germans. The French argued that a two-speed Europe would not be an abandonment of the spirit of Maastricht because the Treaty explicitly predicted several speeds, as only those countries that respected the criteria and wanted to participate in Stage Three could do so (*Le Monde*, 10 February 1993). The French also noted that no minimum date was fixed by the Maastricht Treaty. Correspondingly, they argued that the expansion of the margins of fluctuation in the Brussels compromise was to be seen as a temporary solution and one which would not prevent a rapid move to Stage Three (*Financial Times*, 4 August 1993). At the same time, the French effectively accepted that the widening of the margins provided another reason why Stage Three would have to wait until 1999. The difficulties faced by nearly all the participating countries in respecting the deficit criteria made inevitable the December 1995 decision to delay the move to Stage Three until 1999.

The fourth objective consisted of keeping the ERM intact, which, for French governments, principally centred on increasing the confidence of the international money markets in their ability to maintain the franc–mark parity. In order to build confidence in an increasingly uncertain economic and political situation, several measures were undertaken or proposed at both the domestic and European levels. The pledge of 'unlimited' Bundesbank intervention helped to discourage speculation against the franc. This is further discussed below. The new Minister of Finance, Edmond Alphandéry, also announced shortly after the March 1993 election his decision to make the Bank of France independent more quickly than previously anticipated.[188] However, an independent Bank of France did not compensate for a faltering political commitment.

Another form of confidence building measure that the French pursued sought to reinforce co-operation and co-ordination at the European level with the aim of 'convergence' towards the most 'virtuous' economies. A 'peer pressure' approach to co-ordination had begun in 1990, with the central bank governors meeting once a year to discuss and evaluate the broad compatibility of their monetary policy targets and orientations, and to examine the opportunities for possible corrective measures. These exercises were carried out on the basis of a thorough analysis of national economic and monetary developments. The French sought to develop this co-ordination further by defining a growth norm for a Community monetary aggregate or an inflation target fixed in absolute terms (and not in relative terms, as established in the Treaty) (Jaillet, 1994). The French also proposed greater co-ordination via the placing of representatives of the Bundesbank and the Bank of France in the decisionmaking bodies within the other institution. The Bundesbank opposed this suggestion principally because there was no body equivalent to its Council in the Bank of France, which would render mutual representation unequal. In February 1993, the European finance ministers agreed to accept the Commission's request to prolong the member states' existing economic 'convergence' programmes to 1996 and to set common standards for measuring these economic performance targets.[189] The following May, the finance ministers agreed to Monetary Committee proposals on common confidential indicators to prevent situations of crisis. The French also pursued improved bilateral co-operation with the Germans. Following the July 1993 speculation attacks, the French sought to strengthen their convergence programme with the Germans: starting in August 1993, these were planned in 'tight concertation' and presented to the press simultaneously. The French also sought to expand and clarify the co-ordination role of the EMI (Jaillet, 1994), while the Germans firmly opposed such ambitions. Beyond the taking of necessary measures to meet the Maastricht convergence criteria, there was no agreement as to the details of what should be accomplished during Stage Two.

The widening of the margins of fluctuation to ±15 per cent combined with the adoption of a more flexible attitude towards exchange rates was, ironically, another way to bring about stability and discourage speculation. This was combined with the French determination not to allow a significant devaluation of the franc and to maintain high interest rates.[190] Initially, the French claimed that they would seek to return as soon as possible to the old margins. At a Franco-German summit meeting at the end of August 1993, Prime Minister Balladur announced a more relaxed French position in favour of continuing with the wider margins. Nonetheless, the franc was held to a level just below the floor of its former fluctuation margins *vis-à-vis* the mark and then re-entered these margins by December.

Other confidence building measures were proposed by the French but not acceptable to either the Germans or other member state governments. One was the further tightening of the franc–mark fluctuation margins. The Belgians had announced a unilateral tightening of the bands between their franc and the mark in June 1990. The French chose not to attempt a unilateral move but rather argued in favour of a series of joint Franco-German measures to maintain new margins. The Germans refused and the Bundesbank insisted that a much stronger intellectual case could be made for wider not narrower bands. Indeed, the speculation crisis of July–August 1993 and the subsequent stability of parities in the wider fluctuation margins ended French demands for tighter margins. The French also advocated a tax on speculative capital movements – although they did little to develop this idea, given German and other European opposition.

The Bérégovoy, Balladur and Juppé governments defended themselves against the claims of domestic opponents that the high interest rates combined with the convergence criteria made the EMU project unrealistic given the current economic climate. The typical argument presented throughout this period was that the high level of German rates was due to the very unique inflationary situation created by the German government's reunification policies. The EMU project was not to be scrapped because of an exceptional economic development. French governments also challenged arguments that the EMU project should be postponed. It was not the project but the ERM constraint that required the maintenance of high interest rates. Moving to the single currency was presented officially as the best way to lower interest rates quickly.

Alphandéry, one of the leading proponents of EMU in the Balladur government, himself seriously undermined international confidence in the strength of the franc and the ERM. In a 24 June 1993 radio interview, he argued – the first French minister of finance to do so publicly – that the reduction of French unemployment depended upon the lowering of German interest rates.[191] He also claimed that he had demanded a meeting with Bundesbank officials to discuss the joint lowering of rates.

It is arguable that no confidence building gestures or demonstration of determined political commitment would have been sufficient to stem speculative attacks against the franc and other European currencies. The combination of high real interest rates, low economic growth, growing unemployment, liberalised capital flows and artificially fixed exchange rates was too great a temptation for international financial markets, and ultimately forced the widening of ERM fluctuation margins. By September 1992, market speculators had come to the conclusion that huge profits could be made from attacking the system. The only potentially effective confidence building gesture was the guarantee of unlimited Bundesbank intervention in defence of the franc to prevent it from dropping below its lower fluctuation margin. However, continued speculation until August 1993 demonstrated that international financial markets were only temporarily deterred by the joint Franco-German declarations proclaiming this guarantee.

With the limited success of confidence building gestures, the French also chose to ignore European directives on the freedom of capital movements in order to stem speculation. This was difficult to avoid given the high cost of defending the franc. One example was during the massive outflow of capital immediately following the September 1992 referendum. The Bank of France increased overnight money market rates to 30 per cent, while at the same time offering domestic banks special lending facilities in order to avoid an immediate rise in bank lending rates. In return, French banks agreed not to use these facilities either to attack the franc or to lend to anyone wanting to do so. The Commission did not challenge French actions.

The fifth objective linked to keeping the EMU project on track was to respect the convergence criteria. In 1990, the French had respected all the criteria. By 1993, they well-exceeded the deficit criterion and the national debt was rising rapidly. With the national economic recession – and corresponding pressure to increase government expenditure – prospects of meeting these two criteria by the 1996 or 1998 deadlines declined considerably. This objective involved satisfying the demands of both the German government and mollifying an increasingly sceptical international financial community, on the one hand and demonstrating responsiveness to domestic demands, on the other. The French governments of the post-Maastricht period had to demonstrate their will to meet the convergence criteria necessary to keep the EMU project on schedule, yet also a capacity to stimulate economic growth, protect the welfare state from encroaching cutbacks and demonstrate to French public opinion their ability to stand up to a German 'diktat'. This was as much a political objective as an economic one: to satisfy both domestic and external opinion on the government's ability to keep the EMU project on track without excessive political and economic upheaval in France.

To satisfy international opinion, immediately following the March 1993 elections, the new government adopted contractionary fiscal measures, including a rise in social security taxes. However, the Raynaud Report on public expenditure, published at the start of May 1993, undermined international confidence further by demonstrating that this effort was far from sufficient. The report estimated that the French budget deficit would establish itself for 1992 at 330 billion francs and that it risked reaching 400 billion in 1993, which, in addition to the social security deficit, would reach a total of 6 per cent of GNP, or twice the Maastricht norm. The negative public and political reaction to the new Balladur government's fiscal measures, and notably pressure from within the RPR, encouraged the planning for increases in public spending and subsidies, and the selection of other ways to control the deficit and debt. A bond issue (the Balladur bond) was launched and further privatisations had begun to cover much of the extra costs.[192] Balladur and Alphandéry also argued that the convergence criteria were unrealistically severe given the economic recession facing most of Western Europe (*Le Figaro*, 4 May 1993). With the economic margin of manoeuvre at the national level severely constrained, French governments throughout the post-Maastricht period argued in favour of European growth initiatives.

In 1994, the Balladur government had some success in lowering the deficit to 4.1 per cent. Chirac's election to the presidency initially did not bode well for the deficit, which rose in 1995 and 1996, nor did the withdrawal of the Juppé Plan on social security reform following civil unrest. In 1996, the Juppé government cut social security spending more gradually, lowering the deficit again to 4.1 per cent in 1997. Despite French government complaints about the rigid application of the deficit criterion, it accepted the 'Growth and Stability Pact' – including specific fines and ungenerous exemptions – demanded by the Germans. Chirac's determination to bring about the necessary, but politically difficult, structural reforms in order to meet the 3 per cent criterion for 1997 – as well as incorrect predictions of stalled economic growth for 1997–98 – led him to call the National Assembly elections for the end of May and the start of June 1997, ten months earlier than necessary.

In their joint election manifesto with the other elements of the Plural Left, the socialists demanded the relaxation of the 3 per cent criterion – part of what they called the '*euro social*' – an end to public spending cuts and rather the stabilisation of the deficit. However, within a month of the Plural Left's victory, the new government led by Lionel Jospin had confirmed its commitment to proceeding with EMU and meeting the deficit criterion and cuts continued. Despite the efforts of the Juppé government, the deficit for 1997 was set to rise to between 3.5 and 3.7 per cent. To lower this, the Jospin government decided to discount the future pensions of France Télécom employees, thus lowering the deficit by 37.5 billion francs. While conforming with German demands on the criteria, the Jospin government nonetheless continued to demonstrate publicly its opposition to German diktat. It announced a predicted 3.1 per cent deficit figure for 1997, when it could have certainly 'fixed the books' further as managed by several of the other member states. The Jospin government also continued the privatisation of state-owned companies and banks – the first Socialist-led government ever to do so. This was in part to raise capital in order to lower the deficit in the following years.

In its election manifesto, the Plural Left had also insisted upon the qualification of the Growth and Stability Pact by the creation of a Growth and Employment Pact and the inclusion of the Employment Chapter in the Amsterdam Treaty. Its aim was to increase European spending on projects designed to stimulate employment and compensate for the austerity required at the national level. The Germans had previously refused European involvement in employment policy. They acquiesced to avoid a crisis with the Jospin government and help the Plural Left 'save face'. However, they did so only when they were assured that the new policy would involve no additional spending or binding policy commitments. That the Jospin government accepted such a minimal qualification of the project demonstrated the priority placed on keeping the EMU project on track. The Plural Left was completely successful in obtaining only one of its demands on EMU: that the Germans allow the Italians to participate in Stage Three, despite their difficulties respecting several of the convergence criteria. The insistence placed upon Italian participation demonstrates the continued French emphasis placed upon diminishing, as much as possible, German influence within the eurozone.

The attempt to lower French interest rates

The debate between French governments and the Bundesbank over German interest rates and the anchor issue was essentially about power. In 1993, the Balladur government succeeded in making several small cuts to interest rates. However, given the large drop in inflation, French real short term rates rose. The decline in domestic industrial output in 1992 and 1993 increased pressure on the government to lower rates further. Bérégovoy had argued that a 'yes' vote in the September 1992 referendum would strengthen confidence substantially in the ERM and the EMU project and permit the lowering of interest rates. Some claim that prior to the March 1993 election, Balladur had promised the CNPF that French short term rates would be lowered 4 points by the end of the year (Kaletsky, *The Times*, 28 June 1993). The French did manage to lower rates to levels below those in Germany for several weeks in 1993. However, given the credibility gap between the strength of the mark and the franc, speculation prevented lower rates from being maintained for a prolonged period.

The EMU project increased the pressure on the Bundesbank to incorporate the economic interests of the other ERM countries – at least the economically virtuous and notably France – into the formulation of its interest rate policy. The French and other European governments sought to hold the Bundesbank to this commitment and succeeded in forcing it to accept minor cuts in German interest rates, in spite of persistently high domestic inflation. These cuts were never large enough effectively to stem speculation against the franc and other ERM currencies. Nonetheless, the cuts made were of political importance.

The franc was unable to play the role of the anchor currency in the system, which would have enabled the Balladur government to maintain short term interest rates below those in Germany. A crucial moment came at the end of June 1993. The French had succeeded in maintaining rates below those in Germany for several weeks and lowered rates independently of the Germans on three occasions, the last prior to the Brussels compromise being 21 June. Alphandéry sought to do so again but Treasury and Bank of France officials hesitated because they feared that such a move would look like a bid for the anchor role (interviews with Treasury and Bank of France officials). The decision was reached that both the markets and the Bundesbank would react badly to a further cut. Given that the franc was at the bottom of its fluctuation margins with the mark, French officials feared that the markets would perceive a unilateral cut as a sign of French weakness, of readiness to let the franc fall.

French attitudes on the potential role of the franc as anchor varied over the period and from official to official, although most in the Treasury and the Bank of France felt that the franc still lacked sufficient credibility to play this role. However, the establishment of a joint franc–mark anchor was upheld as a desirable goal by all the key actors. Crucially, this would give the French a say over German interest rates. On 5 April 1993, de Larosière argued that the strong French current account surplus, low inflation and the rapid move to an independent Bank of France, merited a reinforced role in the EMS for the franc via the establishment of a joint mark–franc anchor.[193]

Connolly cites sources that Trichet, the Head of the Treasury, followed Bundesbank Vice-President Tietmeyer's demand on 21 June 1993 that the French not cut rates unilaterally again (1995, p. 304*ff*). In addition to the credibility gap and the negative reaction of the markets, the French were clearly very sensitive to Bundesbank irritation at any perceived attempt to replace the mark as ERM anchor. The French were also fully aware of the Bundesbank's ability to sabotage the EMU project. Some have suggested that Tietmeyer might have claimed to Trichet that some form of secret joint anchoring of the ERM could be arranged, but that it was necessary to wait for the departure of Helmut Schlesinger, the more hawkish Bundesbank President.[194]

For much of the period of speculation and in particular at the time of the July 1993 crisis, when a more substantial modification of the EMS proved necessary, the French presented an argument which would allow the franc to remain in the ERM, permit the lowering of interest rates and bring greater stability to the mechanism. They argued that the mark should leave the mechanism for a brief period, at least while German inflation remained high. This would also in theory permit the franc to become the anchor of the EMS. Delors joined the French authorities in arguing for a mark float during the August 1993 Brussels negotiations. However, the economic feasibility of such a proposal was questionable and German interest rates would likely have continued to have had considerable influence over interest rates in the ERM member countries.

In the Brussels negotiations, the Germans accepted the departure of the mark from the ERM – probably because they recognized that it would not alter monetary realities in Western Europe. Problems arose, however, because the Dutch insisted that the guilder follow the mark. The Belgians were divided and found it politically difficult to follow either the mark or the franc. The Luxembourgeois argued in favour of following the mark which created tension within the Belgo-Luxembourg monetary union. Many Danish officials also preferred to follow the Germans while recognizing the domestic political difficulties of doing so. The departure of the German currency would, therefore, have resulted in the re-establishment of at least most of the mark zone, which existed prior to the creation of the EMS and was preferred by the Bundesbank. The franc would retain as satellites only the peseta, the escudo and perhaps the lira and the punt. Spanish proposals for the recreation of a Latin Monetary Union emphasized this division. The existence of two systems would severely curtail any influence the French had over German monetary policy and likely stall the EMU project. To avoid this scenario, the French opted for enlarged margins. This also enabled them to stem speculation against the franc, avoid an excessively large devaluation and attempt to re-establish the previous franc–mark parity in the near future.

The French decision to maintain high interest rates following the expansion of the margins, consistently above those in Germany, was a crucial means of containing Bundesbank reticence regarding the EMU project. The project was kept on track and the French retained the possibility of continued limited influence over German monetary policy. Nonetheless, French demands to lower European interest rates and modify the ERM constraint continued. They were expressed most notably by Chirac during the months preceding the presidential elections.

Moreover, several of his advisers drew up specific proposals on ERM reform that he could present to the Germans (Aeschimann and Riché, 1996, pp. 284–8). These recommended – unrealistically, given the inevitable Bundesbank opposition – a large co-ordinated drop in French and German interest rates and/or the establishment of a joint anchor.

Finally, an often ignored factor in explaining high French interest rates, was the need to attract foreign capital to finance French company debt (Reland, 1998). France had the highest dependence on foreign capital of all the EC countries, which provided a major economic reason for French opposition both to the revaluation of the mark following German reunification and to the lowering of French interest rates following the widening of fluctuation margins in July 1993. High German rates posed an additional threat to the French economy by attracting capital to finance reunification. As during previous periods, the ERM thus provided a useful external constraint helping to justify high interest rates which were necessary for domestic economic reasons. Nonetheless, the French would have still preferred to lower rates as long as this did not lead to capital flight.

The attempt to ensure unlimited Bundesbank intervention

The establishment and maintenance of the guarantee of unlimited Bundesbank intervention to support the franc was the French governments' second power-related demand during this period. The EMS already required the intervention of strong currency central banks in the event of weak currencies reaching their parity floors and the Basle–Nyborg accords had established the principle of intermarginal interventions. The French sought obligatory unlimited intervention before the franc reached its ERM floor. As opposed to previous attempts to accomplish this, during this period the French had strong arguments to support their position, as well as the full support of the German chancellery. First, the asymmetry of the ERM combined with high German interest rates imposed an unfair burden on France which pursued more virtuous economic policies than did the Germans. Second, the maintenance of the franc–mark parity was crucial to the survival of the ERM and arguably the EMU project. The departure of other currencies from the ERM was more acceptable for political as well as economic reasons.

In September 1992, an agreement – later labelled the 'sweetheart' deal – was established between the two governments and the two central banks, the precise terms of which were never made public.[195] This was restated in January 1993 and supported by numerous statements made by the Bundesbank president and vice-president, Chancellor Kohl and

Minister of Finance Theo Waigel (see, for example, *Financial Times* (12 February 1993)). However, the managers of international capital funds were fully aware of the Bundesbank's reluctance to agree to this guarantee given the inflationary impact of large scale interventions, and thus continued to speculate against the franc. At the end of July 1993 – as speculation reached unprecedented levels – French negotiators at Brussels also sought direct unlimited Bundesbank intervention, buying francs and keeping them, rather than merely lending marks to the Bank of France via the VSTF.[196] This would have transformed the Bundesbank into, in effect, a currency board of the Bank of France and was consequently refused.

The 'German question'

The German chancellery played an ambiguous role in monetary matters during this period, the analysis of which goes beyond the scope of this chapter. On the one hand, it publicly supported French claims for Bundesbank intervention and action on interest rates. Given the central importance of the franc–mark parity to the survival of the EMS, the German government was most insistent upon large scale Bundesbank intervention in defence of the franc. At the end of January 1993, for the first time, Kohl publicly asked the Bundesbank to lower rates to avoid a 'massive recession' in Europe. Prior to this, only the SPD opposition and some German economists dared to demand lower rates. Horst Köhler, the Secretary of State for Finance, stated that the presentation of an austerity budgetary programme for the upcoming years should be met by interest rate cuts (*Le Monde*, 2 February 1993). On the other hand, the German government accepted the terms of the 'Emminger letter' and thus the clear limits placed upon the 'Europeanisation' of both interventions to defend weak currencies and interest rate policy.

As a treaty obligation embraced by the German government, the Bundesbank was expected to accept the EMU project and assist in its completion. The reality was more complex, however, and the Bundesbank continued to place the objective of domestic price stability above European goals although it could not ignore these goals. The period was one of an intense battle for power between the French, on the one hand and the Bundesbank, on the other. Following persistent French demands, the Bundesbank was forced by the German government to accept some support for the franc and to make minor interest rate cuts to demonstrate its acceptance of the importance of considering the economic interests of the other European member states. International speculators were not, however, discouraged from attacking the franc, given their awareness of the 'Emminger letter' which the Bundesbank President Schlesinger waited to invoke.[197] He complained publicly of the massive intervention in September and December 1992 and became increasingly hostile to constant Bundesbank intervention from January 1993 onwards. In July 1993, the Bundesbank Council effectively produced this letter by refusing unlimited intervention in defence of the franc. The Bundesbank was determined to maintain the mark's anchor role in spite of large German budget deficits and high inflation. The French variously accused Bundesbank officials of engaging in activities and making statements to strengthen the mark's anchor role and undermine confidence in the EMS and the EMU project: raising and lowering interest rates at strategic moments, repelling close monetary co-operation with the French, making negative statements about the EMS, the EMU project and the ECU, and thus encouraging negative comments in the German press.[198]

In addition to having to deal with growing domestic political pressure to remove the franc from the ERM constraint (discussed below), the French governments of this period sought to counter strong German public and political opposition to EMU. Leading German politicians, including those in government, continued to demand the delay of the project. In this context, the departure of the franc from the ERM – even temporarily – risked postponing the start of Stage Three *aux calendes grecs*. French policymakers recognized the need to help their German colleagues counter domestic opposition. One factor encouraging French support for the 'Stability Pact', was the intention to send a clear sign to the German public that the euro would be as strong as the mark.

The battle over nominations

The final battle between the French and Germans over monetary power prior to the start of EMU concerned the choice of the first ECB president. In French policymaking circles, it was widely assumed that Jean-Claude Trichet – former head of the Treasury and Governor of the Bank of France since late 1993 – would fill this position. The presidency is an important symbol of monetary power: both the public and international face of the ECB. Placing Trichet in this position was thus of considerable importance to the French. It was also seen as an appropriate compromise given the decisions to establish the ECB in Frankfurt and to replace the ECU with the euro – both loaded with symbolic significance. Moreover, the French disclosed publicly that a secret agreement on Trichet's appointment had been reached with the Germans in

October 1993 when Frankfurt was selected over Lyon. Owing to the important role of the future ECB president, the power motive went beyond the purely symbolic. The assumption was – regardless the autonomy of the Bank of France in relation to the French government – that Trichet's appointment would enhance French influence within the ECB during its crucial formative years and at the international level.

However, German and Dutch central bankers thought otherwise. On 14 May 1996, they succeeded in convincing the other central bank governors to select Wim Duisenberg, the head of the Dutch bank, as the final president of the EMI prior to its transformation into the ECB. Most participating governments assumed that he would stay on for an eight-year term as the first ECB president. The French did not. After a lengthy battle on the matter, a compromise was reached in May 1998 to replace Duisenberg by Trichet after four years. This was, in effect, contrary to the fixed term established in the Maastricht Treaty. Officially, Duisenberg would serve the eight-year term. However, he promised to step down after four years. This compromise was made more palatable for the French by the strategic appointment of the two most recent heads of the Treasury to important European monetary and economic policymaking positions: Christian Noyer as ECB Vice-President and Jean Lemierre as the first president of the Economic and Financial Committee, the rebaptised Monetary Committee.[199]

An 'Anglo-Saxon' conspiracy?

Developments in the international monetary system had little impact upon the basic objectives of French policy on monetary integration during this period. The instability created by the dollar's decline contributed to the waves of speculation against European currencies, although this was only one of several causes. The principally American sources of this speculation – large capital funds – provided an object of criticism against which certain leading French politicians sought to reinforce a European solidarity in defence of the EMS. It was claimed that large scale speculation against ERM currencies amounted to an 'Anglo-Saxon' conspiracy to destroy the EMU project. The leading advocate of these conspiracy claims was former prime minister and leading UDF politician, Raymond Barre.[200] While leading Socialist politicians generally refrained from making these claims, both Balladur and Alphandéry made policy statements along these lines although not as emphatically as Barre. The French were by far the most active proponents of conspiracy theory. Few other leading European politicians reiterated the claims.

Three kinds of conspiracy were variably proposed or claimed. The first amounted to speculation capital funds joining forces to profit from large scale intra-ERM currency turmoil prior to the move to the single currency. This 'conspiracy' simply made good financial and strategic sense: funds had to group together in order to force the devaluation of, and earn money on, the larger European currencies such as the pound, franc, lira and peseta. The second was a deliberate attempt on the part of these funds to destroy the project in order to avoid losing a major potential source of earnings. Most French newspapers and several leading politicians made one or both of these claims.[201]

Some leading French politicians and newspaper columnists also claimed the possible involvement of the American government in encouraging these funds to speculate against ERM currencies. They suggested the opposition of the American Treasury to the creation of the ECU as a reserve currency, which could compete against the dollar as the dominant international reserve currency and consequently decrease the margin of manoeuvre of American monetary and budgetary policymaking. The Europeans would also be in a better position to force the Americans to agree to a new IMS. This element of French conspiracy theory demonstrated French *dirigiste* thinking on economic policy and superimposed on the American Treasury, not implausibly, a considerable capacity and will for such international strategic planning. Arguably, conspiracy theories were particularly attractive to French minds, less familiar with the basic mechanisms of the market. However, from this perspective, it is surprising that one of France's leading economists, Raymond Barre, appealed repeatedly to such theories.

It is unclear to what extent the French proponents of conspiracy theories truly believed their claims or rather presented them solely for strategic reasons: to reinforce European solidarity in the face of aggressive attacks from outside the Community and the determination to continue progress towards EMU. Another possible aim was to appeal to the anti-American prejudice of the French population in order to bolster public support for the sacrifices necessary to keep the project on track. French governments presented the project as the only way to expand European monetary influence in the world, challenge American monetary power and end economically expensive speculative attacks. Conspiracy theories also were an effective means of diverting attention from the fundamental economic reasons for speculation.

The intensification of attitudes against the ERM constraint and the EMU project

The Balladur government manifested an apparent shift in attitudes on both economic policy and German monetary dominance. The new government did not challenge the goals of European integration established by the Socialists. However, it did challenge the imposed economic austerity that the fulfilment of these goals made necessary as well as, implicitly, German monetary leadership. This challenge both reflected and was reinforced by growing opposition in both academic and policy-making circles to the economic impact of the strong franc policy and the need to respect the deficit criterion. In opposition, the Socialists demanded the moderation of austerity and the qualification of the project. In government, these demands were channelled into the establishment of an inefficacious façade of *'gouvernement économique '*.

The growing challenge to the strong franc policy

The decision of the Bérégovoy government to increase the stimulative effect of fiscal policy in 1992 and early 1993 was motivated by the desire to encourage economic growth within the tight constraint of the EMS and the EMU project. With the 1993 legislative elections in sight, it was motivated by political and electoral considerations. The decision, however, does not reflect a significant shift in economic attitudes: given the low level of French inflation, some measure of fiscal stimulation was appropriate and was not considered to be damaging to the strong franc. Nor was the decision to be seen as contrary to the goals of the EMU project: exceeding the convergence criterion on budget deficits was justified as temporary. In order to increase the government's macroeconomic margin of manoeuvre, several of Bérégovoy's advisers – including those who had actively supported the policy of 'competitive disinflation' – also encouraged the Prime Minister to temporarily suspend franc membership from the ERM (interviews with staff members).

The Balladur government's pursuit of an aggressively expansionary monetary policy represents a slight shift in economic attitudes. While the Socialists felt bound by the constraint of the EMS and the EMU project, the RPR–UDF government was willing to ignore this constraint – partially and temporarily – face German criticism, fan unprecedented speculative pressures and test German commitment towards maintaining the franc in the narrow band. The degree of this shift should not be exaggerated: despite considerable opposition and reluctance from within both the RPR and the UDF to the Maastricht Treaty, Balladur and Alphandéry strongly supported the EMU project. They sought, however, to loosen the constraints on economic policy-making as much as possible, even if doing so meant rocking the European boat. The policy shift from the Socialists to the RPR–UDF government was further encouraged by the deepening economic recession. Expansionary policies can also be seen as a response to the demands from within the new government and a reflexion of a certain nationalist pique at the constraint imposed by German monetary dominance.

These attitudes were also fed by growing criticism in academic economic and policymaking circles to the strong franc and the constraints imposed by the EMU project more generally. This opposition did not focus attention upon issues of interest to Anglo-American academics: notably, optimal currency zones and the difficulties of adjusting to cope with internal shocks in the future EMU. French academic opposition was less theoretically advanced, and focused upon more immediate concerns, notably high unemployment and the right policy mix. Most of the leading academic critics – on both the Left and the Right – were former opponents or sceptics with regard to the operation of the EMS.[202] Following the September 1992 referendum, a group of French intellectuals, led by Jean-Claude Guillebaud and Régis Debray, established the group *Phares et Balises* to oppose the strong franc policy and the orthodoxies defended in the forum of the *Fondation Saint-Simon*. Over the next three years, particularly during election campaigns, periods of speculation and the civil unrest of November / December 1995, opposing groups of economists and other intellectuals waged war in the French press.

Typical of the arguments presented by opponents to the strong franc policy, two articles entitled 'The Tragedy of the Strong franc' by an adviser to the UDF minister Alain Madelin were published under the pseudonym of Galilée (1993, 1994). The choice of the name evoked two points: first, opposition to the monetary policies imposed by French governments and certain public officials because such policies did not correspond to good sense; and second, the threat of punishment for opposing the government's line which forced officials and other opponents into pseudonymity in order to express their actual opinions on the matter. For Galilée, the true *'exception culturelle française'* was an inability of much of the economic policymaking élite in France – principally *énarques*, and specifically Trichet – to understand economics. Given the imposition of policy from above, such criticism of the economic henchmen of Mitterrand's European policy is excessive. Their responsibility was to find convincing justifications for EMU not to

criticise government policy. Galilée argued that given the various economically damaging constraints, the EMU project was best abandoned
for the near future.

With the rise of unemployment from mid-1990 after three years of
gradual decline, this became an increasingly important academic concern. Economists disagreed on the extent to which high French unemployment was due to labour market rigidities, a high minimum wage
and lack of company investment. Most agreed, however, that high
interest rates discouraged investment and, consequently, hiring. On
the Left, André Grjebine, for example, focused attention on the long
term impact of high unemployment (both youth unemployment and
long term unemployment) as far more structurally serious for the French
economy than the credibility of the franc (Grjebine, 1992). Given the
lack of alternative approaches to lowering interest rates in the near
future, he argued that floating was the only possible way effectively to
combat unemployment. Expansionary monetary policies, as pursued
somewhat by Bérégovoy and more so by the Balladur government had
a strictly limited impact. This link between the EMS and the EMU
project and rising unemployment was also embraced by several leading
conservative politicians. Most notably, Philippe Séguin, future president
of the RPR, spoke of the failure to adopt a more aggressive stance on
unemployment as a 'Social Munich', a phrase which dramatised the ill
effects of the German dominated EMS and the Maastricht convergence
criteria (Séguin, 1996).

The governments of this period embraced the litany of economic
reasons frequently presented to support the EMU project. In addition
to the Single Market crowning argument, the principle of the 'triangle of
incompatibility' became the major justification for EMU. The argument
was simplistically satisfying: the French supported EMU because they
had no choice but to do so, given liberalised capital movements and
what they argued were fixed exchange rates. The governments' official
response to the complaints about high interest rates was that EMU was
the best way to lower them over the long term (Jacquet, 1992; Lagayette,
1992).

The British precedent was potentially dangerous for French governments. Aided by lower interest rates, by the end of 1992 the British
economy began to rise out of recession. Opponents of the ERM, saw
strong noninflationary British economic growth as an indication of the
economic difficulties created by the constraint. Many French policymakers denied any direct link and claimed that Britain was already set
to emerge from a cyclical recession. Others accepted that lower short

term interest rates and the devaluation of the pound had a stimulatory effect on the British economy but that this would not be the case in France or would not be sufficiently great to compensate for the impact of the loss of credibility upon long term rates. They pointed to the great reliance of the British economy on short term rates and the almost universal use of adjustable mortgage rates, which meant that high interest rates had a significant impact upon home buyers.

Both academics and French policymakers began to question the wisdom of seeing the EMS as a system of fixed rates even though this perception was reinforced by the convergence criterion of no parity realignments for two years prior to the vote on moving to Stage Three.[203] In part, the French defence of the fixed rate system was linked to the policy of 'competitive disinflation' and the strong franc. With low inflation, excessively high real interest rates and low economic growth in France, the logic of fixed rates began to collapse. French governments blocked strategic realignments within the ERM for three principal reasons. First, they opposed the revaluation of the mark on the grounds that this was not economically justifiable because the inflation differential was in France's favour. Second, the maintenance of fixed rates was seen as the best way to discourage speculation and keep the EMU project on track. Third, the French also sought to prevent the devaluation of weak currencies which would damage France's competitive position. Moreover, the forced economic convergence of Spain and Italy – aided by the discipline of ERM membership – was the best way to ensure their participation in Stage Three, without which France would have more difficulty containing German monetary influence in EMU.

In August 1993, many people in France and abroad actively encouraged a franc float, or the full use of the expanded ERM margins, through a substantial cut in French interest rates.[204] In addition to the fear of deflation, the argument in favour of lower rates was that they would not affect the franc–mark parity in the medium term. The franc would drop initially and then, given low French inflation, would rise again, and, depending on the degree to which interest rates were lowered, could rise to its former level. The pound sterling had already started to rise from its postdevaluation low. However, Alphandéry and Treasury officials had decided that lowering interest rates was too much of a risk in terms of weakening the credibility of the franc as a strong currency. Lowered rates would also have strengthened the arguments of those in favour of a more flexible EMS and regular devaluations and would have put the EMU project at risk by damaging claims that fixed exchange rates were ultimately preferable. The French also refused to lower interest rates because they stubbornly upheld the view that the resulting devaluation was not justifiable on economic grounds. French Treasury officials felt that it would simply lead to less confidence in the franc and further devaluations or the necessity to raise rates.

Treasury officials and many liberal politicians appreciated the convergence criteria of the EMU project as a useful tool to justify necessary spending cuts, notably in the area of social security – which French governments found politically hazardous to undertake. This orthodox economic thinking was embodied in the November 1994 Minc Report of the Planning Commission, which was supported publicly by Balladur. Such logic also helps to explain the willingness of Alain Madelin to agree to the condition of continued ERM membership when he accepted the post of minister of finance in the first Juppé government in May 1995. Madelin had previously been a leading advocate of removing the franc from the ERM because of excessively high interest rates. Following his departure from the government at the end of August 1995 – for reasons linked to the pace of the Juppé government's fiscal and budgetary reforms, not the strong franc policy – Madelin and his close supporters moderated their proposals for an 'alternative policy'. They called instead for a devaluation within the ERM permitting lower interest rates combined with the tightening of the fluctuation margins to demonstrate the commitment of the French government to defending the new parity.

All French governments during this period continued to argue in favour of the creation of a *'gouvernement économique'*: the need for a European political counterweight to the ECB to provide economic leadership in Europe. Little real progress was made in this direction. The principal manifestation of this was the creation of the Growth and Employment Pact and the inclusion of the Employment Chapter in the Amsterdam Treaty. However, as noted above, this involved no additional spending or binding commitments. The creation of the Euro-X Council – a special council of economic and finance ministers of the EU member states participating in EMU – was presented by both the Juppé and Jospin governments as a major step towards *'gouvernement économique'*.[205] However, this did not involve the transfer of any new powers: the Euro-X would simply receive the powers granted to the Council (ECOFIN) by the Maastricht Treaty, which included, most significantly, the establishment of exchange rate agreements with countries outside the eurozone – on the condition that the Council respect the goal of price stability. The creation of the Euro-X was logically necessary: the EU member states which did not participate in EMU were not to contribute directly to the discussions of common interest of the countries within the eurozone. Some leading French officials also misleadingly claimed that the creation of the new Economic and Financial Committee, the rebaptised Monetary Committee, helped to reinforce the control of the Euro-XI over the economic framework in which monetary policy was made, and thus was a step closer towards the creation of '*gouvernement économique*'.[206]

Attitudes on European integration

Attitudes on further European integration did not have a profound impact upon French policymaking following the Maastricht summit. As during previous periods, few leading French politicians presented themselves as European federalists. Nationalist opposition to the Maastricht Treaty within the Socialist Party had been effectively quelled and one of the leading opponents, Chevènement, had left the Party upon his resignation from the post of minister of defence during the Gulf War. Opposition within the UDF and, more significantly, the RPR intensified during the Maastricht Treaty referendum campaign. Crucially, the anti-integrationists included several leading members of the RPR, notably Philippe Séguin and Charles Pasqua (Séguin, 1992, 1993). The extent to which opposition was rooted in the loss of autonomous policymaking powers *per se* differed from actor to actor (Benoit, 1997). Séguin and Pasqua – in addition to much of the RPR rank and file – rooted their opposition to the Treaty in a traditional Gaullist vision of Europe. Their opposition to the economic and social ramifications of the EMU project was clearly secondary.

The nationalist bent of the neo-Gaullists likely contributed to the more strident demands of the Balladur government on the reduction of interest rates and the modification of the convergence criteria, but did not touch the core of French support for the project. Following the March 1993 victory, Séguin and Pasqua continued to oppose the project publicly. In mid-1993, Séguin, now President of the National Assembly, launched his offensive on employment and criticism of what he labelled the 'Social Munich' of French economic policy. Chirac declined to silence Séguin or remove him from the party when Balladur publicly asked him to do so. The Minister of the Interior, Pasqua, published a working document in *Le Monde* which, without directly challenging the government, comprehensively contradicted the economic policy pursued by Balladur since his arrival in power (*Le Monde*, 18 February 1994). Séguin began to present a more pragmatic line following the December 1995 Madrid European Council, when it became clear that EMU was going to proceed and that his opposition would prevent him from being nominated prime minister. Pasqua's opposition was considerably more immutable. His refusal to support the Amsterdam Treaty led to his departure from the RPR executive in December 1998 and his formation of a more Eurosceptic neo-Gaullist party in June 1999. In 1997, the Euroscepticism of the PCF and *Chevènementist* coalition partners was reflected in the demands presented in the Plural Left's election manifesto but was not sufficiently influential to prevent the Jospin government from proceeding with the project.

Domestic political motives

Several domestic political developments affected French policy on monetary integration during this period. First, the difficult campaign on the ratification of the Maastricht Treaty and the narrow 'yes' vote in the September referendum raised the spectre of a popular backlash against the EMU project and encouraged the continued efforts of anti-EMU politicians and the demands to modify the project. The Socialist government had relatively little trouble ensuring parliamentary support for the Treaty. On 13 May 1992, the National Assembly voted to approve the constitutional revisions necessary for the TEU by 398 to 77, with 99 abstentions. Most of the RPR members either abstained or voted against.[207] The leaders of the three largest parties all voted 'yes' in the referendum, although Chirac refused to discourage the majority of RPR supporters from voting against the Treaty and did not campaign against the 'no' lobby led by Pasqua and Séguin.

Opposition leaders – notably Séguin who performed strongly in a televised debate with Mitterrand – played an important role in swinging a significant number of the erstwhile undecided and supporters against the Treaty in the final weeks prior to the referendum. However, the success of the negative campaign owes as much to opposition to the Treaty itself as to general discontent with the Socialist government, opposition to Mitterrand's presidency, the worsening economic situation and, in the case of French farmers, concern with CAP reforms. Rural and poorer France voted overwhelmingly against the Treaty while urban and wealthy areas voted in favour. A majority of supporters of the Socialists, the UDF, *Génération Ecologie* and the Greens voted in favour of the project, while the large majority of RPR, PCF and National Front supporters voted against.[208]

A second major political development during this period was the swing in business attitudes against the ERM constraint. Most business leaders supported the Maastricht Treaty, with the notable exceptions of

Pierre Suard, chairman of Alcatel Alsthom, and Jacques Calvet, chairman of Peugeot (Benoit, 1997, pp. 39–41). Following the referendum, business opposition to the high interest rates necessary to keep the franc in the ERM increased considerably (Aeschimann and Riché, 1996, pp. 177–83). By the start of 1993, a majority of the leaders of large French businesses argued in favour of temporarily floating the franc in order to lower rates, although few challenged the EMU goal itself. Their influence encouraged several leading political supporters of the EMS and EMU to call for a temporary float – in spite of the risks that this posed for the continuation of the EMU project – including Alain Madelin and *even* Barre and Giscard (Bauchard, 1994, p. 125). The CNPF officially maintained its support for continued participation in the ERM and the EMU project, even though its president, François Périgot – in a personal capacity – recognized that the price to pay might be excessively high. With the gradual lowering of French interest rates from the start of 1996, business opposition to the ERM constraint declined. Moreover, it should be noted that public acceptance or support for the strong franc policy and the EMU project – in spite of their close association with the country's economic difficulties – remained relatively high throughout the period.[209]

A third major political development affecting French policy during this period was the massive success of the RPR–UDF in the March 1993 National Assembly elections and the strongly divided RPR leadership, which potentially menaced the project. To maintain international confidence in the franc, Balladur appointed the Barrist Alphandéry as minister of finance but retained for himself responsibility for monetary policy. Balladur was one of the seven RPR National Assembly members who had voted 'yes' in the 13 May 1992 vote. The large RPR–UDF majority encouraged a change in French policy for several reasons. As noted above, most RPR National Assembly members and a substantial number of the UDF members opposed the project. This imposed a shift in general tone. Moreover, the large size of the RPR–UDF majority created considerable potential for backbench revolt on the issue. The opposition expressed during the 1992 referendum campaign could only be partially contained once in government. The substantial opposition towards further European integration within the RPR, encouraged negative comments from certain party leaders on the EMU project and the nature of the EMS constraint.

Most significantly, Chirac made several negative statements on the operation of the EMS during the period leading to the Brussels compromise. Moreover, during the presidential campaign his comments on the

EMS were persistently ambiguous – he was surrounded by several advisers known for their hostility to both the ERM constraint and EMU – and he made repeated criticisms of the economic orthodoxy as expressed in the Minc Report. Chirac sought to position himself in relation to the more liberal Balladur, the other leading right-wing presidential candidate (Biffaud and Mauduit, 1996). Following his election, Chirac even began publicly to criticise the tight monetary policy of the Bank of France, in order to shift the blame for France's economic difficulties. This ended when massive speculation sanctioned the 1996 budget and Trichet – now the Governor of the Bank of France – made a secret deal with Chirac and Prime Minister Alain Juppé to start lowering interest rates in exchange for the government's strong commitment to cut the deficit (Aeschimann and Riché, 1996, pp. 316*ff*). Despite his former ambiguity on the strong franc, Chirac was not willing to jeopardise the project. By the start of 1996, he had transformed himself into a strong supporter of the strong franc policy.

Following the August 1993 Brussels compromise, an intense battle was waged within the government and the administration on making use of the greater flexibility permitted by the widened fluctuation margins, by lowering interest rates and pursuing a more expansionary fiscal policy. In order to check the influence of RPR dissent and Galilée-type attitudes in the administration, several top civil servants under the name Jean-Claude Le Franc submitted a letter in the 10 August edition of *Le Monde*. In this they criticised the Balladur government for *not having* sufficiently defended the franc, lamented the 'dislocation of the EMS' and advocated continued adherence to a strong franc policy. The letter also praised Bérégovoy who defended the franc against two major assaults in 1992 and appeared critical of Balladur for failing to do so. It is likely that the letter was an attempt to support Balladur against the demands from within his own party.

Balladur also had to work within the constraints of the French political system and the powers conferred upon the president, notably in determining the major objectives of European policy. In a 29 March meeting between the head of Mitterrand's staff, Hubert Vedrine and Balladur, and in his speech to the nation later the same day, the President insisted that the new government support the Maastricht Treaty and, more specifically, the maintenance of the franc–mark parity within the ERM (Aeschimann and Riché, 1996, p. 191). Moreover, Mitterrand exerted influence on Balladur indirectly through Chancellor Kohl, who met with the future prime minister prior to the March elections. Some have also claimed that President Chirac insisted that the new Jospin government should not jeopardise the project with its demands for a '*euro social*'. Neither Balladur nor Jospin intended to put the project at risk. However, the presidential constraint was useful in terms of countering the opposition of other government members.

Conclusion

The pertinence of European power motives was reinforced during this period. The French were given additional reasons to support EMU as a means of ending German monetary dominance in Europe. The evidence of EMS asymmetry became all the more publicly obvious in the context of speculative attacks against the franc and other European currencies in 1992 and 1993, despite French inflation levels well below those in post-reunification Germany. Moreover, the economic difficulties created by the asymmetry had a greater impact during this period than at any time previously. For a growing number of leading politicians from the mainstream political parties, their advisers, high level bureaucrats, well-known academics, business leaders and bankers, gaining an increased margin of manoeuvre in monetary and economic policymaking was more important than European commitments. They stressed negative European monetary power motives, rather than the positive power motives and temporary economic sacrifice which underlay French policy on EMU. As during previous periods, economic attitudes shaped European power motives.

In response to these demands, all governments during this period sought immediately to increase France's positive monetary and economic power in relation to the Germans: through demands for 'unlimited' Bundesbank intervention in defence of the franc and lower German rates, and through attempts to lower French rates below those in Germany and to reflate the French economy regardless of the convergence criteria. For some, the failure or limited effect of these efforts to stimulate economic growth and stop the rise in unemployment demonstrated the need to leave the ERM and even to cancel the EMU project. For others, the failure simply reinforced the logic behind EMU. Following the Brussels Compromise, the debate continued to rage within administrative, political, academic and business circles, despite the attempted imposition of '*la pensée unique*'. The civil unrest unleashed by the announcement of the Juppé Plan and subsequent deficit cutting helped to maintain the intensity of this debate, as did the demands presented by the Plural Left during the 1997 election campaign.

To what extent was French policy during this period rooted in economic attitudes rather than European monetary power motives: that is,
what was the relative importance of the belief in the economic merits of
the strong franc policy in itself in relation to the desire to end Bundesbank monetary dominance in Europe? Of the political leaders, Balladur
was motivated by both economic attitudes and the desire to enhance
French European monetary power. The decisions by Chirac and Jospin
to keep the franc in the ERM and pursue the necessary economic reforms
to keep the EMU project on track were determined principally by power
motives, in addition to the more general desire not to be blamed for the
destruction of the EMU project. Neither Chirac nor Jospin were convinced by the economic arguments presented to them in favour of the
strong franc policy.

The financial administrative élite's support for the project was rooted
in both enduring attitudes and power motives. The French government
accepted the convergence criteria in 1991 with little hesitation, both
because their inclusion in the Treaty was a necessary condition to end
Bundesbank dominance and because the French had no trouble meeting
them. With the strong franc apparently unshakable and reforms to
government spending of no pressing necessity, power objectives were
most important. The subsequent economic difficulties, made worse by
the operation of the ERM, and demands for an alternative economic and
monetary policy, demonstrated the necessity of the EMU project both to
end Bundesbank monetary power as well as to push through the liberal
economic reforms favoured by the financial administrative élite. The
project thus became the means by which this élite – and now, more
specifically, top officials in the Bank of France – enhanced its power at
both the European level and within France.

Few opponents of the strong franc policy proposed an alternative
which could satisfy, even partially, French European power motives.
The temporary removal of the franc from the ERM would have likely
destroyed the EMU project.[210] Moreover, the departure of the franc
would return monetary Europe to 1978. The Bundesbank would dominate, less fettered by French political pressure, and twenty-five years of
efforts to increase the responsibility of the German central bank to help
defend weak currencies would have been largely in vain. Likewise,
certain economic attitudes – notably, the well-entrenched opposition
to floating – strongly discouraged removing the franc from the ERM. A
float was supported by many proponents of an 'alternative policy',
especially in light of the British and Italian precedents, where
economic growth improved while inflation was contained following

the September 1992 devaluations. However, floating was anathema to the French financial administrative élite.

At the same time, it would have been both economically and politically difficult to return the franc to the unreformed ERM, without the continuation of the EMU project. Economically, liberalised capital flows ensured the continuation of periodic massive speculation against the franc within the ERM. Politically, the French could not have continued going cap-in-hand to the Germans in order to obtain assistance and waiting for the Bundesbank to lower short term interest rates. The difficulty of defending the franc during the 1990s demonstrated that the ERM was only acceptable to the extent that it was soon to be abandoned. In other words, in order to satisfy their power motives, French policymakers were left with little alternative but to continue the EMU project.

Conclusion

Monetary power motives

This analysis of the thirty-year period between 1968 and 1999 demonstrates the central importance of international and European power motives in determining French policy on monetary co-operation and integration. This policy reflects all three forms of power motives in relation to the United States and Germany: negative, positive and veto.[211] Each French initiative was a product of either negative or positive power motives in relation to both countries. In relation to the United States, most initiatives reflected negative power motives – to decrease the impact of dollar fluctuations upon the domestic economy. While the French continually sought to influence American international monetary policy, their positive power motives in relation to the Americans were realistically limited. Most initiatives also reflected both positive and negative power motives in relation to Germany. The principal objective was to influence German policy, although in doing so the French sought to diminish the external constraint of having to follow this policy. The formation of monetary policy after the establishment of EMU was to be a kind of veto power or shared power at the European level: in the ECB monetary policy is decided by majority voting. The independence of the ECB and the Bank of France also qualified this power considerably. At the international level, a common monetary policy and currency represented considerable potential for the expansion of European positive power which would at least take into consideration French economic needs.

The expression of French negative power must be qualified further. In certain periods French governments sought to impose an external constraint upon themselves in order to diminish the impact of another

177

external constraint: in the case of the Snake and the ERM, the impact of American economic and monetary policies. Also, other motives contributed to the decision to impose an external constraint, the most important being to control domestic inflation and reform the 'overdraft' domestic economy. This could be considered a fourth form of power: using international monetary policy to strengthen the position of the government in pursuing domestic economic objectives against opposing entrenched interests, which is both an expression of economic attitudes and domestic political motives.

International monetary power involved increasing French control over domestic monetary and economic policy via increasing French power in the international system and shielding the French economy from the impact of foreign, non-European, notably American monetary and economic policies. This meant three specific objectives. First, as French control over the domestic economy was damaged by the floating dollar, French governments sought to prevent this fluctuation via exchange rate agreements with the Americans. Limited progress was due to an American ideological and economic aversion to fixed and moving peg systems and then an inability – for economic reasons – or lack of commitment to maintain target zones. Second, the failure of such efforts encouraged the French to seek greater stability at the European level. Third, the French sought to challenge the role of the dollar in the international system. In part this was a reaction to American policies which failed to take into consideration French economic concerns. In part this also reflected the objective of increasing French positive monetary power – via the European Community/Union – in relation to the United States. French concerns would have to compete with other European member states' concerns in the determination of common European monetary policies. Nonetheless, French interests could potentially have more impact on the United States through a common European monetary policy, than they could have unilaterally on American policy.

French European monetary power motives reflected at least four inter-related objectives.[212] The French sought to contain the expression of German monetary, economic and potential political power within the European Community. Many French policymakers saw the EMU project as the best way to restrict the power of reunified Germany. In this regard, increased German foreign policy confidence in the 1970s and 1980s had already worried the French. They also sought to limit German monetary dominance within the European Community. Through the establishment of the Snake and the EMS, they hoped to prevent the creation of a deutschemark zone. Through the EMU project, the French intended to end German dominance by sharing monetary policymaking power at the European level.

Correspondingly, the French sought monetary co-operation and integration as the best way of maintaining French influence over German and other European monetary and economic policy. Principally, the French demanded that German monetary policy incorporate the interests of other EMS member states, notably French interests. Specifically, this meant lowering German interest rates. In the context of the asymmetric operation of the EMS, the French sought maximum German financial support for the defence of the franc–mark parity. These three objectives relate directly to the international monetary power motive of maximising French power at the international level. Containing German monetary power in a European framework was deemed the only way to avoid the creation of a tri-polar world of monetary power around Germany, Japan and the United States. Finally, and most crucially, the French sought to maximise national control over domestic monetary and economic policy. The first three positive power objectives are closely linked to the fourth negative power objective. Given German monetary dominance and the asymmetrical operation of the EMS, limiting German monetary power was the only way for the French to increase national control over domestic monetary policy.

Both international and European power motives explain the drive behind French support for each development of European monetary co-operation and then integration. They were closely interlinked. French interest in international monetary stability was due in large part to the weakness of the franc in relation to the mark and the resulting impact of capital flows on the stability of the franc–mark parity, while the interest in European monetary co-operation was to limit the economic impact of both American and German monetary policy. Initially, international power motives created interest in European monetary co-operation. European interests were present but secondary, and in fact discouraged support for a joint European float of currencies. Negative international power – establishing a European zone of monetary stability in an unstable monetary world – formed the basis for French interest in remaining in European monetary arrangements. It also explains French support for an expanded use of the ECU during the 1980s and 1990s. However, from 1974 onward, the logic of reforming European monetary arrangements was principally concerned with minimising German monetary power in Europe and maximising French control over German and European monetary and economic decisions.

In terms of achieving stability, international monetary co-operation with the Americans was more important than intra-European co-operation. The latter could not provide the stability of the former, given that the principal source of instability was capital flowing in and out of the dollar. The former could only provide stability if the Americans were restrained in allowing the dollar to fluctuate. Intra-European co-operation was a second best option. No system could provide stability without economic convergence and no system, short of EMU, could ensure *complete* stability in the context of growing capital flows.

The emphasis on power motives places this analysis within the realist/neo-realist tradition of the study of international relations which has been applied to explain co-operation between states.[213] However, the analysis here escapes the limitations of realism which focuses upon informed and rational state actors and state preferences as being driven purely by the acquisition of power. Moreover, it also seeks to go beyond the framework of those neo-realist writers who:

> adhere to a common systemic level of analysis; a common treatment of states as the most important actors; and a methodological affinity for deducing state motivations from their systemic position, and hence analysing all behavior in light of the circumstances surrounding the actors   (Haas, 1990, p. 37).

The analysis here is inspired by more sophisticated versions of neo-realism which expand notions of actors, goals and rationality. The emphasis placed upon economic and monetary power also corresponds to liberal intergovernmentalism's focus upon macroeconomic preferences and flexibility (Moravcsik, 1998).[214]

The importance of attitudes

Power motives alone cannot explain French willingness to participate in constraining European monetary arrangements and the details of French policies. It is equally important to place emphasis upon the attitudes of leading policymakers. Five closely linked monetary and economic policy attitudes which encouraged support for European monetary co-operation were outlined in Chapter 1: opposition to floating currencies; support for a strong currency; preference for low inflationary economic growth; emphasis placed upon a trade and balance of payments surplus and support for an interventionist role of the State in the economy. Opposition to floating limited options. However, given the asymmetry of European arrangements and the 'sound money' bias of the EMU project, French willingness *and ability* to participate in monetary co-operation and integration was determined above all by the pursuit of anti-inflationary policies. With the EMU project, attitudes on the institutional control of monetary policy also shaped the perception of desirable integration. While European monetary co-operation fit well into the context of the French tradition of state intervention in the economy, the EMU project did not.

Attitudes on the overall process of European integration also shaped French policy on monetary co-operation and integration. The support of most policymakers for monetary co-operation and integration was not based on any enthusiasm for European integration and the necessary loss of either *de facto* or *de jure* policymaking autonomy. These attitudes were normally linked to those on desirable economic policy: the restriction or loss of national policymaking powers was tolerated to the extent that European arrangements would either ensure or enable the adoption of certain economic policies. In the 1970s, European monetary arrangements were considered unacceptable by most policymakers because they implied the loss of *de facto* autonomy and forced convergence towards German economic policies. In the 1980s, this loss of autonomy was only somewhat more acceptable given the change in French economic attitudes. The loss of *de jure* autonomy in the EMU project met considerable opposition and was only accepted to the extent that it was the price for ending German monetary dominance in Europe. While many academics and politicians in other European countries claimed that EMU would necessarily lead to the creation of a European federal state, no leading French politician in favour of the project ever presented such a claim, except in terms of a long term possibility.

What is more important in terms of French support for European monetary co-operation and integration is that most leading politicians – while far from supporting Euro-federalism – were less opposed to European developments and using positive European rhetoric than was de Gaulle. As was argued in Chapter 2, it is possible that de Gaulle himself would have called for French initiatives on European monetary co-operation. However, the arrival of Pompidou permitted the radical EMU initiative which implied French support – however tentative and temporary – for further European integration. In all the major mainstream parties, there remained determined opponents to further integration. However, government leaders were consistently pragmatic on European developments, albeit cautiously so.

French support for the EMU project in the 1990s and the most far-reaching European integration to date, can also be seen as a reaction to the near collapse of traditional sources of French international and European political power (Hoffmann, 1992). Since World War II, France's position in the international hierarchy and her leadership in Europe relied upon Cold War power dynamics, an independent nuclear deterrent and postcolonial leadership in Francophone Africa. The end of the Cold War diminished the relevance of these sources of power and placed increased emphasis upon economic and financial strength. The corresponding rise of reunified Germany would inevitably challenge French influence both within Europe and at the international level. In Chapter 5, it was explained how French support for EMU pre-dated German reunification and the end of the Cold War. Nonetheless, these developments clearly reinforced the support of many French policy-makers for EMU – and encouraged a change in position of some erstwhile opponents. The project was seen as an effective means of containing growing German monetary power within a European framework and ensuring continued French leadership on economic affairs – through European institutions – at the international level.

Changes in government and rhetorical shifts on desirable economic policies and European monetary co-operation and integration affected only modestly the overall direction of French policy. The most significant change was from the Chirac government of 1974–76 to the Barre government. However, the demands on Snake reform made by Jean-Pierre Fourcade between 1974 and 1976 corresponded to those made by all French governments on the Snake or the EMS. The 1981 election of the Socialists augured considerable change. However, within a year of the elections, Delors succeeded in modifying the Socialists' reflationary policies. The core demands on EMS remained the same. In the four subsequent changes of government following elections (1986, 1988, 1993 and 1997), the rhetoric of opposition (normally more reflationary and critical of the external constraint) did not transform itself into a correspondingly dramatic policy shift on monetary co-operation. This demonstrates the degree to which the core power motives were shared by all governments. Moreover, the differences between factions within governing parties on policy were always greater than the differences between governments. Few leading politicians in the RPR, UDF and Socialist Party opposed French participation in monetary arrangements *per se*. However, because of their attitudes on desirable economic policy and European integration, they were more or less willing to accept the European constraint upon domestic economic policymaking.

Moreover, it is problematic to attach changes in policy to changes in government rather than other political and economic developments, for example in comparing the post-1983 Socialist governments and the 1986–88 Chirac government. The former focused upon the pursuit of anti-inflationary policies and strengthening the franc. The latter placed greater emphasis on making the EMS less asymmetric by increasing the obligatory support by strong currency countries for weak currencies. Upon their return to power in 1988, the Socialists moderated these demands. It has been claimed that the different focus reflected different economic and political attitudes (increased emphasis on moderately reflationary policies and a neo-Gaullist nationalistic pride). However, it is difficult to determine the extent to which these differences were due to the change in government as opposed to other political and economic developments. Between 1983 and 1986, the Socialists could not have expected the German government to have accepted demands for a more symmetric system, given the lack of economic convergence between the two countries. Once the inflation differential had been substantially reduced by 1986, French demands for greater symmetry became more credible. Equally, when the Socialists returned to power in 1988, asymmetry was less of an issue because of strong economic growth, monetary stability and the renewed focus upon the EMU project.

The central role of the technocratic élite

The degree to which there was consistency in French policymaking also indicates the importance of both the common and persisting attitudes of the financial administrative élite. This élite consisted of current and former Treasury officials – notably, members of the élite Financial Inspectorate – financial policy advisers to the president, the prime minister and the minister of finance, and leading Bank of France officials working on external monetary policy. Dyson (1994) examines the importance of an 'epistemic community'[215] to the spread of 'sound money' ideas across several countries, concluding that this approach to policymaking fails to explain the decision by key member state governments to support the EMU project. Rather 'the national basis for economic policy ideas remained solidly entrenched' (p. 251). The analysis here stresses the influence of a nationally-based 'epistemic community' – the financial administrative élite – upon the development of French policy on monetary co-operation and integration. This community extended into the academic sphere and involved the participation of a handful of leading politicians: most importantly, Barre, a former academic economist; Giscard, a member of the Financial Inspectorate; and Delors, a former Bank of France official. It included policy advisers and politicians belonging to different parties who nonetheless shared similar reflexes to monetary developments and similar goals in terms of policy on European monetary co-operation.

Given its technical understanding of monetary and financial matters and its proximity to power, the financial administrative élite had considerable influence over policymaking. It consistently demonstrated a core feature of an epistemic community in that it '[delimited] the dimensions of policy [and established] the boundaries within which ritual policies would be considered' (Haas, 1990, p. 56). Pompidou's EMU initiative in 1969, Giscard's efforts to create the EMS, the decisions to keep the franc in the ERM in 1983 and 1993 and the consistent pursuit of anti-inflationary policies all demonstrate the influence of this community. Competing sources of information on monetary and other economic matters were limited to a small number of left-wing and liberal academics which possessed sufficient knowledge to challenge participation in European arrangements on technical grounds. However, most competition to the influence of the financial administrative élite was political: non-technical, ideologically-based opposition on the Left and the Right.

The influence of the financial administrative élite cannot explain all developments in French policy or their timing. Most importantly, this élite was divided on the EMU project, given its institutional implications. Political, normally presidential, leadership remained crucial. On most major policy decisions, the decisive actor was the president because of the high politics nature of European monetary co-operation and integration and because these developments fell within the 'reserved domain' of foreign and European policy established by the Constitution of the Fifth Republic and the precedent set by de Gaulle. The motives and attitudes of de Gaulle, Pompidou, Giscard, Mitterrand and Chirac were thus crucial to the policies finally adopted.

Economic ideas as justification of policy

Although certain economic attitudes clearly shaped French policy on European monetary co-operation and integration, it is important to emphasize that economic ideas were often used by policymakers to justify decisions taken for non-economic, principally power, reasons. This was notably the case with regard to EMU, the economic justifications for which were formulated *after* Mitterrand's decision to support the project. This is not to claim that support for EMU did not follow an economic logic: it appealed to the well-entrenched desire for monetary stability and low inflation. However, EMU was not necessary to maintain 'sound money' economic policies and the project was also highly questionable on economic grounds and directly contradicted French economic policymaking tradition. Citing Lindblom (1968), Dyson (1994) emphasizes the important role performed by institution-based economists in providing partisan analysis to support the positions of those in power. However, referring to the prevalence of 'sound money' ideas in the 1980s, he asserts that the 'direction of influence was not simply linear': 'economic ideas are not powerless in their own right' in that 'policymakers must arm themselves' (p. 253). In France, it is clear that they did so selectively and in such a way as to satisfy their power motives.

Domestic political motives

Domestic political motives had considerable influence on official government rhetoric – thus frequently convincing many observers of non-existent dramatic policy shifts – and determined the timing of particular French policy developments. However, these motives did not fundamentally shape French policy. Government leaders involved directly in monetary policymaking had to demonstrate some responsiveness to the demands and opinions of other leading politicians of the party or parties in government, the National Assembly party members and grassroots support. In right-wing and left-wing governments, there was both active support for, and strong opposition to, European monetary co-operation and integration. Grassroots sentiment in these parties often opposed European monetary developments for economic, political or nationalist reasons. Opposition – notably during the first Socialist government, the RPR–UDF governments of 1986–88 and 1993–97 and the Socialist-led coalition from 1997 – encouraged the governing leadership to question policies embraced by previous governments. Gaullist opposition to the EMU project in the early 1970s forced an about turn in Pompidou's pro-EMU rhetoric and led to French opposition on developments which eroded national policymaking autonomy. French policy on monetary co-operation and integration was always élite driven, led by a small number of governing politicians with the support of their advisers and top Treasury and/or Bank of France officials. Both the Socialist and RPR leaderships had to drag important sections of the leadership and most of their rank and file down the path towards further co-operation and integration.

Party competition and party political strategy (linked closely to electoral considerations) shaped policymaking. However, the evidence suggests that in most cases the influence of such considerations was limited to the timing of, or added justification for, particular initiatives. It was probably greatest in the case of Pompidou's EMU announcement at The Hague summit of December 1969, which was motivated in part by his goal to maintain and attract the support of pro-European centrists. In other cases, the impact of party political strategy is less clear. Giscard perhaps saw a major European monetary initiative with Germany as a possible way to establish common ground between his UDF and the more pro-Community socialists, while isolating the neo-Gaullists and the Communists (Story, 1988, p. 401). Equally, Mitterrand's support for the EMS helped attract centrist voters to the Socialist Party, while Balladur's calls for 'the rapid pursuit of the monetary construction of Europe' was possibly linked to the RPR's effort to attract centrist support to Chirac's candidacy in the upcoming May 1988 presidential elections. In other respects, party political strategy appears to have been irrelevant in terms of shaping French policy. The opposition of the RPR to the austerity necessary to lower French inflation made participation and then re-entry into the Snake mechanism politically difficult but did not prevent this. Moreover, during the 1970s, there was no firm support for monetary co-operation – let alone integration – beyond the UDF. However, this did not prevent Giscard from establishing the EMS.

The government's margin of manoeuvre within the constraints of party competition occasionally shaped policy. The re-election of a conservative coalition majority in the March 1978 National Assembly elections placed Giscard in a position of political strength (Story, 1988, p. 401). This was sufficient to overcome RPR opposition to economic adjustment policies, the external aspect of which was the establishment of the EMS. Mitterrand's re-election in May 1988 and the subsequent election of the Socialist government, gave the President the political space in which to pursue a major European initiative. Moreover, policy on monetary co-operation and integration was not greatly influenced by electoral considerations. Indeed, despite the tendency to reflate the economy prior to elections, governments sought to avoid devaluation in the final months of their electoral mandate, as this was perceived as a sign of political weakness and managerial incompetence.

The ERM provided a useful political, as well as psychological, constraint on economic policymaking, which better enabled French governments to impose anti-inflationary measures. For Giscard, this was one explicit motivating factor of several behind his efforts to return the franc to a European monetary mechanism. Between 1981 and 1983, those leading Socialist politicians who placed emphasis on controlling inflation – notably Delors – recognized the bulwark that the EMS provided against the tide of Socialist reflationary demands. Moreover, Treasury and Bank of France officials advocated support for arrangements which would bind the hands of all politicians.

Interest group activity was of limited importance in shaping French policy. Until the post-Maastricht period, no major French economic interest group campaigned actively against or in favour of progress on monetary co-operation and integration, although business, banking and farming interests were generally favourable. French governments, therefore, had considerable room to manoeuvre on the issue. No group considered the problems associated with floating, currency realignments within the ERM or the gains from monetary co-operation sufficiently great to mount an organised campaign in favour of new European initiatives. Agricultural interests, led by the FNSEA, initially placed some pressure on French governments to maintain intra-European monetary stability in order to ensure the survival of the CAP, and supported both the Snake and the EMS. However, with the successful operation of the MCAs in maintaining agricultural prices, European monetary arrangements were no longer perceived to be essential to these interests. The opposition of French farmers to Maastricht had less to do with the content of the accord – which, given the operation of the CAP, likely would be beneficial – than frustration with CAP reform and opposition to the Socialist government more generally. Trade unions tended to oppose monetary co-operation, although – until the post-Maastricht period – not actively so. Until then, the foci of their attention were the austerity measures pursued by governments, not the external constraint. Although in favour of exchange rate stability, the high interest rates necessary to maintain the strong franc weighed heavily on many French companies. Starting in 1991, with the rise in real interest rates following German reunification, some leading French manufacturers mounted a campaign against the ERM constraint. However, the movement was insufficiently organised to force a change in policy. Moreover, the most important institution representing manufacturing interests, the CNPF, continued officially to support the government.

Public opinion had little direct influence on substantive government policy on monetary co-operation and integration. Until the post-

Maastricht period, the French public was largely ignorant, favourable or indifferent, thus leaving governments large room to manoeuvre. The link between domestic economic austerity and monetary co-operation was not drawn. Public opinion may have been reluctant to support the economic policies necessary to keep the franc in European monetary arrangements but did not criticise the external constraint itself. From the start of 1992, and in particular during the referendum campaign, when excessively high short term interest rates were increasingly associated with EMS membership, the French public became more hostile towards both the system and the EMU project. Nonetheless, during this period to the start of 1999, polls consistently showed that a majority of the voting public continued to support the core elements of the project.

There was continuity in the core French demands on European monetary co-operation over the thirty-year period covered in this study, from the growing instability in the Bretton Woods system in the late 1960s to the start of Stage Three of the EMU project. These demands were shaped by international and European power motives. While most French governments complained of the asymmetry of European exchange rate mechanisms, the preference for monetary stability encouraged continued French participation. However, the willingness and ability of French governments to keep the franc in these mechanisms depended upon their pursuit of low inflationary economic policies. The failure to create a symmetric EMS helped convince some French policymakers to support the move to EMU. However, opposition to the institutional implications of the EMU project also discouraged others from doing so. President Mitterrand played a central role in imposing the project upon a reluctant Treasury and Socialist government. The asymmetric operation of the EMS in the post-Maastricht period and the high interest rates required to prevent speculation against the franc, reinforced the monetary power motives that encouraged support for proceeding with EMU.

Notes

1 The analytical and conceptual framework

1 There is no French language study of the different factors influencing the development of French foreign monetary policy (European or international). Aeschimann and Riché (1996), in their journalistic account of French policy on EMU and the strong franc, come closest. Valance (1996) and Develle (1988) provide useful – if non analytical – overviews of the history of French monetary policy. Bauchard (1994) provides the most insightful examination of the commitment of Pierre Bérégovoy and Edouard Balladur, respectively Socialist and RPR minister of finance and prime minister, to the policy of 'competitive disinflation' and the strong franc, but fails to extend this effectively to French policy on the EMS and EMU. The most exhaustive study of the economic history of French external monetary policy is to be found in the series of papers presented at the December 1992 conference *Du franc Poincaré à l'écu*. However, the papers which cover the period between 1968 to 1992 are principally economic analyses of French policy. Material in French on European monetary co-operation and integration tends either to be journalistic, descriptive and focused on particular periods, or a presentation of the economic arguments in favour or against the EMS and EMU (see, for example, Wyplosz and Riché (1993)). The relevant economic literature includes, notably, the work of Fitoussi and Grejbine which explains and criticises the economic logic behind 'competitive disinflation'.

The English language literature on French foreign monetary policymaking (again European or international) is even less extensive and limited to particular periods and policy initiatives. Bordo (1994) examines the economic motives behind French policy on the operation of Bretton Woods System. Dyson and Featherstone (1996) analyse the roles and the policy positions of the different French actors in the 1988–91 negotiations leading to EMU. Their study of motives is, however, principally limited to the opinion of policymakers concerning the impact of the EMU project upon the French State and the monetary policymaking roles of the different institutions. Of greatest relevance to this study, Story (1988) examines the different economic and political factors which led the French and Germans to establish the EMS in 1979.

There are several English language studies which examine the economic and political motives of the major Community member states in pursuing European monetary co-operation and integration. Tsoukalis (1977), Ludlow (1982) and Kruse (1980) outline some French political and economic motives relating, respectively, to the early 1970s negotiations on EMU, the establishment of the EMS and monetary developments during the 1970s more generally. However, they do so in the context of a larger study of the negotiating positions of the different member states and fail to explore these motives.

Dyson (1994) examines the logic behind European monetary integration without fully exploring the motives behind French policymaking. Moravcsik (1999) applies liberal intergovernmentalism to European monetary co-operation and integration in the context of a larger study of European integration. In spite of his two-tiered approach and focus upon France as one of the crucial motors of European integration, Moravcsik's analysis of French motives is superficial. Several articles discuss the political and or economic motives of major states in relation to particular European monetary policy developments. However, none provides a detailed examination of French motives.

2   Odell draws directly from Bergsten's factors, in particular his discussion of the elements of power.

3   Odell presents an ideas perspective (1982, pp. 58–75) which for Story 'holds that policy is shaped by changes in reigning ideas, by the general ideas that statesmen have acquired over time and by their specific attitudes to events. Their intentions may be gauged by what they say, or omit, and by the advisers they choose or confide in' (1988, p. 398).

4   Michel Develle cited in Valance (1996, p. 339) (author's translation).

5   In the 1930s, the financial élite in the Treasury and the Bank of France saw devaluation as a heresy and to the great detriment of lenders (Carré de Malberg, 1993).

6   Plessis (1993) divides the history of the strength of the franc – in relation to the dollar and pound – into four periods: first, the repeated devaluations of 1914–26; second, the stability of the franc Poincaré, 1926–36; third, the repeated devaluations of 1936–58; and fourth, the relative stability of the period since 1958. The overall drop of the franc's value in relation to the dollar was from 490 (old francs) in 1914 to 530 at the end of 1992.

7   Blum's reckless campaign pledge 'Neither deflation, nor devaluation' was to haunt the new Socialist government (Halimi, 1996).

8   This incorrect association was drawn by the then finance minister Michel Sapin in his closing remarks at a December 1992 ministry of finance conference on monetary policy (1993, p. x). The importance of the devaluation to subsequent economic growth is emphasized by Saly (1987).

9   For a detailed study of French monetary history and inflation see Patat and Lutfalla (1986; 1990).

10 At the start of 1945, a major debate took place between Pierre Mendès France, the minister of economics and René Pleven, the minister of finance. Mendès sought to break inflation through strong controls on wage increases and other austerity measures. Pleven advocated a 'policy of confidence', arguing that the growth in industrial production would help to calm inflation. For political reasons, de Gaulle supported Pleven and Mendès resigned. This set the stage for high inflation and frequent franc devaluations throughout most of the term of the Fourth Republic.

11 Jacques Rueff, a leading advocate of anti-inflationary policies, also sought – unsuccessfully – to reform the provision of State credit in order to eliminate this important structural source of French inflation (Rueff, 1977, pp. 244–56). See also Valance (1996, p. 327).

12 Cohen writes of the 'inflationist social compromise' which involved 'the consensual refusal of the state, the trade unions and the employers to control

nominal changes in incomes and prices' (Cohen in Hayward, 1995, p. 27, note 8).

13 The French economist Jacques Rueff complained of this assumption in the 1930s ('De quelques hérésies économiques qui ravagent le monde', paper presented at the Sorbonne, 27 February 1933; reprinted in Rueff (1977, Annexe IV, pp. 321–32)).

14 Upon assuming office in 1958, de Gaulle declared that he would 'give to France a model franc, the parity of which [would] not change as long as [he was] in power' (Charles de Gaulle, *Mémoires d'espoir* (Paris: Plon, 1970); cited in Aeschimann and Riché (1996, p. 26; author's translation)).

15 Likewise, the extension of QMV in the Treaty of European Union (TUE) to the establishment of certain social rights at the European level was seen as necessary in order to build a European social policy along French lines.

16 This can be compared to 51 per cent in the US, 55 per cent in the UK, 68 per cent in Japan and 86 per cent in Germany. The German percentage is high, but it must be remembered that the banks obtained one fifth of their capital on the bond market and another 10 per cent on the stock market (Loriaux, 1991, p. 59).

17 For an overview of the financial reforms of the mid-1980s, see Loriaux (1991) and Mamou (1988).

18 This made realignments more difficult, both economically and politically, than previously. The Commission eagerly claimed that realignment was made 'impossible' and that the next logical step was to move towards a single currency, to which Giscard, minister of finance from 1962, agreed in principle (Tsoukalis, 1977, p. 60).

19 Moreover, during the 1970s, the French concluded that the provision of MCAs, in the event of franc devaluations, made French agricultural exports less competitive. At the end of December 1978, the French delayed starting the operation of the EMS by demanding – unsuccessfully – that the MCAs be gradually phased out (Kruse, 1980, p. 245).

2 The first steps to monetary co-operation

20 There was a widespread belief, 'at least in Community circles, that a *de facto* monetary union had already been achieved' (meaning fixed intra-EEC exchange rates) (Bloomfield, 1973, p. 7).

21 From 1958 to 1968, French gold reserves increased from 500 tonnes to 4600.

22 *Le Monde*, 16 October 1963; Tsoukalis, 1977, p. 58. In its October 1963 report, the National Assembly commission also recommended the adoption of 'fire extinguishers', for example, the creation of a gold pool, in order to prolong the survival of the system.

23 De Lattre was moved to the 'dignified but harmless post' of deputy governor at the Bank of France. He later played an important role during the 1970–71 negotiations on EMU (Tsoukalis, 1977, p. 61).

24 Decision of the Council of 6 March 1970, Annex 2 in Council-Commission of the European Communities, 1970.

25 This was adopted by the Werner Group (*Interim report*, p. 17 and Annex 4).

26　In March 1968, for example, de Gaulle and Debré refused to endorse the final plan allowing for the eventual creation of Special Drawing Rights (SDRs) even though all the other participating states supported this development. The French also opposed a joint float, sought by the Germans, because they refused any revaluation of the franc in relation to the dollar. Following the announcement of the Nixon administration's measures, the French blocked the opening of commercial discussions hoped for by the United States, insisting that they re-establish acceptable fluctuation margins for the dollar.

27　French ambitions to re-establish an IMS based on the gold standard became increasingly unrealistic with the gradual elimination of the remaining features of this standard following the end of the convertibility of the dollar in August 1971. In 1974, SDRs ceased to be defined in relation to gold but rather in relation to a basket of sixteen important currencies. The Commission followed by abandoning the gold reference of the European Unit of Account (0.8886 grams) which became the weighted average of member state currencies in 1975. Finally, in January 1976, the IMF Jamaican Agreement finished officially all reference to the gold standard and floating currencies were formally legalised.

28　The principle of a European realignment, a devaluation of the dollar and a return to fixed parities were all accepted.

29　Certain accounts stress the purely bilateral nature of the agreements. The Americans wanted to negotiate with the French because they blocked progress on trade talks. As the European partners were presented with a Franco-American *fait accompli* they had little choice but to agree.

30　Esambert (1994). Pompidou fully recognized that the realities had not changed and that the establishment of tighter European fluctuation margins would likely be necessary (Roussel, 1984, pp. 452–3; Valance, 1996, p. 344). The Smithsonian agreement represented a temporary and fragile agreement between the partisans of a return to fixed parities and the advocates of floating exchange rates. The new system established the dollar as its standard while imposing no obligations on the Americans to stabilise their currency.

31　This is discussed in the European monetary power section below.

32　The French had difficulty convincing the other member state governments of the wisdom of such action. The Werner Group explicitly endorsed the objective of eventually increasing the use of EEC currencies in order to decrease dependence on the dollar. However, it recommended continuing with the dollar in most interventions for the time being (Werner Group, *Interim Report*, pp. 13–14). Following the collapse of Bretton Woods and the loss of confidence in the dollar, the German position on using dollars for intra-EEC interventions changed, largely because the Germans had dangerously large dollar reserves and sought to convert these gradually. The Germans accepted French demands that only Community currencies be used for interventions within the Snake-in-the-tunnel, while the dollar would be used only when the Snake reached the ceiling or the floor of its tunnel.

33　The average annual GNP growth during the period between 1968 and 1973 in France was 5.8 per cent versus 4.9 per cent in West Germany. Average annual rates of inflation for the period between 1961 and 1974 were 5.3 per cent in France and 3.9 per cent in Germany, with a considerably higher margin of difference during the early 1970s (Commissariat Général au Plan, 1983, p. 114).

34 De Gaulle's decision not to devalue the franc was largely due to his anger with the indiscretions of German finance minister Strauss to the German press following the meeting to discuss realignment.

35 This was even though 'consultation frequently took the form of each minister defending at great length the policies adopted by his government, while having very little, if any, knowledge of the problems faced and the policies pursued by the other EEC governments' (Tsoukalis, 1977, p. 141). Moreover, member states, including the French, occasionally ignored the obligation to consult, or consulted selectively. Neither the French devaluation of August 1969 nor the German revaluation of October were preceded by consultations. However, it was useful in limiting the public demonstration of tensions between EEC member states and avoiding the collapse of monetary relations in a period of considerable instability. The co-ordination of exchange rate intervention did promote some intra-EEC stability and several realignments were successfully co-ordinated.

36 The French also requested improved balance of payments support.

37 The Germans and Dutch floated their currencies in May 1971, after the French refused to accept demands for a joint European float. This was part of a compromise which involved the introduction of new capital controls in most of the EEC member states.

38 For a discussion of the divergence indicator see Chapter 4.

39 It was later revealed that Chancellor Schmidt promised President Emminger of the Bundesbank (in the so-called 'Emminger letter') that Bundesbank intervention was not unlimited and would never prevent the maintenance of price stability in Germany. This is discussed further in Chapters 4 and 6.

40 Many observers claimed that the French deliberately sought an undervalued currency.

41 In his memoirs, Giscard goes so far as to blame the French population for the inflationary economic policies in order to excuse the governments of the early 1970s (Valéry Giscard d'Estaing, *Le Pouvoir et la Vie*, tome II: *L'Affrontement* (Paris: Cie 12, 1991); quoted in Valance, 1996, p. 351).

42 Such measures reflected a widespread practice in the industrialised world for dealing with the problem of stagflation during the mid-1970s.

43 It might also be argued that by politicising the debate, the EMU discussions prevented progress on monetary co-operation.

44 It has also been suggested that Pompidou launched his initiative on EMU to balance his more positive policy on British entry: to balance enlargement with deepening European integration (Tsoukalis, 1977, p. 83). Given Pompidou's limited interest in further European integration, such claims are probably exaggerated. Rather Pompidou's interest in both British entry and monetary co-operation can best be explained by the motive of containing German economic and diplomatic influence within an enlarged Community.

45 France and the other four member states opposed German demands on independence. The debate on independent monetary authorities in the early 1970s was almost identical to the one leading to the Maastricht Treaty, although the outcome was very different.

46   Former chancellor Schmidt has since noted that he and Giscard decided in a private interview at the end of 1977 to restart the path to European economic and monetary union (interview, in *Die Zeit*, August 1990, cited in Valance, 1996, pp. 360–1). The EMS was to be the first stage of this development. If this was the case, Giscard sought to avoid the difficulties of the previous EMU discussions by not raising the nature of the final goal in domestic public discussion.

47   The five other member states opposed but had little choice other than to accept. The position of the Commission (which was frequently accused of taking the French line, given Raymond Barre's position as Commissioner responsible for economic and financial affairs) was also modified to focus on Stage One and avoid any elaboration on EMU in order to meet with the approval of French nationalist opinion (*Agence Europe*, 16 November 1970).

48   The weight of the UDF/centrists increased from 114 versus 173 neo-Gaullists and 11 'other Right' in 1973, to 119 versus 145 neo-Gaullists and 12 'other Right' in 1978.

3   The decision to keep the franc in the ERM

49   These include Attali, 1992; Bauchard, 1986; Colombani, 1985, Estier and Neiertz, 1987; Favier and Martin-Roland, 1990; July, 1986; and Pfister, 1985. Relevant academic works on the period include Cameron, 1996; Elgie, 1993; Friend, 1989; Hall, 1986; Haywood, 1989; Loriaux, 1991.

50   Between the start of February and 10 May, the haemorrhage amounted to $5 billion, while an equal amount left the country during the ten-day interim following the second ballot and Mitterrand's investiture on 21 May, increasing to $1 billion a day by 18 May. On the day that Mitterrand assumed the presidency, 21 May, capital flows from France reached a new daily record of $1.5 billion.

51   The 'collective' decision not to devalue following the elections was made prior to Mitterrand's second ballot victory in a meeting of Mitterrand, Mauroy, Delors, Bérégovoy and Mauroy's close friend Jean Deflassieux, a pro-Socialist banker (interviews with ministerial staff members).

52   The dollar rose from 5.30 francs in May 1981, to 6 francs in March 1982 and 6.65 in mid-June. According to one surprising estimate 64 per cent of the increase in French inflation from 1981 to 1982 could be directly attributed to the strength of the dollar (*Le Monde*, 24 March 1983; *Prévision et Analyse économique*, 4, 1, 1983). See also the comments by Riboud (1983, p. 54).

53   Despite considerable opposition from within the Socialist government, Mitterrand accepted a freeze of 15 billion francs of expenditures, which evidently satisfied the Germans.

54   The inflation differential between France and the average of her six largest trade partners had increased from 3.5 per cent during the first six months of 1981 to 5.5 per cent in June 1982.

55   These included the presentation of the 1983 government budget in September, which announced no spending increases; the success of wage and price freezes in lowering inflation to the target of 10 per cent (still twice that of Germany); convincing the unions to accept the deindexation of wages; and

the reintroduction of a two-tiered money market (different current account and capital rates).

56 Although there was positive news regarding economic growth and unemployment, the financial indicators encouraged a continued attack on the franc (Hayward, 1986, p. 219). GDP growth was 2.3 per cent in 1982, the highest of the large European countries, and unemployment had stabilised at around 2 million, whereas British and German unemployment continued to rise. However, the government deficit for 1982 had also reached a record 2.6 per cent of GDP, the trade deficit reached 93 billion francs, and France's current account deficit with Germany had tripled in 1982 over the previous year.

57 Fourteen banks provided a total of 28 billion francs (Bauchard, 1986, p. 124).

58 Total French reserves – both currency and gold – dropped to 260 billion francs by the end of 1982, which represented a total loss of 65 billion francs.

59 In total, the three realignments (8.5, 10 and 8 per cent), in addition to the 24 September 1979 revaluation of the mark by 2 per cent, resulted in a *de facto* 28.5 per cent devaluation of the franc against the mark. Taken in total, the realignment only put French and German industrial competitiveness at roughly the same level as the start of 1979, given the accumulated inflation differential of 29.4 per cent (and not considering changes in labour productivity) (Petit, 1989, p. 258).

60 The VSTF loan was agreed when France formally applied for it in May (*Agence Europe*, 3606, 11 May 1983).

61 See, for example, Jean Louis Bianco's comments in Favier and Martin-Roland (1990, p. 462).

62 Didier Maus, ed., *Textes et Documents relatifs à l'élection présidentielle des 26 avril et 10 mai 1981* (Paris: Documentation Française, 1981), p. 158.

63 See, for example, 'M. Delors demande l'adoption d'une attitude commune et ferme', *Le Monde*, 13 June 1981.

64 Because most international loans were denominated in dollars, the burden increased whenever the dollar increased in value – which was the case until 1985. France had asked for, but not made use of, an ECU loan facility to coincide with the two previous realignments. It has been claimed that the acceptance of the May 1983 loan was also politically motivated in that Delors was in effect further tying France to the EMS (*Le Monde*, 19 May 1983).

65 According to those policy advisers interviewed. The idea of expanding the use of the ECU to challenge the preeminence of the mark (European monetary power motives) was not an important theme of the period. However, Delors' ideas regarding a tri-polar IMS around the dollar, the yen and the ECU, did effectively assume a much less important role for the mark.

66 For example, 'Delors s'explique', in *L'Expansion*, 4–7 August 1981, p. 57. When Bundesbank President Karl Otto Pöhl dismissed Delors' proposals as unrealistic, the French minister of finance struck back by challenging Pöhl's commitment to European 'solidarity' and by claiming that his comments damaged the strength of the EMS.

67 A leading member of Delors' staff, interview.

68 Mitterrand's intervention in the Bundestag to influence the West German debate on the Cruise missile issue – immediately following the March 1983 decision – suggest another interest in not upsetting close Franco-German

relations. Mitterrand sought to counter the growing 'Euroscepticism' within the German government and the rising neutralist tendencies in German public opinion, principally through his more flexible approach to the major European problems of the period. For a description of Mitterrand's efforts at the European level see Haywood (1989) and Howarth (1991).

69 In his 23 March 1983 television address, Mitterrand justified his decision by the will not to 'isolate France from the European Community'. He subsequently stated on numerous occasions that the continued pursuit of Chevènement-type economic policies would have damaged France's relations with her European partners (for example, Favier and Martin-Roland, 1990, p. 462).

70 Mauroy and other leading Socialists denied the liberal character of the government's post-March 1983 economic policies. The Prime Minister claimed that rigour was not to be confused with liberalism (Favier and Martin-Roland, 1990, p. 450).

71 CERES, *L'Enlévement de l'Europe*, (Paris: Entente, 1979).

72 Bauchard (1986) uses this label. Here it is applied loosely to politicians who, at the time, would never have described themselves as 'Social Democrats', considered a negative epithet by most socialists.

73 Indeed, it is arguably, the sound economic logic of their approach which in part explains the necessity of silencing all opposition to EMS membership following the March 1983 period.

74 'Delors s'explique', *op. cit.*, pp. 53–8.

75 See, for example, 'Delors s'explique', *op. cit.*. His stated objective shortly after his selection as minister was to achieve what Barre could not accomplish: to lower inflation to between 7 and 8 per cent in three years.

76 Delors, statements on *Grand Jury RTL-Le Monde* (29 November 1981), cited in Estier and Neiertz (1987, p. 149).

77 Mauroy's financial adviser, Daniel Lebègue – a Treasury official and a self-described 'man of the Left' – had been directly involved in the negotiations to establish the EMS in 1978.

78 At the time of each of the four decisions (May 1981, October 1981, June 1982 and March 1983) a float likely only would have worked with large international loans or the selling of gold reserves.

79 The financial advisers to the president, prime minister and minister of finance stressed this point (interviews).

80 This is outlined by Philippe Simonnot, '1983: comment la ruse de la raison européenne a triomphé de l'"autre politique"', in *Le Monde*, 29 June 1993, pp. 25,30 and 31, p. 30; Simonnot, interview, 23 March 1994.

81 In a July 1983 interview he admitted that he accepted many of the reflationary economic policies of the first year of Socialist government for very non-economic reasons (*Témoinage Chrétien*, 11 July 1983, quoted in Hall, 1986, p. 195).

82 Favier and Martin-Roland, 1990, p. 462. Mitterrand later claimed to have regretted consulting so many people and to have under-estimated the risk of leaving the system (*ibid.*, p. 465).

83 See, for example, Pierret (1983, pp. 48–50). Pierret was a Socialist member of the National Assembly and the *rapporteur général* of the finance committee National Assembly – therefore, a prominent defender of Socialist government's economic and monetary policies.

84 *Cahier et Revue de L'OURS*, 96, January 1979.
85 In 1985, even after several years of austerity, the French were generally favourable to the ECU and the EMS (roughly 65 per cent), more than the citizens of any other Community member state with the exception of Belgium and Luxembourg (*Eurobarometer*, 1985).
86 Mauroy, 1990, p. 19. De Gaulle devalued the franc 17.7 per cent in December 1958; Pompidou did so in August 1969 by 12.5 per cent; and Giscard devalued outside the Snake as minister of finance in January 1974 and again, as president, in March 1976.
87 As Jean Denizet notes: 'it is not the political gesture which will be remembered, but rather the gesture of weakness and surrender in the face of external attacks' (J. Denizet, 'L'Arme du Système monétaire européen' in *L'Expansion*, 174, 3–16 July 1981, p. 46).
88 Mauroy, 1982, p. 25. Expecting an immediate devaluation of the franc, the Governor of the Bank of France, Renaud de La Genière, tendered his resignation on 21 May and had to be persuaded to stay on (Pfister, 1985, p. 246).
89 This statement at the 16 June 1982 Council of Ministers meeting encouraged action on the part of Delors and Mauroy, but also gave hope to the adversaries of deflation that they could continue to prepare their 'other policy' (Favier and Martin-Roland, 1990, p. 429).
90 Y. Roucaute, *Le Parti Socialiste* (Paris: Bruno Huisman, 1983), p. 178.
91 Cameron, 1996, pp. 73–6.

4   The French challenge to German monetary dominance

92 On economic and European policymaking during this period see Bauchard (1994), Cameron (1996), Loriaux (1991) and Mamou (1987). On élite policymaking more generally see Attali (1994) and Favier and Martin-Roland (1990).
93 This progress in fact preceded the March 1983 decision. The ECU had increased its share of Eurobond issues from eighth place (0.3 per cent of the total) in 1980, to third place (3.6 per cent of the total) in 1982 behind the mark at 4.9 per cent and the dollar at 85.2 per cent (Bundesbank report on the ECU, 18 August 1987 and *Agence Europe*, 3967, 12/13 November 1984 and 3969, 15 November 1984). ECU loans jumped from 0.8 billion in 1981 to 9.2 in 1985, at which time they represented 4 per cent of total international issues.
94 By the end of 1983, bank and savings deposits in ECU reached an estimated 3 billion, with banks increasing their ECU loans.
95 Germany was the only Community country in which ECU transactions were not authorised or even quoted in the mid-1980s. The Bundesbank and the ministry of finance argued that the increased use of the ECU would weaken the mark and import inflation.
96 *Le Monde*, 15 May 1984. Delors insisted upon the expansion of the VSTF in May 1984, once France had exhausted two-thirds of its funds with a 4 billion ECU loan.
97 Indeed, since the realignment of April 1986, French unit wage costs had risen more slowly than those in West Germany.

98   Balladur, 1988. The tenses have been changed.
99   The French authorities continued to impose restrictive exchange controls on the strength of a 1968 Commission directive. At the time, the Commission agreed to the controls, given the deteriorating balance-of-payments situation in France. Although the measures were meant to be temporary, they remained in place for over 15 years. Moreover, the Commission allowed a number of controls on the condition that governments consult the Commission prior to their establishment.
100   For example, Francesco Giavazzi and Alberto Giovannini, *Limiting Exchange Rate Flexibility: The European Monetary System* (Cambridge, Massachusetts: MIT Press, 1989). Between 1983 and 1988 France, Italy, Belgium, Luxembourg and Ireland all maintained some form of capital controls.
101   This was in spite of the conference that took place on the subject in Brussels during the SEA negotiations.
102   The 'triangle of monetary incompatibility' is often attributed to Padoa Schioppa who postulated the 'inconsistent quartet', the fourth side being free trade, although there are older theoretical sources. T. Padoa Schioppa, 'Squaring the circle, or the conundrum of international monetary reform', *Catalyst*, 1, Spring (1985). It is actually the implication of the simplest version of the Mundell–Fleming model (Begg and Wyplosz, 1992, pp. 20–2).
103   *The Economist*, 22 November 1986, p. 84. The agreement effectively implemented a plan that had been proposed by the European Commission six months earlier (Commission of European Communities, *Programme for the Liberalisation of Capital Movements in the Community*, Brussels, 23 May 1986).
104   See, for example, the demands presented at the 4–6 October 1984, annual meeting of the French Chambers of Commerce and Industry, in *Le Figaro*, 8 October 1984; and *Les Echos*, 8 October 1984.
105   Delors first publicly argued for promoting the ECU in a 9 September 1983 *Le Monde* article.
106   At this meeting Delors fought to increase the acceptability of exchanges in ECU between the central banks. He sought the 100 per cent repayment in ECU of loans made in the context of the VSTF; to enable the holding of ECUs by the central banks of non-Community European countries, notably Switzerland and Austria; to increase the private use of the ECU; to facilitate the transaction of ECU bonds by banks and other financial institutions; and to permit the remuneration of holdings in ECU at market rates, as opposed to the existing calculation on the basis of central bank discount rates.
107   For example, Edouard Balladur, 'The EMS: advance or face retreat', *Financial Times*, 17 June 1987.
108   See, for example, Fabius (1985, p. 157) and *Financial Times* (15 November 1985).
109   These factors are explored in the next chapter in the context of an examination of the French rejection of the British proposal for a hard ECU, which was not unlike the proposals of this period made by both the Socialist and RPR–UDF governments on the parallel currency.
110   In a 14 January 1988 interview in *Le Figaro*, Balladur asked the following: 'In relation to what is the value of the ECU to be calculated? In relation to the weighted average of the other European currencies like today? In relation to

other criteria, and what will these be? Will the ECU be the single currency of Europe, or will it circulate at the same time as the other currencies? What will be the amount of ECUs in circulation (author's translation)?

111 Interviews with Balladur and Bérégovoy staff members. The size of the combined European gold reserves also indicated the potential strength of a common European currency. In 1988, the EMS countries together held 432 million ounces of gold while the Americans held only 262 million ounces. The Germans alone held only 119 million ounces, while the French held 102 (*Le Monde*, 26 January 1988).

112 In 1986, President Reagan surprised the international community by proposing to return to a system of 'predicted' exchange rates.

113 France was one of the few countries that respected the monetary and economic engagements defined for the G-7 in the Louvre accords of 22 February 1987, including reduced deficit and rate of inflation (*Le Monde*, 7 November 1987).

114 Bundesbank President Pöhl argued that 'over-ambitious commitments to peg certain exchange-rate levels or target zones run the risk not only of clashing with domestic monetary objectives but of collapsing when the markets test them'. Bundesbank opposition to the creation of the EMS was expressed in similar terms (*The Economist*, 7 November 1987).

115 This was the principal objective of the September 1986 Gleneagles meeting of the Community finance ministers (*Le Monde*, 14 September 1987).

116 Balladur's frustration at German and American stubbornness also encouraged him to be the first official from the participating countries to announce publicly that the secret target controls did in fact exist (*La Tribune de l'expansion*, 4 January 1988).

117 For a full description of this policy, its success and its impact on the French economy see Fitoussi (1993).

118 See *Economie et Statistiques*, 108, June 1985; and *Economie et Statistiques*, 203, November, 1987.

119 See, for example, the comments of Pierre Netter, President of the Permanent Assembly of the Chambers of Commerce, following the March 1986 legislative elections (*Le Monde*, 23/24 March 1986).

120 Begg and Wyplosz, 1992. IMF reports of 1984 and 1986 also confirmed the significant benefits of the EMS (Ungerer *et al.*, *The European Monetary System: Recent Developments* (Washington: IMF, December 1986)).

121 For example, André Grjebine, 'Contre la dictature du mark', *Libération*, 29 January 1988; and Serge Federbusch, 'Les faiblesses du franc fort', *Le Monde*, 12 January 1988.

122 For example, the IPECODE (close to the CNPF) study which recommended an 8 or 9 per cent devaluation in the second trimester of 1986 (*Le Monde*, 3 July 1985).

123 On the Right, see the writings of Jean-Jacques Rosa in *Le Figaro* and on the Left, see the writings of André Grjebine.

124 See, for example, Fabius (1985).

125 Both Banque Indosuez and Crédit Lyonnais presented studies in 1984 on the need to promote the use of the ECU and to remove existing national obstacles to its increased use (*Financial Times*, 10 July 1984 and *Les Echos*, 7 August 1984).

126   It was during this period that Bérégovoy established himself as the great defender of the strong franc policy. For the development of Bérégovoy's economic thinking see Aeschimann and Riché (1996) and Bauchard (1994, 'Deuxième Partie: Pierre Bérégovoy').

127   However, as late as June 1983, Prime Minister Mauroy launched a public attack on the 'Solemn Declaration on European Union', the Stuttgart Declaration, which advocated, among other demands, the reinforcement of the EMS (Robin, 1985, p. 219).

128   Dyson claims that the inclusion of the EMU goal in the SEA represents a success for the French (1994, p. 117). The analysis here demonstrates that none of the leading French policymakers sought EMU. Delors did so only once he had become Commission president. Giscard d'Estaing, while influential, was not a member of the RPR–UDF government during this period.

129   Numerous articles in the French press, on both the Left and the Right, argued in favour of the ECU along these lines. See, for example, 'L'Ecu, rival du dollar?', in the conservative weekly *La Vie Française*, 6 June 1983 and 11–17 May 1984; and 'L'Ecu "über alles"', *Le Monde*, 30 September 9/1 October 1984).

130   For example, the comments of the left-wing nationalist Chevènement in *Financial Times*, 10 May 1983 and *Le Monde*, 2 June 1983. For details on the internal Party debate on the EMS between 1984–86, see Haywood, 1989, pp. 246–50.

131   The CERES faction decided to campaign in the June 1984 European elections for renegotiation of French EMS membership (D. Motchane, *Le Monde*, 17 March 1984).

132   Starting in September 1987, Balladur and other RPR members of the government began to call the EMS a 'mark zone'.

133   Interviews with former members on the Bérégovoy and Balladur staffs.

134   While it is necessary to confirm the impact of Genscher's diplomatic sensitivity upon the formation of German policy with German officials, it is interesting that many French policymakers and observers agree that this was likely the most important German motive (interviews). Dyson (1994, p. 255) and De Grauwe (1993) argue that the Maastricht Treaty should be seen 'as a political exercise in postponing conflict between two key interests,' those of Germany and the soft currency countries. However, it is crucial to emphasize that the French, alone among the European partners, were able to force the Germans to the negotiating table.

5   Negotiating the EMU project, May 1988 to December 1991

135   While there have been numerous studies on the Maastricht Treaty, only a handful of authors have specifically analysed French motives and the development of French policy during the negotiations leading to the Maastricht Summit: most notably, Aeschimann and Riché (1996), Balleix-Banerjee (1997, 1999), Dyson (1994), Dyson and Featherstone (1999), Moravcsik

(1998), and Ungerer (1993). Dyson (1997) provides a synoptic account of the inter-institutional dynamics of French policymaking on EMU and the institutional implications of the project for the French State.

136 On this accomplishment see 'Un franc fort ne fait pas le printemps', *L'Evène-ment du jeudi*, 21–27 May 1992. The drive to replace the mark as the EMS anchor currency is discussed in Chapter 6.

137 France succeeded in abolishing capital controls from 1 January 1990, six months in advance of the 30 June deadline.

138 For a more detailed summary of the conclusions of the Delors Report see D. Gros and N. Thygesen, 1992, pp. 317–23.

139 The European ministers of finance had agreed to proceed with the IGC over a year earlier (*Agence Europe*, 15 November 1989, 5131).

140 This motive is also emphasized by Dyson (1994), Dyson and Featherstone (1999), Eichengreen and Frieden (1993), Fitoussi (1995), Garrett (1993), Grieco (1995), Moravcsik (1998) and Sandholtz (1993).

141 This is incorrectly claimed by numerous scholars including, for example, Vernet (1992).

142 For an analysis of French policy see *Agence Europe* (7 March 1991, 5446) and Balleix-Banerjee (1997, pp. 461–518). While the details of French policy were determined principally by Bérégovoy and Treasury officials, the Ministry of Foreign Affairs and the President's general secretariat had some input.

143 The French draft treaty (article 5–10) proposes that at the subsequent vote to determine which countries would participate in the final stage, the member states would decide by qualified majority to determine if at least eight of the member states were able to proceed.

144 The role of the EMI, it was finally agreed, was to reinforce the co-ordination of monetary policies, oversee the operation of the EMS, promote the development of the ECU, and prepare for a single monetary policy. On the European currency, article 109f.2 of the Treaty states that the EMI should 'facilitate the use of the ECU and oversee its development, including the smooth functioning of the ECU clearing system'. Meeting in Basle on 29 October, the Central Bank Governors left open certain aspects of the statutes of the EMI, including the structure of the direction; the voting procedures within the Institute; the constitution of its capital; and its location. Given the considerable disagreement between member states, decision on these matters was left until later.

145 According to French negotiators, even without qualified majority, several countries wishing to move to Stage Three could not be prevented from doing so (interview).

146 Other aspects of economic performance could be taken into account, such as the balance of payments and unit labour costs (article 109j, 1&2).

147 See the French draft treaty, *Agence Europe*, 28–29 January 1991, 5419.

148 This was later confirmed by an October 1993 ruling of the German Constitutional Council.

149 Interviews with members of Bérégovoy's support staff.

150 *Financial Times*, 8 June 1988, confirmed by Treasury officials.

151 P. Fabra, *Le Monde*, 30 May 1989. Moreover, the Louvre accords requested Germany and Japan to stimulate their economies, with lower interest rates, at the worst possible moment (P. Fabra, *Le Monde*, 10 April 1990).

152 See, for example, Jean Denizet, 'Mondialisation de l'économie et changes flottants sont inconciliables', *La Tribune de l'expansion*, 16 June 1989.

153 The imposition of low inflationary growth throughout the Community would undermine much of the competitive element of the policy of 'competitive disinflation'!

154 Bérégovoy was very critical of post-reunification German policy: 'The Germans seem to want to ask all from monetary policy and nothing from budgetary policy, which compromises growth in Europe and in Germany.' (*Le Quotidien de Paris*, 20 December 1990, author's translation)

155 For example, regarding the claim that the single market depends upon exchange rate stability, a large number of studies fail to show any significant effect of exchange rate volatility on the volume of foreign trade or on the prices used in foreign trade (Begg and Wyplosz, 1992). Most of the studies have been produced since 1988. However, prior to 1988, there were also very few studies demonstrating the economic benefits of EMU and there were numerous articles expressing scepticism as to the economic impact of monetary union prior to the move to the IGC (Begg and Wyplosz, 1992).

156 At the European level, this *a posteriori* economic justification came in the form of the Commission's *One Market , One Money* (1990).

157 For a more detailed account of this opposition see Aeschimann and Riché (1996) and Balleix-Banerjee (1997;1999).

158 Moreover, it should be recalled that French monetary history was considerably different from that of Germany. Although inflation had repeatedly been a problem both prior to and since World War II, the Laval Deflation of the mid-1930s was generally perceived to be the most economically disastrous monetary development in the twentieth century – and this was strongly associated with Bank of France 'independence'.

159 See, for example, the writings of J.-P. Patat, Deputy Director of Studies at the Bank of France (including 1992); also interview, 21 March 1994. Bank of France officials resorted on numerous occasions to writing anonymous articles in support of independence on economic grounds. See, for example, 'La réforme du pouvoir monétaire en France', *Commentaire*, 31, Autumn 1985, pp. 788–96.

160 Aglietta (1988) claims that the relationship between the state and the central bank is not the real problem.
'Monetary systems each have their own particular history. It is only in federal countries that central banks need to be independent of government. To create such a relationship in a highly centralised nation would be totally artificial and would not at any rate provide a real guarantee of anti-inflationary monetary policies, which is economic not juridicial. What is essential is that the central bank is not the prisoner of a financial structure that requires it, under pain of destabilising this structure, to monetise public or private debts. It is the financial structure which must be transformed so that the central bank is not required to finance financial institutions. The policy must define the general conditions of the liquidity for all of the national economy. To achieve this judicial change is insufficient: what is needed is financial deregulation. This has been achieved in France. . . . The dependence that existed was not *vis-à-vis* government but rather a structural dependence which limited the Bank of France's margin of manoeuvre. . . .

The aim was to organise an open financial market in which the banks could lend without perturbing excessively the interest rates.... Internal deregulation and the raising of the external controls on capital movements go together.' (p. 19, author's translation)

161 Delors himself did not believe in central bank independence when the Committee was established in June 1988 (Dyson, interview, 26 June 1998).

162 De Larosière also defended the idea of '*gouvernement économique*', although he made it clear that his vision was decidedly different from that advocated by Bérégovoy and Mitterrand, and more in line with that of the Bundesbank. De Larosière sought to grant the Council the power to survey national budgets, make public recommendations on adjustments to member states not respecting the convergence criteria and impose fines on recalcitrant member states (de Larosière, *Banque de France-Info*, 90–08, 1 March 1990 and 90–30, 22 October 1990).

163 The Dutch presidency presented a couple of texts (*Agence Europe*, 9 May 1990, 5250) as did the Commission (*Agence Europe*, 18 May 1990, 5257).

164 These include: deficit at less than 3 per cent of GDP; debt at less than 60 per cent; an average rate of inflation, over a period of one year before the examination, at no more than 1.5 points above the average of the three best performing member states; and an average long term interest rate, over a period of one year before the examination, that does not exceed by more than 2 percentage points that of the average of the three best performing member states in terms of price stability (*Treaty on European Union*, Article 109j).

165 One of the leading French negotiators, interview.

166 However, even then, the French also argued in favour of the possible imposition of sanctions against countries which failed to adopt economic policies which maintained monetary stability (draft treaty article 1–3.3).

167 For example, Mitterrand confirmed that he hoped that Europe was moving towards 'a system that would eventually be federal' (*Agence Europe*, 28 June 1990). In his April 1988 election campaign document, *Lettre à tous les Français*, Mitterrand stated his commitment to a 'United States of Europe' but did not clarify what this meant in institutional terms.

168 See, for example, Bérégovoy's comments in *La Tribune de l'Expansion* (8 October 1990): 'It is very important to accompany EMU with a true political union. If not, democracy would be excluded.' (author's translation)

169 The French recognized that it was necessary to accept some political integration in order to give the German government something to present to the German population, resolutely hostile to EMU. Knowing full well the extent of French reticence on political integration, the Bundesbank played publicly with the idea of PU, repeatedly raising the necessary link between EMU and PU. See Marsh (1992) and the comments made by Pöhl (1989) in a paper attached to the Delors Report.

170 See, for example, Tiersky (1992) who claims simplistically that there were tit-for-tat advances: the Germans accepted EMU while the French accepted the establishment of a Common Foreign and Security Policy (CFSP).

171 Delors argued on several occasions – *even after* the Mitterrand and Kohl initiative on PU in April 1990 – that the Europeans should focus their efforts entirely on EMU and leave PU until a later date (for example, his speech to the European Parliament in May 1990 (*Agence Europe*, 31 May 1990, 5266).

172   For clues on Delors' attitudes see Ross (1995, notably 'Conclusions') and Grant (1994).
173   For a good example of the differences, see the interview published in the *Le Figaro* (4 December 1990) with Michèle Alliot-Marie, RPR Assistant General Secretary responsible for European Affairs, and the former minister of european affairs in the 1986–88 Chirac Government, Bernard Bosson (UDF).
174   See, for example, Balladur's comments in *Le Monde*, 26 May 1990. The depth of Balladur's opposition to a single currency must be questioned, given his rapid conversion in favour of the EMU project early in the 1992 referendum campaign (Balleix-Banerjee, 1993).
175   'Qui a peur de l'Ecu?', *Le Nouvel Observateur*, 12 April 1990. Balladur lent full support to British Chancellor of the Exchequer, John Major's plan for a parallel currency and claimed that their projects corresponded exactly (*Agence Europe*, 29 June 1990, 5285).
176   See, for example, Eichengreen and Frieden (1993).
177   Moravcsik (1998, p. 380) correctly challenges claims that business support did not exist. However, this should not lead to the conclusion that business interests created the momentum behind the project (Sandholtz, 1993).
178   Former high level Bank of France official, interview; Dyson *et al.*, 1994.
179   For a discussion of the impact of EMU upon the economic policymaking power structure of the French State see Dyson *et al.* (1994).
180   These are drawn in part from Dyson (1997, pp. 64–8) and Balleix-Banerjee (1997, 1999).

6   After Maastricht, December 1991 to January 1999

181   Accounts of French policymaking during this period include Abdelal (1998), Aeschimann and Riché (1996), Balleix-Banerjee (1997, 1999), Bauchard (1994), Connolly (1995), and Mélitz (1994). Abdelal provides an account of French 'followership' in the EMS in the post-1993 period which stresses French power motives and the French desire to keep the EMU project on track in order to share monetary power with the Germans. Although he does not enter into a detailed study of French motives, his thesis corresponds closely to the arguments made in this chapter. Studies of Franco-German monetary relations during this period include Andrews (1995), Cameron (1993) and Wood (1995). German motives and attitudes are explored in Loedel (1993, 1999) and Smith and Sandholtz (1995). Busch (1994) and Dyson (1994), Sandholtz (1995, 1996) attempt to interpret the impact of currency turmoil upon the monetary integration process.
182   All figures cited in this section are drawn from OECD (1994 and 1999).
183   Bérégovoy was on the verge of devaluing the franc on 22 September 1992, when speculation subsided (Aeschimann and Riché, 1996, pp. 153–7).
184   The French public deficit rose from 2.0 per cent of GDP in 1991 to 3.2 in 1992 and 4.5 in 1993.
185   French foreign currency reserves fell by more than ff100 billion (£13 billion) in the week prior to 29 July (according to Bank of France figures released on 5 August 1993 and quoted in *Financial Times*, 6 August 1993).

186   The Germans lowered their repo rate by 0.15 points to 6.8 per cent which helped the French avoid a large devaluation of the franc.

187   These are outlined in article 109f and the Protocol on the Statute of the European Monetary Institute annexed to the Treaty.

188   Sapin had previously recommended an early move to independence in order to stem speculation against the franc, but Bérégovoy opposed the move, fearing that it would damage Socialist chances in the upcoming legislative elections (interviews; Aeschimann and Riché, 1996, p. 164).

189   This decision to extend the convergence programmes to 1996, gave Germany an extra year to cope with the huge cost of unification and provided the French with increased room to manoeuvre on its deficit.

190   Dyson (1994, p. 253) claims that the decision to maintain high interest rates and not to take advantage of the new scope for flexibility in monetary policies, provides an example of how economic policy ideas – in this case the policy of 'competitive disinflation' – 'imprison policy actors'. This ignores the French desire to ensure the survival of the EMU project.

191   Aeschimann and Riché, 1996, pp. 208–11; Connolly, 1995, pp. 308*ff*. Alphandéry's 'gaffe' provoked the hostile reaction of the Bundesbank which, a week later, lowered its repo rates 50 basic points, below short term French rates, thus challenging French efforts to maintain lower rates than the Germans. The timid French response – lowering rates to exactly German levels – was seen as a sign of French weakness on the currency markets, and sparked off the July speculation crisis which led to the near collapse of the ERM.

192   The issue brought in a vast sum – 110 billion francs, or more than 1 per cent of GDP.

193   De Larosière, interview in the newsletter of the French banking association (AFB), 5 April 1993; cited in Connolly, 1995, p. 301. De Larosière confirmed this claim when interviewed (26 August 1994).

194   Trichet did not confirm this when interviewed but other Treasury and Bank of France officials did.

195   Chancellor Kohl played a crucial role in imposing this deal upon a reluctant Bundesbank in part in exchange for an agreement that Germany would insist upon the devaluation of the lira. Köhler and Tietmeyer met with Sapin and Trichet in Paris on 12 September to arrange the details of the deal (Aeschimann and Riché, 1996, pp. 142–75).

196   French government demands were supported intellectually by numerous academics including André Grjebine (see, for example, *Le Monde*, 6 October 1992 and *Le Figaro*; 8 January 1993, interviews, 3 and 10 April 1994).

197   While the Bundesbank officially denied the existence of the letter, Schlesinger partially invoked it in public on numerous occasions (see, for example, *Libération*, 3 October 1992).

198   Connolly (1995), Loedel (1999) and Marsh (1992) outline the various manoeuvres of the Bundesbank to preserve its autonomy and the dominant position of the mark.

199   Noyer, with no previous experience working in a central bank and not trained as a monetary economist, was a unique appointment to the ECB. Rather his background was typical of heads of the French Treasury: general

training in public administration at the *Ecole Nationale d'Administration* and then in financial management in the Financial Inspectorate.

200   See, for example, Barre's comments at the February 1993 Davos meeting (*La Croix*, 2 February 1993).

201   These claims were also frequently made, in the context of interviews, by Treasury and Bank of France officials, journalists, support staff members and politicians.

202   On the Left these academic critics included André Grjebine, Jean-Paul Fitoussi (1995) and Emmanuel Borgues; while on the Right, Jean-Jacques Rosa (1998) and Alain Cotta were two of the leading liberal critics. Fitoussi (1995) accepted that the long-term objectives of the report were desirable, but felt that the underlying obsession with inflation – which had ceased to be a problem – was misguided and excessively reduced the money supply. Moreover, he argued that the social impact, in terms of unemployment, was too high a price to pay, and required the adoption of a more moderate policy.

203   Raymond Barre, argued that it was a mistake to see the ERM prematurely as a *de facto* MU (*Financial Times*, 4 February 1993). The Germans and British also consistently argued in favour of a more flexible EMS which worked to undermine international confidence in the ERM parities.

204   A group of well-known MIT professors argued this point in an article published simultaneously in the *Financial Times* (6 August 1993) and *Le Monde*.

205   At the Dublin European Council, Chirac claimed that the Germans agreed to create the Euro-X in exchange for the French accepting the 'Growth and Stability' pact. European ministers of finance reached agreement on the powers and operation of the Euro-X in October 1997. It was relabelled the Euro-11 following the determination of the number of countries able and willing to participate in Stage Three of the EMU project.

206   'On n'est plus très loin du gouvernement économique', interview with Jean Lemierre in *Libération*, 13 January 1999. Jean Lemierre, former head of the French Treasury and the first president of the Economic and Financial Committee, made such announcements to the French press upon the creation of the council at the start of 1999. The powers of the new Economic and Financial Committee do not reinforce those of the Euro-11. Like the former Monetary Committee, this new body includes leading central bank officials and the heads of national treasuries. It incorporates the principal responsibilities of the former Monetary Committee, placing emphasis upon economic policy co-ordination (which explains the change in name). Like its predecessor, the new Economic and Financial Committee was to be the principal body in which detailed negotiations and decisions take place, leaving Ecofin to ratify the decisions or to negotiate and make decisions in those situations in which the treasury officials and bank governors are not able to reach agreement. In June 1998, the Commission's proposals to strengthen economic policy co-ordination in the context of the new Committee and the Euro-11, were rejected by the member states.

207   On the 13 May 1992 vote in the National Assembly, 88 members of the RPR (including Chirac) abstained and 31 voted against. Only seven RPR members voted in favour.

208 In a pre-referendum poll (cited in *Financial Times*, 3 September 1992), two-thirds of RPR members were shown to be against the Maastricht Treaty, 39 per cent of the UDF, 88 per cent of the National Front, at least 19 per cent of the Socialists, 61 per cent of the PCF, 38 per cent of the *Génération Ecologie* (officially yes) and 47 per cent of *Les Verts* (the leadership of which was unable to adopt an official position).

209 For a detailed description of the development of French public opinion see the annual surveys in Sofres (1990–99); and Balleix-Banerjee (1997, pp. 146*ff*). Precise poll results depended upon the wording of the question but support for both the EMS and the EMU project remained consistently above 50 per cent.

210 This was due principally to the strong opposition in Germany to EMU. It would have been very difficult for Kohl to sell the re-establishment of the project to the German population or to ignore the Maastricht rule of no realignments for two years.

Conclusion

211 See the section on international and European monetary power in Chapter 1.

212 This widens Story's (1988) 'power politics' perspective. One of the best studies of Franco-German relations and their importance to European integration is Simonian (1985).

213 For a brief survey of realist and neo-realist explanations of co-operation between states, see Haas (1990, pp. 39–47).

214 Moravcsik effectively recognizes the importance of economic and monetary power when he writes: 'The central French economic goal – greater macro-economic *flexibility* through restraints on the Bundesbank and multilateral financing of central bank intervention – remained the same regardless of whether the forum was regional, bilateral or multilateral' (Moravcsik, 1998, p. 412) (italics added). However, Moravcsik confuses goals with power. To be precise, the French sought the economic (monetary) *goal* of lowering domestic interest rates (and related goals) by increasing their economic and monetary *power* (flexibility) in relation to the Germans. The commercial interests of powerful economic producers – which, according to liberal intergovernmentalism, are the principal factor determining national preferences – are shown to be of *secondary* importance in the development of French policy on monetary co-operation and integration. This is explained in the domestic politics section below.

215 Haas (1990) provides a useful definition of this concept. 'An epistemic community is a professional group that believes in the same cause-and-effect relationship, truth tests to assess theory and shares common values. As well as sharing an acceptance of a common body of facts, its members share a common interpretative framework, or "consensual knowledge", from which they convert such facts, or observations, to policy-relevant conclusions. . . . An epistemic community's power resource, domestically and internationally, is its authoritative claim to knowledge. To the extent that its members can penetrate the walls of government and maintain their authority, new orders of behavior are possible' (p. 55).

Bibliography

BOOKS

Abadie, F. and Corcelette, Jean-Pierre, *George Pompidou, 1911–1974* (Paris: Editions Ballard, 1994).

Aeschimann, E. and Riché, P., *La guerre de sept ans: histoire secrète du franc fort, 1989–1996* (Paris: Calmann-Lévy, 1996).

Aglietta, M. and Orléans, A., *La violence de la monnaie* (Paris: PUF, 1982).

Attali, J., *Verbatim I, II, III* (Paris: Fayard, 1993, 1994, 1995).

Balleix-Banerjee, C., *La France et la Banque Centrale Européenne* (Paris: PUF, 1999).

Banuri, T. and Schor, J. B., eds, *Financial Openness and National Autonomy : Opportunities and Constraints (Oxford: Clarendon Press, 1992).*

Batten, D. S. and Michael P. B., *The Conduct of Monetary Policy in the Major Industrial Countries*: *Instruments and Operating Procedures* (Washington: IMF, July 1990).

Bauchard, P., *Deux ministres trop tranquils* (Paris: Belfond, 1994).

Bauchard, P., *La Guerre des Deux Roses* (Paris: Grasset, 1986).

Bell, D. and Criddle, B., *The French Socialist Party* (Oxford: Oxford University Press, 1988).

Benoit, B., *Social-Nationalism: an Anatomy of French Euroscepticism* (Aldershot: Ashgate, 1997).

Bergsten, C. F., *The Dilemmas of the Dollar: The Economics and Politics of United States International Monetary Policy* (New York: New York University Press, 1975 and second edition, London: M. E. Sharpe, 1996).

Biffaud, O. and Mauduit, L., *La Grande Méprise* (Paris: Grasset, 1996).

Boissonnat, J., *La révolution de 1999. L'Europe avec l'Euro* (Paris: Sand, 1998).

Carr, E. H., *Twenty Years' Crisis 1916–1936, an introduction to the study of international relations*, 2nd edn (London: Macmillan, 1946).

Cloos, J., *Le traité de Maastricht. Genèse, analyse, commentaires*, (Brussels: Etablissements Emile Bruylant, 1993).

Cobham, D., ed., *European Monetary Upheavals* (Manchester: Manchester University Press, 1994).

Coffey, P., *Europe and Money* (London: Macmillan, 1977).

Cohen, Samy and Smouts, Marie-Claude, eds, *La politique extérieure de Valéry Giscard d'Estaing* (Paris: Presses de la Fondation nationale des sciences politiques, 1985).

Colombani, J.-M., *Portrait du Président* (Paris: Gallimard, 1985).

Commissariat Général au Plan, *Quelle Stratégie Européenne pour la France dans les Années 80?* (Paris: La Documentation Française, 1983).

Connolly, B., *The Rotten Heart of Europe, The Dirty War for Europe's Money* (London: Faber and Faber, 1995).

Cousté, P. B., Visine, F. and Chirac, J. *Pompidou et l'Europe* (Paris: Librairies Techniques, 1974).

Delors, J., *La France par l'Europe* (Paris: Bernard Grasset, 1988).

Delwit, P., *Les partis socialistes et l'intégration européenne* (Brussels: Université de Bruxelles, 1995), Chapitre 2, 'La SFIO et le parti socialiste face aux Communautés européennes', pp. 55–127.

Denizet, J., *Le Dollar* (Paris: Fayard, 1985).

Develle, M., *Vive le franc* (Paris: Olivier Orban, 1988).

Droulers, F., *Histoire de l'écu européen* (Paris: Aria-Créations, 1990).

Du franc Poincaré à l'écu (Paris: Cheff, 1993).

Dyson, K., *Elusive Union: The Process of Economic and Monetary Union in Europe* (London: Longman, 1994).

Dyson, K and Featherstone, K., *The Road to Maastricht: Negotiating Economic and Monetary Union* (Oxford: Oxford University Press, 1999).

Eichengreen, B. and Frieden, J., *The Political Economy of European Monetary Unification* (Boulder, Colorado: Westview, 1994).

Eichengreen, B. and Frieden, J., eds, *The Political Economy of European Integration: The Challenges Ahead* (Ann Arbor: Michigan University Press, 1997).

Elgie, R., *The Role of the Prime Minister in France 1981–91* (London: Macmillan Press Ltd., 1993), 'Crisis Policy-Making (II): The Politics of Devaluation, March 1983', pp. 122–39.

Esambert, B., *Pompidou, capitaine d'industries* (Paris: Odile Jacob, 1994).

Estier, C. and Neiertz, V., *Véridique Histoire d'un septennat peu ordinaire* (Paris: Grasset, 1987).

Fabius, L., *Le Coeur du Futur*, (Paris: Calmann-Lévy, 1985).

Favier, P. and Martin-Roland, M., *La Décennie Mitterrand, I, Les ruptures (1981–1984)* (Paris: Editions du Seuil, 1990).

Favier, P. and Martin-Roland, M., *La Décennie Mitterrand, II, Les épreuves (1984–1988)* (Paris: Editions du Seuil, 1991).

Featherstone, K., *Socialist Parties and European Integration, a Comparative History* (Manchester: Manchester University Press, 1988).

Atkinson, A. B., Flemming, J. S., Fitoussi, J.-P., Blanchard, O. and Malinuaud, E., *Competitive Disinflation. The mark and budgetary politics in Europe* (Oxford: Oxford Univeristy Press, 1993).

Fitoussi, J.-P., *Le Débat Interdit, Monnaie, Europe, Pauvreté* (Paris: Arléa, 1995).

Frears, J. R., *France in the Giscard Presidency* (London, George Allen and Unwin, 1981), Chapter 7, 'The Economy', pp. 128–37.

Fridenson, P. and Straus, A, eds, *Le Capitalisme français* (Paris: Fayard, 1987).

Friend, J., *The Long Presidency* (Oxford: Westview, 1998).

Friend, J., *Seven Years in France: François Mitterrand and the Unintended Revolution, 1981–1988* (London: Westview, 1989).

Fonteneau, A. and Muet, P.-A., *La Gauche face à la crise* (Paris: Presse de la FNSP, 1985).

Gauron, A., *Années de rêve, années de crises*, tome II (Paris: La Découverte, 1988).

Genscher, H.-D., *Rebuilding a house divided: a memoir by the architect of Germany's reunification* (New York: Broadway, 1998) (translated from the 1995 original in German).

Georges Pompidou et l'Europe (Paris: Complexe, 1995).

Giovannini, A. and Mayer, C., *European financial integration* (Cambridge: Cambridge University Press, 1991).

Goodman, J. B. *Monetary Sovereignty: the Politics of Central Banking in Western Europe*, (Ithaca: Cornell, 1992).

Grant, C., *Delors. Inside the House that Jacques Built* (London: Nicholas Brealey Publishing, 1994).

Gretschmann, D., ed., *EMU: Implications for National Policy-Makers* (The Hague: Martinu and Nijhoff, 1993).

Gros, D. and Thygesen, N., *European Monetary Integration, From the European Monetary System to European Monetary Union* (Harlow, Essex: Longman Group UK Limited, 1992).

Guerrieri, P. and Padoan, P. C., *The Political Economy of European Integration* (London: Harvester Wheatsheaf, 1989).

Guyomarch, A., Machin, H. and Ritchie, E., *France in the European Union* (London: Macmillan, 1988).

Hall, Peter, *Governing the economy, the politics of state intervention in Britain and France* (Cambridge: Polity Press, 1986).

Haas, P. M., *Saving the Mediterranean* (New York: Columbia University Press, 1990).

Harrop, J., *The Political Economy of Integration in the EC* (Aldershot: Edward Elgar, 1992), 2nd edn.

Hayward, J., *The State and the Market Economy* (Brighton: Wheatsheaf, 1986).

Heclo, H., *Modern Social Politics in Britain and Sweden* (New Haven: Yale University Press, 1974).

Hodgman, D. R., *National Monetary Policies and International Monetary Cooperation* (Boston: Little, Brown and Company, 1974).

Jacquet, P., ed., *Europe 1992: L'intégration financière, Enjeux internationaux*, travaux et recherches de l'IFRI (Paris: Masson, 1989).

Jean, A., *L'écu, le SME et les marchés financiers* (Paris: Organisation, 1990).

Jeanneny, J.-M., ed., *L'Economie Française depuis 1967* (Paris: Seuil, 1989).

July, S., *Les Années Mitterrand* (Paris: Grasset, 1986).

Jurgensen, P., *Ecu: naissance d'une monnaie* (Paris: J. C. Lattès, 1991).

Keeler, J. and Schain, M., *Chirac's challenge: liberalisation, Europeanisation and malaise in France* (Basingstoke: Macmillan, 1996).

Kenen, P. B., *EMU in Europe: moving beyond Maastricht* (Cambridge: Cambridge University Press, 1995).

Kennedy, E., *The Bundesbank: Germany's Central Bank in the International Monetary System* (London: Royal Institute for International Affairs, 1991).

Kingdon, John, *Agendas, Alternatives and Public Policies* (New York: Harper Collins College, 1995).

Koch, H. (1983) *L'histoire de la Banque de France et de la monnaie sous la IV République* (Paris: Dunod).

Kruse, D. C., *Monetary Integration in Western Europe: EMU, EMS and Beyond* (London: Butterworths, 1980).

Lauber, V., *The Political Economy of France from Pompidou to Mitterrand* (New York: Praeger, 1983).

Lauber, V., *The Politics of Economic Policy, France 1974–1982*, The Washington Papers, Vol. XI, 97 (New York: Praeger, 1983).

Laughland, J., *The Death of Politics. France under Mitterrand* (London: Michael Joseph, 1994).

Lindblom, C., *The Policy-making process* (Englewood Cliffs: Prentice-Hall, 1968).

Loedel, Peter, *Deutsche Mark Politics: Germany in the European Monetary System* (Boulder, CO: Lynne Rienner, 1999).

Loriaux, M., *France After Hegemony* (Ithica: Cornell University Press, 1991).

Ludlow, P., *The Making of the European Monetary System: A case study of the politics of the European Community* (London: Butterworth Scientific, 1982).

Lynch, F., *France and the International Economy* (London: Routledge, 1997).

Kuisel, R. F., *Capitalism and the State in Modern France* (Cambridge: Cambridge University Press, 1981).

Marsh, D., *The Bundesbank* (London, Mandarin, 1992).

Mamou, Y., *Une machine de pouvoir, la Direction du Trésor* (Paris: La Découverte, 1987).

Mauroy, P., *C'est ici le chemin* (Paris: Flammarion, 1982).

McNamara, K., *The Currency of Ideas: Monetary Politics in the European Union*, (London: Cornell University Press, 1988).

Mitterrand, F., *Ici et Maintenant*, (Paris: Fayard, 1980).

Moravcsik, A., *The Choice for Europe* (London: University College London Press, 1998).

Nay, C., *Les Sept Mitterrand, ou les métamorphoses d'un septennat* (Paris: Grasset, 1988).

Odell, J. S., *U.S. International Monetary Policy: Markets, Power and Ideas as Sources of Change* (Princeton: Princeton University Press, 1982).

Patat, J. P. and Lutfalla, M., *Histoire monétaire de la France au XXe siècle* (Paris: Economica, 1986), *A Monetary History of France in the Twentieth Century*, translated edition (London: Macmillan, 1990).

Pébereau, M., *La Politique Économique de la France: Les relations économiques financières et monétaires internationales* (Paris: Armand Colin, 1990).

Pedersen, T., *Germany, France and the Integration of Europe: a realist interpretation* (London: Pinter, 1998).

Pfister, T., *La vie quotidienne à Matignon au temps de l'Union de la Gauche* (Paris: Hachette, 1985).

Prate, A., *La France et sa Monnaie: Essai sur les relations entre la Banque de France et les gouvernements* (Paris: Julliard, 1987).

Reuters, *Euro: Les enjeux pour la France* (Paris: Economica, 1998).

Riché, P. and Wyplosz, C., *L'Union monétaire de l'Europe* (Paris: Editions du Seuil, 1993).

Robin, G., *La diplomatie de Mitterrand ou le triomphe des apparences* (Les-Loges-en-Josas, Bièvre, 1985).

Rosa, J.-J., *L'Erreur Européenne* (Paris: Grasset, 1998).

Ross, G. Hoffmann, S. and Malzacher, S., *et al.*, *The Mitterrand Experiment, Continuity and Change in Modern France* (Cambridge: Polity Press, 1987), esp. 'Introduction', pp. 3–16, and 'The difficult Economics of French Socialism', pp. 17–54, with articles by Richard F. Kuisel, Robert Boyer and Peter A. Hall.

Ross, G., *Jacques Delors and European Integration* (Cambridge: Polity Press, 1995).

Roussel, E., *George Pompidou* (Editions Jean-Claude Lattès, 1984), esp. Chapter 22, 'Effort industriel et ouverture européenne', pp. 437–53.

Rueff, J., *L'age de l'inflation* (Paris: Payot, 1963).

Rueff, J., *Le péché monétaire de l'occident* (Paris: Plon, 1971).

Rueff, J., *Oeuvres Complètes I, De l'aube au crépuscule, Autobiographie* (Paris: Plon, 1977).

Séguin, P., *Ce que j'ai dit* (Paris: Grasset, 1993).

Séguin, P., *Discours pour la France* (Paris: Grasset, 1992).

Simonian, A. H., *The Privileged Partnership* (Oxford: Clarendon Press, 1985).

Sofres, *L'Etat de l'opinion* (Paris: Editions du Seuil, 1990–94).

Steinherr, A., ed., *30 Years of European Monetary Integration: From the Werner Plan to EMU* (London: Longman, 1994).

Sutton, M., *France and European Union 1944–2000* (London: Longmans, forthcoming).

Swoboda, A. K., ed., *Europe and the Evolution of the International Monetary System* (Paris: Institut Universitaire de Hautes Etudes Internationales, 1973).

Tsoukalis, L., *The New European Economy, The Politics and Economics of Integration*, 2nd revised edn (Oxford: Oxford University Press, 1993).

Tsoukalis, L., *The New European Economy Revisited* (Oxford: Oxford University Press, 1997).

Tsoukalis, L., *The Politics and Economics of European Monetary Integration* (London: George Allen and Unwin, 1977).

Ungerer, H., *A Concise History of European Monetary Integration* (London: Quorum Books, 1997).

Valance, G., *La Légende du franc* (Paris: Flammarion, 1996).

Van Ypersele, J. and Koeune, J.-C., *The European Monetary System* (Luxembourg: Office for Official Publications of the EC, 1985).

Vesperini, J. P., *Le franc dans le Système Monétaire International* (Paris: Economica, 1989).

Welfens, P. J., ed., *European Monetary Integration: from German Dominance to an EC Central Bank?* (Berlin: Springer- Verlag, 1991).

Woolley, J. T., *Monetary Politics: The Federal Reserve and the Politics of Monetary Policy* (New York: Cambridge University Press, 1984).

Articles and chapters in edited books

Abdelal, Rawi, 'The Politics of Monetary Leadership and Followership: Stability in the European Monetary System since the Currency Crisis of 1992', *Political Studies*, XLVI, pp. 236–59.

Aglietta, M., 'L'Evolution du SME vue par un expert français', *Documents*, 4, October 1988, pp. 14–19.

Aglietta, M., 'Etat, monnaie et risque de système en Europe', in Bruno Théret, ed., *L'Etat, la finance et le social, souveraineté nationale et construction européenne* (Paris: Editions de la Découverte, 1995), pp. 432–49.

Aglietta, M., 'L'indépendence de la Banque de France', *Banque*, May 1993, pp. 64–7.

Aglietta, M. and Baulant, C., 'Contrainte extérieure et compétitivité dans la transition vers l'Union économique et monétaire', *Observation et Diagnostics économiques*, 48, January 1994, pp. 7–54.

Aglietta, M. and Mendelek, N., 'Politiques économique nationales et évolution du Système monétaire européen', *Economie perspective internationale*, 4e trimestre, 32, 1987, pp. 43–68.

Albert, M., 'La Désunion Monétaire Européenne', *Revue français de Science Politique*, 22, 2, April 1972, pp. 382–90.

Alphandery, E., 'Le franc contre Mauroy?', *Revue Politique et Parlementaire*, May–June, 1983, pp. 44–7.

Andrews, D. M., 'European Monetary Diplomacy and the Rolling Crisis of 1992–1993', in S. Mazey and C. Rhodes, eds, *The State of the European Community*, Vol. 3 (Boulder, Colorado: Lynne Rienner, 1995), pp. 159–76.

anonymous, 'La Peur du Colosse: en France, La Défiance s'accroît à l'égard des allemands réunifiés, surtout par peur d'une perte d'influence', *Documents*, 3, 1993, pp. 34–7

anonymous, 'La réforme du pouvoir monétaire en France', *Commentaire*, 31, Autumn 1985, pp. 788–96.

Arnould, D., 'Le Nouveau Système Monétaire Européen: seule solution au problème des montants compensatoires?', *Banque* (Paris), 381, February 1979, pp. 161–5.

Artis, M. J., 'The Maastricht Road to Monetary Union', *Journal of Common Market Studies*, 30, 3, September 1992, pp. 299–309.

Artus, P., 'La politique monétaire en France', *Revue français d'économie*, 2, 3, Summer 1987, pp. 165–223.

Balleix-Banerjee, Corinne, 'Libéraux et centristes [français] face au projet de Banque central européenne', *Revue du Marché commun et de l'Union européenne*, 1995, 387, pp. 228–37.

Balleix-Banerjee, Corinne, 'Discours politique et intégration européenne : les gaullistes face au projet de Banque central européenne, *Revue d'Intégration européenne*, 1993, 17, 1, pp. 7–52.

Baslé, M. A. 'Economics and economists in France today', in J. Howorth and G. Ross, eds, *Contemporary France*, Vol. 3 (London: Pinter Publishers, 1989), pp. 205–19.

Baun, M. J., 'The Maastricht Treaty As High Politics: Germany, France and European Integration', *Political Science Quarterly*, 110, 4, 1995–96.

Baverez, N., 'Sur deux erreurs de politique économique: 1. La politique du bloc-or; 2. Le franc fort', *Commentaire*, 66 and 67, 1994.

Beaulieu, P., 'Implications monétaires de l'intégration européenne, *Projet*, février 1971, no. 52, pp. 185–200

Beaulieu, P., 'A propos de la situation monétaire internationale', *Projet*, May 1971, no. 55, pp. 613–17.

Beck, N., 'Domestic Political Sources of American Monetary Policy: 1955–82', *The Journal of Politics*, 46, 3, 1984, pp. 786–817.

Berger, G, 'Le Conflit entre l'Europe et les Etats-Unis', *Revue Française de Sciences Politiques*, 22, 2, April 1972, pp. 348–58.

Bertram, C., 'Le géant qui voulait se faire aussi petit que le nain', *Cadmos*, Winter/Spring, 1992–93, 60–61.

Bloomfield, A., 'The historical setting', in B. Krause and W. Salant, eds, *European Monetary Unification and its Meaning for the United States* (Washington: Brookings, 1973).

Boissieu, C. de, 'French Monetary Policy in the light of European Monetary and Financial Integration', *Tokyo Club Papers*, no. 3, 1989.

Boissieu, C. de, 'Chronique de la rédaction, la nouvelle politique monétaire française', *Revue d'Economie Politique*, 2, February 1987, pp. 156–64.

Boissieu, C. de and Biacabe, J.-L., 'L'Evolution du rôle international du franc et la transition vers l'Union Economique et Monétaire', in *Du franc Poincaré à l'écu* (Paris: CHEFF, 1993), pp. 687–707.

Boissieu, C. de and Pisani-Ferry, Jean, 'The Political Economy of French Economic Policy and the Perspective of EMU', in B. Eichengreen *et al.*, *The Political*

Economy of European Integration: The Challenges Ahead (Ann Arbor: Michigan University Press, 1997).

Bordes, C. and Mélitz, J. 'La coordination des politiques monétaires', *Revue économique politique* (special edition), 101 (1) January–February 1991.

Bordo, M. D., Simard, D. and White, E. N. 'La France et le système monétaire international institué par Bretton Woods', in *Du franc Poincaré à l'écu* (Paris: CHEFF, 1993), pp. 639–75.

Bourel, F., 'Les montants compensatoires et le système monétaire européen', in *Documents: revue des questions Allemandes*, 3, September 1979, pp. 30–8.

Boyer, R., 'The Current Economic Crisis: Its Dynamics and its Implications for France', in G. Ross *et al.*, eds, *The Mitterrand Experiment*, (Cambridge: Polity Press, 1987), pp. 33–53.

Bouvier, J., 'The Banque de France and the State from 1850 to the Present Day', in G. Toniolo, ed., *Central Banks' Independence in Historical Perspective* (Berlin: de Gruyter, 1988), pp. 73–104.

Branca, E., 'Maastricht attérit à Francfort', *Valeurs actuelles*, 8 November 1993.

Brown, W. M., 'World Afloat: National Policies Ruling the Waves', *Essays in International Finance*, 116, May 1976, (Princeton, 1976).

Bruclain, C., 'La Désunion monétaire Européenne', *Chroniques d'Actualité de S.É.D.É.I.S.*, June 1971, 4, 6, pp. 321–31.

Busch, A., 'The Crisis in the EMS', *Government and Opposition*, 29, 1, Winter 1993, pp. 80–96.

Calleo, D. P., 'The Franco-German Partnership in the New Europe', *SAIS Review*, Summer–Autumn, 1993, 13, 2, pp. 25–39.

Cameron, D., 'Economic Policy in the Era of the EMS', in Gregory Flynn, ed., *Remaking the Hexagon, The New France in the New Europe* (Oxford, Westview Press, 1995), pp. 117–57.

Cameron, D., 'Transnational Relations and the Development of European Economic and Monetary Union', in Thomas Risse-Kappen, ed., *Bringing Transnational Relations Back In: Non-State Actors, Domestic Structures, and International Institutions* (Cambridge: Cambridge University Press, 1995).

Campanella, M. L., 'Getting to the Core: A Neo-institutionalist Approach to the EMU', *Government and Opposition*, 30, 3, 1995, pp. 347–69.

Carré de Malberg, N., 'Les inspecteurs des finances et la défense du franc, 1934–36', in *Du franc Poincaré à l'écu* (Paris: CHEFF, 1993), pp. 125–69.

Cobham, D., 'European Monetary Integration: A survey of Recent Literature', *Journal of Common Market Studies*, 29, 4, June 1991, p. 363–83.

Cohen, B. J., 'European Financial Integration and National Banking Interests' in Paulo Guerrieri and Pier Carla Padoa, eds, *The Political Economy of European Integration* (London: Harvester Wheatsheaf, 1989), pp. 144–69.

Cohen, D., Mélitz, J. and Oudiz, D., 'Le système monétaire européen et l'asymétrie franc-mark', *Revue économique*, May 1988, pp. 667–77.

Cohen, E., 'L'Union Economique et Monétaire ou l'échec d'un procès fédératif subreptice', in Bruno Théret, ed., *L'Etat, la finance et le social, souveraineté nationale et construction européenne* (Paris: Editions de la Découverte, 1995), pp. 458–82.

Cohen, E., 'France: National Champions in Search of a Mission', in J. Hayward ed., *Industrial Enterprise and European Integration: from National to International Champions in Europe* (Oxford: Oxford University Press, 1995).

Cole, A., 'Looking on: France and the New Germany', *German Politics*, 2, 3, December 1993, pp. 358–76.

Cross, S. Y., 'Following the Bundesbank: The Spread of Central Bank Independence', *Foreign Affairs*, 73, 2, March/April 1994, pp. 128–35.

Crouhy-Veyrac, L. and Saint-Marc, M., 'Le couple Franc-Mark du SME à l'UEM', in *Du franc Poincaré à l'écu* (Paris: CHEFF, 1993), pp. 707–37.

De Cecco, M., 'The European Monetary System and National Interests', in Paulo Guerrieri and Pier Carla Padoa, eds, *The Political Economy of European Integration* (London: Harvester Wheatsheaf, 1989), pp. 85–99.

De Grauwe, P., 'The Political Economy of Monetary Union in Europe', *The World Economy*, 16, 6 November 1993.

Denizet, J., 'Nécessité d'une Monnaie Européenne', *Revue d'économie politique*, Summer–August 1970, 4, pp. 589–607.

De Porte, A. W., 'France's New Realism', *Foreign Affairs*, 63, 1, Autumn 1984, pp. 144–66.

Dornbusch, R. and Jacquet, P., 'La France et l'Union économique et monétaire européenne', *Observations et diagnostics économique*, 39, 1991, pp. 31–73.

Drain, M., 'La France et la construction européenne: de l'accélération aux-incertitudes', *Rélations Internationales et Stratégiques*, 9, Spring, 1993, pp. 135–46.

Dyson, K., 'EMU, Political Discourse and the Fifth French Republic: Historical institutionalism, path dependence and "craftmen" of discourse', *Modern and Contemporary France*, 7, 2, May 1999.

Dyson, K., 'La France, L'Union économique et monétaire et la construction européenne: renforcer l'exécutif, transformer l'Etat', *Revue Politiques et Management Public*, 13, 3 September 1997, pp. 57–77.

Dyson, K., Featherstone, K. and Michaelopoulos, G., 'Strapped to the mast: EC central bankers between global financial markets and regional integration', *Journal of European Public Policy*, 2, 3 September 1995, pp. 465–87.

Eichengreen, B. and Frieden, J., 'The Political Economy of European Monetary Unification: An Analytical Introduction', *Economics and Politics*, 5, 2, 1993, pp. 85–103.

Fonteneau, A. and Muet, P.-A., 'Reflation and Austerity: Economic Policy under Mitterrand', *Economic Policy*, 16 April 1993.

Frisch, A., 'Les exigences d'une coopération exemplaire', *Documents, Revue des questions allemandes*, 3, 1993, pp. 7–12.

Gabriel, F., 'La Politique Monétaire Française en question', *La Revue Banque*, 522, décembre 1991, pp. 1106–9.

Galilée, 'La Tragédie du "franc fort"', *Revue des deux mondes*, September 1993, pp. 16–27.

Galilée, La Tragédie du "franc fort" II', *Revue des deux mondes*, March 1994.

Garcin, T., 'L'unification allemande et la classe politique française', *Hérodote*, 68, January–March, 1993, 112–24.

Garret, G., 'The Politics of Maastricht', *Economics and Politics*, 4, 2, 1993, pp. 105–23.

Giavazzi, F. and Giovannini, A., 'Modèles du SME: l'Europe n'est-elle qu'une zone deutsche mark?', *Revue économique*, 1988 May, pp. 641–66.

Giavazzi, F. and Pagano, M., 'The advantage of tying one's hands', *European Economic Review*, 32, 1988, pp. 1055–82.

Goodman, J. B., 'Monetary Politics in France, Italy, and Germany: 1973–85', in Paolo Guerrieri and Pier Carla Padoa, eds, *The Political Economy of European Integration* (London: Harvester Wheatsheaf, 1989), pp. 171–201.

Goodman, J. B., 'The Politics of Central Bank Independence' in *Comparative Politics*, 23, 3 April 1991, pp. 329–49.

Goodman, J. B. and Pauly, L. W., 'The Obsolescence of Capital Controls? Economic Management in an Age of Global Markets', *World Politics*, 46, October 1993, pp. 50–82.

Grieco, J. M., 'The Maastricht Treaty, Economic and Monetary Union and the neo-realist research programme', *Review of International Studies*, 21, 1995, pp. 21–40.

Grjebine, A., 'Après Maastricht: des écus et des chômeurs?', *Le débat*, September–October, 1992, 71, pp. 16–42.

Grjebine, A., 'Les trois voies de la construction européenne', *Le débat*, September–October, 1992, 71, pp. 55–7.

Gros, D. and Thygesen, N., 'Vers l'Union monétaire européenne, pourquoi et comment?', *Observation et diagnostics économiques*, 33, October 1990, pp. 131–53.

Haas, P., ed., 'Knowledge, Power and International Policy Co-ordination', special issue of *International Organisation*, 46, 1992.

Halimi, S., 'Less Exceptionalism than meets the eye', in Anthony Daley, *The Mitterrand Era* (London: Macmillan, 1996), pp. 83–96.

Hall, P. A., 'The Evolution of Economic Policy under Mitterrand, in G. Ross *et al.*, *The Mitterrand Experiment* (Cambridge: Polity Press, 1987), pp. 54–74.

Henderson, D., 'International economic integration: progress, prospects and implications', *International Affairs*, 68, 4, 1992, pp. 633–53.

Hirsch, F., 'The political economics of European monetary integration', *The World Today*, 28, 10 October 1972, pp. 424–33.

Hoffmann, S., 'Dilemmes et stratégies de la France dans la nouvelle Europe', *Politique Etrangère*, Winter, 4, 1992.

Huntzinger, J., 'La politique extérieure du parti socialiste', in *Politique étrangère*, 1, 1981, pp. 33–44.

Ikenberry, G. J., Lake, D. A. and Mastanduno, M. 'Introduction: approaches to explaining American foreign economic policy', *International Organization*, 42, 1, Winter 1988, pp. 1–32.

Italianer, A., 'Mastering Maastricht: EMU issues and how they were settled', in K. Gretschmann, ed., *Economic and monetary union. Implications for national policy-makers* (Dordrecht: Martinus Nijhoff Publishers, 1993), pp. 149–67.

Jacquet, P., 'Maastricht, ou la souveraineté retrouvée: Réponse à André Grjebine', *Le débat*, September–October 1992, 71, pp. 43–7.

Jochimsen, R., 'Current Issues on the Policy of the Bundesbank', *German Politics*, 2, 3, December 1993, pp. 341–57.

Kaelble, H., 'Allemagne-France: convergences et divergences', *Le débat*, September–October, 1992, 71, pp. 58–65.

Karailiev, E. and Williams, P., 'La France dans le Système monétaire européen: les incertitudes de la stabilité', *Economie et Finances Agricoles*, 1979 July/December, Caisse National de Credit Agricole, pp. 1–11.

Kassim, Hussein, 'French autonomy and the European Union', *Modern and Contemporary France*, 1997, 5, 2, pp. 167–80.

Kaufmann, H. M., 'The Importance of Being Independent: Central Bank Independence and the European System of Central Banks', in A. M. Sbragia, ed., *Euro-politics: Institutions and Policy-making in the 'New' European Community* (Washington: Brookings Institution, 1992), pp. 267–91.

Kuisel, R. F., 'French Post-War Economic Growth, A Historical Perspective on the *Trente glorieuses*', in G. Ross *et. al.*, eds., *The Mitterrand Experiment*, (Cambridge: Polity Press, 1987), pp. 18–32.

Labarde, P., 'L'Echec du Pari Economique', *Revue des Deux Mondes*, May 1995, pp. 97–111.

Lagayette, P., 'Commentaire' in *Revue d'Economie Financière*, 8/9, March–June, 1989, pp. 129–31.

Lagayette, P., 'Pour l'union monétaire européenne: Réponse à André Grjebine', *Le débat*, September–October, 1992, 71, pp. 48–54.

La Genière, R. de, 'Aspects Monétaires de l'Echéance 92', *La Revue Banque*, April 1989, no. 493, pp. 361–5.

La Genière, R. de, 'Vingt-Cinq Ans de Coopération Monétaire Européenne', *Bulletin Trimestriel de la Banque de France*, 50, March 1984, pp. 23–8.

La Genière, R. de, 'Aspects Extérieurs de la Politique Monétaire Française', *Bulletin Trimestriel de la Banque de France*, 51, June 1984, pp. 25–30.

Landau, J. P., 'Table Ronde: L'union économique et monétaire européenne' (réunissant: P. Artus, C. de Boissieu, G. Etrillard, J. P. Fitoussi, J. P. Landau, P. A. Muet and N. Thygessen) in *Revue française d'économie*, 4, 3, Summer 1989, pp. 157–68.

Lattre, A. de, 'Problèmes posés à un Institut d'émission par la création d'une monnaie commune', *Revue d'économie politique*, July–August, 1970.

Le Cacheux, J. and Lecointe, F., 'La politique de change', Chaptre 16, in J.-M. Jeanneny, ed., *L'Economie Française depuis 1967* (Paris: Seuil, 1989).

Le Gloannec, A.-M., 'Mitterrand et l'Allemagne', *French Politics and Society*, 9, no. 3–4, Summer/Autumn, 1991, pp. 121–9.

Léonard, J., 'Integration financière et union monétaire: la divergence des attitudes nationales', *Revue d'Économie Financière*, 8/9, March–June, 1989, pp. 187–202.

Loriaux, M., 'French Financial Interventionism in the Seventies', *Comparative Politics*, January 1988, pp. 175–93.

Louis, J. V., 'Le lien entre les conférences intergouvernementales sur l'union économique et monétaire et sur l'union politique', in J. Monar *et al.* eds, *The Maastricht treaty on European Union. Legal complexity and political dynamics* (Brussels: European Interuniversity Press, 1993), pp. 163–72.

Main de Boissière, J.-B., 'Vers l'union monétaire', *Defense Nationale*, April 1989, pp. 95–107.

Martin, L., 'International and Domestic Institutions in the EMU Process', *Economics and Politics*, 5, 2, 1993, pp. 125–43.

Marx, B., 'La Relance de l'intégration monétaire européenne', *Economie et Politique*, December 1978, pp. 46–52.

McCarthy, P., 'Can France Survive German Reunification?', *SAIS Review*, Winter–Spring, 1992, 12, 1, pp. 85–100.

Mélitz, J., 'French Monetary Policy and the Recent Speculative Attacks on the franc', in Cobham, D., ed., *European Monetary Upheavals* (Manchester: Manchester University Press, 1994).

Mentré, P., 'Unité monétaire allemande et Union monétaire européenne', *Commentaire*, 13, 50, Summer 1990, pp. 319–22.

Ménudier, H., 'La France et le problème allemand', *Revue française de science politique*, 37, 3, June 1987, pp. 358–70.

Mingasson, J.-P., 'Du Système monétaire européen à l'Union économique et monétaire', *Commentaire*, 13, 50, Summer 1990, pp. 311–17.

Moïsi, D., 'French Foreign Policy: The challenge of Adaptation', *Foreign Affairs*, 67, Autumn 1988, pp. 151–64.

Moïsi, D., 'Mitterrand's Foreign Policy: The Limits of Continuity', *Foreign Affairs*, 60, 2, Winter, 1981/1982, pp. 347–57.

Moravcsik, A., 'Liberal Intergovernmentalism and Integration: A Rejoinder', *Journal of Common Market Studies*, 33, 4 December 1995, pp. 611–28.

Moravcsik, A., 'Preferences and Power in the European Community: A Liberal Intergovernmentalist Approach', *Journal of Common Market Studies*, 31, 4, December 1993, pp. 473–524.

Moravcsik, A., 'Negotiating the Single European Act: national interests and conventional statecraft in the European Community', *International Organization*, 45, 1, Winter 1991, pp. 19–56.

Moreau Defarges, P., 'L'Allemagne et l'avenir de l'unification européenne', *Politique Etrangère*, no. 4, Winter, 1991, 849–57.

Mossé, R., 'La révision du système monétaire international', *Revue politique et parlementaire*, 827, December 1971, pp. 4–19.

Noyer, C., 'A propos du statut et de l'indépendance des banques centrales', *Revue d'économie financière*, September 1992, pp. 13–18.

Paolini, J., 'Les deux politiques européennes de François Mitterrand', *Rélations Internationales et Stratégiques*, 9, Spring, 1993, pp. 124–34.

Parry, G., 'The Interweaving of Foreign and Domestic Policy- Making', *Government Opposition*, 28, 2, 1993, pp. 143–51.

Patat, J.-P., 'Quelques remarques sur la question de l'indépendance de la banque centrale', *Revue d'économie financière*, September 1992, pp. 5–12.

Pelkmans, J., 'Is Convergence Prompting Fragmentation?: The EMS and national protection in Germany, France, and Italy' in Paulo Guerrieri and Pier Carla Padoa, eds, *The Political Economy of European Integration* (London: Harvester Wheatsheaf, 1989), pp. 100–43.

Petit, P., 'Expansionary Policies in a Restrictive World: The case of France' in Paulo Guerrieri and Pier Carla Padoa, eds, *The Political Economy of European Integration* (London: Harvester Wheatsheaf, 1989), pp. 231–63.

Peyrelevade, J., 'Témoignage: Fallait-il dévaluer en mai 1981?', *Revue Politique et Parlementaire*, No. 916, May–June, 1985, pp. 128–31.

Pierret, C., 'Oui au SME, pour l'emploi', *Revue Politique et Parlementaire*, May–June, 1983, pp. 48–50.

Plessis, A., 'Rapport introductif', in *Du franc Poincaré à l'écu* (Paris: CHEFF, 1993), pp. 5–12.

Plihon, D., 'Indépendance ou autonomie de la Banque de France?', *Regards sur l'actualité*, September–October, 1994, pp. 3–23.

Pollin, J.-P., 'Coordination des politiques économiques: les facettes d'un mythe', *Revue d'Économie Financière*, March–June 1989, no. 8/9, pp. 247–58.

Reland, J., 'France', in J. Forder and A. Menon, eds, *The European Union and National Macroeconomic policy*, (London: Routledge, 1998), pp. 85–104.

Riboud, J., 'Quelques enseignements d'une fausse dévaluation', *Revue politique et parlementaire*, 797, March 1969.

Riboud, J., 'Vers un autre Bretton Woods', in *Revue Politique et Parlementaire*, May–June 1983, pp. 51–6.

Rimbert, P., 'Le Problème Monetaire Européen' in *Cahier et Revue de l'OURS* (Organisation universitaire de la recherche socialist), 123, oct. 1981, pp. 34–53.

Rueff, J., 'Préface', in Emile Moreau, *Souvenirs d'un gouverneur de la Banque de France* (Paris: Génin, 1954).

Russell, R., '*L'engrenage*, collegial style and the crisis syndrome: lessons from monetary policy in the European Community', *Journal of Common Market Studies*, 1/2, 1975.

Saly, P., 'Poincaré keynésien?', in P. Fridenson and A. Straus, eds., *Le Capitalisme français* (Paris: Fayard, 1987).

Sandholtz, W., 'Choosing union: monetary politics and Maastricht', *International Organization*, 47, 1, Winter 1993, pp. 1–39.

Sandholtz, W., 'Monetary bargains: the treaty on EMU', in A. W. Cafruny and G. G. Rosenthal, *The state of the European Community, Vol. 2, The Maastricht debates and beyond* (Boulder, Colorado: Lynne Rienner Publishers, 1993) pp. 125–42.

Sandholtz, W., 'Money troubles: Europe's rough road to monetary union', *Journal of European Public Policy*, 3, 1, March 1996, pp. 84–101.

Sapin, M., 'Discours de M. Michel Sapin', *Du franc Poincaré à l'écu* (Paris: Cheff, 1993), pp. IX–XIII.

Schumacher, A., 'Germany and France: A new Partnership? Franco-German relations since unification', *Journal of Area Studies*, 2, 1993, pp. 53–65.

Séguin, P., 'Jacques Rueff contre la politique du coup par coup', *Revue des deux mondes*, 12, December 1996, pp. 18–29.

Smeets, H.-D., 'Does Germany Dominate the EMS?', *Journal of Common Market Studies*, 29, 1, September 1990, pp. 37–52.

Smith, M. E. and Sandholtz, W., 'Institutions and Leadership: Germany, Maastricht, and the ERM Crisis', in S. Mazey and C. Rhodes, eds, *The State of the European Community*, Vol. 3 (Boulder, Colorado: Lynne Rienner, 1995), pp. 245–65.

Stéphane, D., *La leçon d'autuomne: Jeux et enjeux de François Mitterrand* (Paris: Albin Michel, 1983).

Story, J., 'The Launching of the EMS: An Analysis of Change in Foreign Economic Policy' in *Political Studies* (1988), 36, pp. 397–412.

Strange, S., 'Risque de Système ou Vulnérabilité à l'Egard des Etats-Unis', in Bruno Théret, ed., *L'Etat, la finance et le social, souveraineté nationale et construction européenne* (Paris: Editions de la Découverte, 1995), pp. 450–7.

Sur, E., 'Maastricht, la France et l'Allemagne', in *Hérodote, revue de géographie et géopolitique*, special edition 'La Question Allemande', 68, January–March 1993, pp. 125–37.

'Table Ronde: Quelles perspectives pour la politique monétaire?', *Revue français d'économie*, 2, 3, Summer 1987, pp. 221–31.

Taylor, P., 'Interdependence and Autonomy in the European Communities: The Case of the European Monetary System', *Journal of Common Market Studies*, 18, 4, June 1980, pp. 370–87.

Thygesen, N., 'Community Decision-Making on Exchange Rates and Money' in *Journal of Common Market Studies*, 17, 4, June 1979, pp. 313–31.

Tiersky, R., 'France in the New Europe', *Foreign Affairs*, Spring, 1992, pp. 131–46.

'Le Traité de Maastricht: Quelles conséquences pour l'Europe financière?', *Revue d'Economie Financière*, hors série, September, 1992.

Trichet, J.-C., 'Installation du Conseil de la Politique Monétaire', *Bulletin de la Banque de France*, 1, January 1994, pp. 79–95.

Tsoukalis, L., 'Economic and Monetary Union: the primacy of high politics', in H. Wallace and W. Wallace, *Policy-Making in the European Union*, 3 edn, Oxford University Press, Oxford, 1996, pp. 279–99.

Tsoukalis, L., 'Economic and Monetary Union', in L. Tsoukalis, ed. *The New European economy: the politics and economics of integration* (Oxford: Oxford University Press, 1991).

Tsoukalis, L., 'Responsibilities of the International Reserve Centre, European Monetary Personality and Other Fairy Tales', *Journal of Common Market Studies*, 17, 1, September 1978, pp. 45–61.

Ungerer, H., 'The European Monetary System and the International Monetary System', *Journal of Common Market Studies*, Vol. 17, 3, March 1989, pp. 231–48.

Valin, G., 'Deutsche Mark et Franc Français: deux politiques monétaires divergentes', *Allemagnes d'Aujourd'hui*, April–June 1983, 84, pp. 195–203.

Verdun, Amy, 'An "Assymetrical" Economic and Monetary Union in the EU: Perceptions of Monetary Authorities and Social Partners', *Journal of European Integration*, 20, 1, Autumn 1996, pp. 59–82.

Vernet, D., 'The dilemma of French foreign policy', *International Affairs*, 68, 4, 1992, pp. 655–64.

Vers l'union économique et monétaire européenne (Paris: La documentation française, 1990) published papers presented at a colloquium held at the French Ministry of Finance, 21 June 1990.

Virard, M.-P., *Comment Mitterrand a découvert l'économie* (Paris: Albin Michel, 1993).

Vissol, T., 'Enjeux et risques d'une politique monétaire européenne', *Cadmos*, 12, 1989, pp. 56–74.

Wincott, D., 'Institutional Interaction and European Integration: Towards an Everyday Critique of Liberal Intergovernmentalism', *Journal of Common Market Studies*, 3, 4, December 1995, pp. 597–609.

Wood, P. C., 'The Franco-German Relationship in the Post-Maastricht Era', in S. Mazey and C. Rhodes, eds, *The State of the European Community*, Vol. 3 (Boulder, Colorado: Lynne Rienner, 1995), pp. 221–43.

Woolley, J. T., 'Policy Credibility and European Monetary Institutions', in A. M. Sbragia, ed., *Euro-politics: Institutions and Policy-making in the 'New' European Community* (Washington: Brookings Institution, 1992), pp. 157–90.

Woolley, J. T. and LeLoup, L. T., 'The Adequacy of the Electoral Motive in Explaining Legislative Attention to Monetary Policy, A Comparative Study', *Comparative Politics*, 22, 1, October 1989, pp. 63–82.

Yost, D. S., 'France in the New Europe', *Foreign Affairs*, Winter, 1990/91, pp. 107–28.

Zis, G., 'The European Monetary System 1979–84: An Assessment', *Journal of Common Market Studies*, 23, 1, September 1984, pp. 46–72.

Theses

Brandt, Stephen, incomplete D.Phil. thesis on a rational choice approach to French and German policy on EMU, Oxford University.

Balleix-Banerjee, C., *La France et la Banque Centrale Européenne : débats politiques et élaboration de la décision, January 1988–September 1992*, Doctoral thesis, Université de Paris II, 1997.

Dillingham, Alan James, *Shielding the Franc: French Diplomacy and European Monetary Integration, 1969–1988*, D.Phil. thesis, Georgetown University, 1991.

Featherstone, K., *Socialists and European Integration: a comparison of the attitudes held within the British Labour Party, the French Socialist Party and the Belgian Socialist Parties*, Ph.D. thesis, Manchester University, 1987, p. 425.

Haywood, E., The French Socialists and the European Community 1981–1986, Ph.D. thesis, University of Swansea, 1989, especially Chapter V: *Monetary Policy and The European Monetary System*, pp. 220–54.

Howarth, D., *French Policy on European Monetary Co-operation and Integration, 1968 to 1994*, D.Phil. thesis, Oxford University, 1998.

Howarth, D., *The French Socialist Government and the European Relance*, M.Phil. thesis, Oxford University, 1991.

Discussion papers

Arrowsmith, J., 'Pitfalls on the Path to a Single European Currency', EUI Working Group, RSC, 96/21 (San Dominico, EUI, 1996).

Artus, P., 'La politique monétaire dans les années 1990', Document de travail, no. 1990.04/E (Paris: Caisse des dépots et Consignations, 1990).

Bean, C., 'Economic and Monetary Union in Europe', Centre for Economic Performance Discussion Paper, 86 (London: LSE, July 1992).

Bordo, M. D., Simard, D. and White, E. N., 'France and the Breakdown of the Bretton Woods International Monetary System', IMF Working Paper (Washington: IMF, November 1994).

Bordo, M. D. Simard, D. and White, E. N., 'France and the Bretton Woods International Monetary System: 1960 to 1968', NBER Working Paper Series, 4642 (Cambridge, MA: National Bureau of Economic Research, February 1994).

Christiansen, T., 'European Integration Between Political Science and International Relations Theory: the End of Sovereignty', EUI Working Paper, RSC, 94/4, (San Domenico: EUI, 1994).

Cohen, D., Mélitz, J. and Oudiz, G., 'The European Monetary System and the Franc-Mark asymmetry', Discussion Paper, no. 245 (London: Centre for Economic Policy Research, June 1988).

Friend, J. W., 'The Linchpin, French-German Relations, 1950–1990', The Washington Papers 154 (Washington: Praeger, 1992).

Henry, J. and Weidmann, J., 'The French-German Interest Rate Differential since German Unification: the Impact of the 1992–1993 EMS Crisis', EUI Working Paper, RSC, 95/16, (San Domenico, EUI, 1995).

Jochimsen, R., 'The Bundesbank and European Economic and Monetary Union', Discussion Paper, 21 (Oxford: Nuffield College, Centre for European Studies, February 1993).

Marks, G., Hooghe, L. and Blank, K., 'European Integration and the State', EUI Working Paper, RSC, 95/7, (San Domenico: EUI, March 1995).

Melitz, J., 'Monetary Policy in France', Discussion Paper Series, 509 (London: Centre for Economic Policy Research, January 1991).

Østrup, F., 'Economic and Monetary Union', CORE working paper 6/1995, (Copenhagen: CORE, 1995).

Saint-Marc, M., 'The New French Monetary Policy in the Context of the EMS and of financial innovation', Research Papers in Banking and Finance (Bangor: University College of North Wales, 1991).

Staden, B. von, 'The Politics of European Integration', Jean Monnet Chair Papers, 5 (San Domenico: EUI, April 1991).

Ungerer, H., 'Political Aspects of European Monetary Integration', EUI Working Paper, 93/2, (San Domenico: EUI, 1993).

Ungerer, H., 'The EMS – the First Ten Years: Policies – Developments – Evolution', EUI Working Paper, ECO, 90/2, (San Domenico: EUI, 1990).

Ungerer, H. and the European Department of the IMF 'The European Monetary System: Recent Developments', International Monetary Fund, Occasional Paper, 48 (Washington: IMF, 1986).

Unpublished papers

Begg, D. and Wyplosz, C., 'The European Monetary System: Recent intellectual history', unpublished paper, presented at the Conference on 'The Monetary Future of Europe', La Coruna, 11–12 December 1992.

Cameron, D., 'British exit, German voice, French loyalty: defection, domination and cooperation in the 1992–93 ERM crisis', paper presented at the Annual Meeting of the American Political Science Association, Washington, DC, September, 1993.

Dyson, K., 'France, Germany and the Euro-Zone: From "Motor" of EMU to Living in an ECB-Centric Euro-Zone', paper presented at conference France, Germany and Britain–Partners in a Changing World, University of Bradford, UK, 21 May 1999.

Dyson, K. and Featherstone, K., 'France, EMU and Construction Européenne: Empowering the Executive, Transforming the State', paper presented to the Eight International Conference of the Journal 'Politiques et Management Public', 20–21 June 1996, Paris.

Dyson, K. and Featherstone, K., 'Britain and the Relaunch of EMU: Just say "No"?', Paper delivered at the Political Studies Association Conference, 10–12 April 1996, University of Glasgow.

Dyson, K. and Featherstone, K., 'Interlocking Core Executives: Explaining the Negotiation of Economic and Monetary Union', paper for the 24th European Consortium of Political Research, Joint Sessions of Workshops, Oslo, 29 March–3 April 1996.

Dyson, K. Featherstone, K and Michaelopoulos, G., *Reinventing the French State*, Report Number 2, unpublished, European Briefing Unit, Department of European Studies, University of Bradford, UK, August 1994.

Jaillet, P., 'From the EMI to the ESCB, A Survey of Options for the passage to Stage 3 of EMU and the Single Monetary Policy', paper presented at the workshop on

Economic Policy Formulation in Interdependent Markets organised by the European Economic and Financial Center, London, 2–4 February 1994.

Loedel, P., 'German Monetary Policy, EMS Turmoil and European Integration: After 'Imperfect' Hegemony', paper presented at the Columbia University Graduate Student Conference on the 'New Europe', April 1994.

Tyrie, A., 'A Political Economy of Economic and Monetary Union', unpublished paper, Nuffield College, Oxford, 1992.

Official documents

Balladur, E., 'Europe's Monetary Construction', Memorandum to Ecofin Council (Paris: Ministry of Finance and Economics, 8 January 1988).

Chambre de Commerce et d'Industrie, ed., *Politique monétaire pour 1990: pour une politique économique cohérente avec le franc fort*, Alain Bizot, rapporteur, (Paris: Chambre de Commerce et d'industrie, 1990).

Commission des Finances de l'Economie Générale et du Plan, Assemblée Nationale, *Rapport d'information*, presented by Edmond Alphandéry, 2402, First ordinary session of 1991–1992, registered 4 December 1991.

Committee for European Monetary Union, 'Action programme', 1988.

Committee for the Study of Economic and Monetary Union, *Report on Economic and Monetary Union in the European Community* (Delors Report), 1989.

Council-Commission of the European Communities, *Report to the Council and the Commission on the Realisation by Stages of Economic and Monetary Union in the Community – 'Werner Report'*, Supplement to *Bulletin*, November 1970.

CNPF, *Avis sur le project de traité rélatif à l'union économique et monétaire*, November 1991.

EC Commission (Commission for the European Communities), 'One market, on money – An evaluation of the potential benefits and costs of forming an economic and monetary union', *European Economy*, 44, October 1990.

Genscher, H.-D., 'A European Currency Area and a European Central Bank', Memorandum to the General Affairs Council (Bonn: Ministry of Foreign Affairs, 26 February 1988).

Ministère de l'Economie, des Finances et du Budget, 'La contribution française aux progrès de l'union économique et monétaire', (French draft treaty) 16 January, 1999. In English see *Agence Europe*, 28/29 January 91, 5419.

Mitterrand, F., *Lettre à tous les Français*, in *Europe Documents*, no. 1502, 14 April 1988.

Mitterrand, F., *L'Unité*, 29 June 1979.

OECD, *Economic Surveys, France*, Paris (several years).

Parti Socialiste, *Projet Socialiste pour la France des années 80*, 1979.

Newspapers and magazines consulted

French

Le Monde
Le Figaro
Les Echos

Libération
Humanité
L'Express
Le Nouvel Observateur
Le Point
L'Evènement du Jeudi
La Croix
La Vie Française

British

The Times
Financial Times
Guardian
Independent
The Economist
The Economist Intelligence Unit, *Country Report, France*, London, 1968–94.

Other

Die Zeit
International Herald Tribune
Agence Europe
EC Bulletin

People interviewed
(classified according to most pertinent post)

Politicians

Fabius, Laurent, minister for the budget, 1981–84, Prime Minister, 1984–86, and so on.

Guigou, Elisabeth, adviser to President Mitterrand on financial and monetary matters, 1982–85, and European economic co-operation, 1985–88; minister for european affairs, 1990–93.

Sapin, Michel, Socialist minister of finance, 1992–93; member of the Monetary Policy Committee of the Bank of France, 1994–96.

Ministerial support staff

Bert, Thierry, adviser in the SGCI responsible for financial questions, 1986–87; adviser to Edouard Balladur on European economic co-operation, 1987–88; deputy SGCI, 1989–92; adviser to President Mitterrand on European economic co- operation, 1992–95.

Gauron, André, political adviser to Pierre Bérégovoy, minister of finance, 1984–96 and 1988–December 1991; *Directeur-général*, Conseil supérieur d'audiovisuel, 1992–.

Hannezo, Guillaume, adviser on monetary affairs to Pierre Bérégovoy, minister of finance, 1988–92; adviser to President Mitterrand on monetary affairs, 1992–93; *Directeur-général*, Assurance Générale Française, 1993–.

Jolivert, Benoit, adviser to Jacques Delors, minister of finance, 1981–84; deputy director, financial services, Treasury, 1984–85.

Lagayette, Philippe, director of staff, Jacques Delors, minister of finance, 1981–84; *2ème Sous Gouverneur*, Bank of France, 1984–90; *1ère Sous Gouverneur*, 1990–92; *Directeur-général* of the Caisse des dépots et consignations, 1993–.

Lebègue, Daniel, French negotiator during the EMS negotiations, 1978; adviser on monetary policy to Prime Minister Pierre Mauroy, 1981–84; director of the Treasury, 1984–86; *Directeur-général*, BNP.

Peyrelevade, Jean, economic adviser and deputy directeur in Prime Minister Mauroy's staff, 1981–83; author: *La Mort du dollar*, (1974), *L'Economie de spéculation* (1978), *Pour un capitalism intelligent* (1993); currently President, Crédit Lyonnais.

Vial, Patrice, director of Edmond Alphandéry's (minister of economics) staff, 1994–95.

Villeroy de Galhau, François, head of the European Affairs Office, Treasury, 1990; adviser to Pierre Bérégovoy, minister of finance and then Prime Minister, 1990–93; chef du bureau de la trésorie et de la politique monétaire, Treasury, 1993–.

Treasury officials

(Several treasury officials interviewed also served in ministerial staffs.)

Deforges, Sylvain, *adjoint au chef du bureau* responsible for monetary affairs, Treasury, 1981–83; chef du bureau responsible for European affairs, 1987–90; deputy director responsible for monetary affairs, 1990–.

Ducerne, Gilles, *chef du bureau* responsible for monetary affairs, Treasury.

Bank of France officials

Boissonnat, Jean, journalist, member of the Monetary Policy Committee of the Bank of France.

Cordier, M. J., *Chef du service macro-économique*; Paris, 16 May 1994.

Jaillet, Pierre, economist, Bank of France.

Larosière, Jacques de, director of Valéry Giscard d'Estaing's (minister of finance) staff, January–May 1974; director of the Treasury, 1974–78; director-general of the IMF, 1978–86; governor of the Bank of France, 1987–1993; director of the EBRD, 1993–98.

Moutot, François, director of foreign relations, Bank of France, 1990–; French representative on the EMU negotiations concerning the ESCB and the EMI.

Patat, Jean-Pierre, economist at the Bank of France since 1962 and monetary economist since 1970; professor at ENSAE and IEP; author; deputy director-general of studies at the Bank of France, 1990–.

Redouin, Jean Paul, director responsible for credit policy, Bank of France; participant in the negotiations on EMU.

Trichet, Jean-Claude, director of Edouard Balladur's (minister of finance) staff, 1986–87; director of the French Treasury, 1987–92; governor of the Bank of France, 1993–.

CNPF

Lepinay, M., assistant director responsible for monetary affairs, CNPF.

Vever, Bruno, director responsible for monetary affairs, CNPF.

Academics/advisers

Aglietta, Michel, economist at CEPII (Centre d'Etude Prospective et Information Internationale).

Boissieu, Christian de, monetary economist; economist at the Paris Chamber of Commerce.

Brendon, Anton, monetary economist; former president of CEPII (Centre d'Etude Prospective et Information Internationale); chief economist for CPR.

Cotta, Alain, economist, Dauphine (Paris IX).

Dyson, Kenneth, Professor of European Studies, University of Bradford.

Fitoussi, Jean-Paul, economist; President, OFCE (Observatoire Français des conjonctures économiques), professor at IEP, Paris.

Goldey, David, Fellow of Lincoln College, Oxford.

Grjebine, André, economist; professor at IEP, Paris; researcher at CERI (Centre d'études et de recherche internationale); former adviser to Jean-Pierre Chevènement.

Grosser, Alfred, expert on Franco-German relations, professor at IEP.

Jacquet, Pierre, deputy director, IFRI (Institut français des relations internationales).

Pisani-Ferry, Jean, president of CEPII (Centre d'Etude Prospective et Information Internationale), the *rapporteur* on the working group on Europe of the Eleventh Plan.

Riboud, Jacques, monetary economist, director of the *Centre Jouffroy pour la réflexion monétaire*.

Rosa, Jean Jacques, economist, professor and thesis director at IEP, Paris; director of the economic *rubrique* in *Le Figaro*.

Story, Jonathon, professor at INSEAD, Fontainebleu, France.

Wyplosz, Charles, monetary economist, professor INSEAD.

Journalists

Izraelewicz, Erik, journalist on monetary policy, *Le Monde*.

Mezarovich, Yves, journalist on economic and monetary affairs, *Le Figaro*.

Simonnot, Philippe, journalist, monetary economist and author of *L'avenir du système monetaire* and *Crise pour le system monétaire*.

Name Index

Subject Index

.